ABSOLUTISM IN SEVENTEENTH-CENTURY EUROPE

Each volume in the 'Problems in Focus' series is designed to make available to students important new work on key historical problems and periods that they encounter in their courses. Each volume is devoted to a central topic or theme, and the most important aspects of this are dealt with by specially commissioned essays from scholars in the relevant field. The editorial Introduction reviews the problem or period as a whole, and each essay provides an assessment of the particular aspect, pointing out the areas of development and controversy, and indicating where conclusions can be drawn or where further work is necessary. An annotated bibliography serves as a guide for further reading.

PROBLEMS IN FOCUS SERIES

TITLES IN PRINT

Church and Society in England: Henry VIII to James I
edited by Felicity Heal and Rosemary O'Day

The Mid-Tudor Policy c.1540–1560
edited by Jennifer Loach and Robert Tittler

The Reign of Elizabeth I
edited by Christopher Haigh

The Origins of the English Civil War
edited by Conrad Russell

Reactions to the English Civil War 1642–1649
edited by John Morrill

The Interregnum: The Quest for Settlement 1646–1660
edited by G. E. Aylmer

Britain after the Glorious Revolution 1689–1714
edited by Geoffrey Holmes

Absolutism in Seventeenth-Century Europe
edited by John Miller

Britain in the Age of Walpole
edited by Jeremy Black

British Society and Politics from Walpole to Pitt 1742–1789
edited by Jeremy Black

Enlightened Absolutism: Reform and Reformers in later Eighteenth-Century Europe
edited by H. M. Scott

Slavery and British Society 1776–1846
edited by James Walvin

Popular Movements, c.1830–1850
edited by J. T. Ward

Britain and the French Revolution 1789–1815
edited by H. T. Dickinson

British Imperialism in the Nineteenth Century
edited by C. C. Eldridge

Later Victorian Britain, 1867–1900
edited by T. R. Gourvish and Alan O'Day

The Revolution in Ireland, 1879–1923
edited by D. G. Boyce

Absolutism in Seventeenth-Century Europe

EDITED BY

JOHN MILLER

MACMILLAN

First published 1990

Published by
MACMILLAN EDUCATION LTD
Houndmills, Basingstoke, Hampshire RG21 2XS
and London
Companies and representatives
throughout the world

Printed in Singapore

British Library Cataloguing in Publication Data
Absolutism in seventeenth century Europe.
1. Europe. Absolutism, history
I. Miller, John II. Series
321.6094
ISBN 0–333–46113–4
ISBN 0–333–46114–2 pbk

Contents

Introduction

JOHN MILLER

THE TERMS 'absolutism' and 'absolute monarchy' are all too often used uncritically and pejoratively, so they may indicate only 'that the historian who uses them is thinking of a regime where the king has more power than twentieth-century scholars think a seventeenth-century king ought to have had'.[1] Even the *Shorter Oxford English Dictionary* baldly equates 'absolutism' with 'despotism', although theorists of absolutism were usually careful to distinguish between the two.[2] The English especially, proud of their ancient 'liberties', regarded absolutism as both alien and abhorrent and credulously swallowed stories of the tyrannous behaviour of continental rulers. As the seventeenth century wore on, indeed, English political writers increasingly fought shy of the word 'absolutism', which they had earlier used freely; Hobbes, especially, helped to endow it with sinister connotations.[3] The aim of this collection of essays is to examine the reality of absolutism, in theory and in practice, to strip away the distortions created by both the hyperbole of its propagandists and the caricatures of its critics. The authors of the chapters that follow consider first the theory of absolutism, then the experience of most of the major European monarchies. They ask how far (and why) these were strengthened in this period and assess the effectiveness of, and limitations on, royal power. The purpose of this introduction is not to summarise what follows, but to raise more general questions about the nature of absolutism.

Most seventeenth-century monarchs ruled agglomerations of diverse territories, multinational states accumulated gradually through conquest, marriage and inheritance and held through a multiplicity of titles; as one Spaniard wrote in 1647: 'The kingdoms [of Spain] must be ruled and governed as if the king who holds them all together were king only of each one of them.'[4] This was especially true of the two branches of the House of Habsburg. In the first half of the seventeenth century, the Spanish branch ruled not only the whole of Spain but also Portugal (until 1640), Naples, Sicily, Sardinia, Franche Comté (on France's eastern frontier) and the southern Netherlands, not to mention vast colonies in the New World. In addition, it was only in 1648 that Spain finally relinquished any title to the northern Netherlands. Even within Spain itself, the king's power was much greater in Castile than in Aragon or Catalonia, joined to Castile by the union of crowns of 1492. In the same period the Austrian branch ruled a great swathe of territory from Croatia (now part of Yugoslavia) in the south through Austria, Bohemia and western Hungary to Silesia, now part of Poland. In the last years of the century they made huge gains to the east, capturing from the Turks the remainder of Hungary and also Transylvania, thus extending their rule to embrace most of modern-day Romania. Ruling this heady mixture of nationalities was far from easy: Bohemia and Hungary especially had fiercely independent nobilities and differences of language and culture were compounded by those of religion, as the Habsburgs' militant Catholicism came up against the stubborn Protestantism of the Bohemians and Hungarians. To complicate matters still further, the head of the Austrian Habsburgs was invariably (but not automatically) elected Holy Roman Emperor – the process of election in itself a reminder of the more conditional sovereignty of earlier times. This title carried with it a broad suzerainty over most of the German-speaking lands of Europe, a suzerainty often (as in Alsace) contested with others, but which gave the Emperor some claim to the leadership of Christendom, especially against the threat from the Ottoman Turks in the east. At times, as in the early 1680s, this threat became a real source of power for the Emperor and the normally ineffectual Diet of the Empire took practical steps to raise men and money for the common cause.

The Habsburgs were not alone in ruling a multiplicity of peoples. From a small area around Moscow, the tsars of Muscovy and then of Russia had by 1700 come to rule a vast empire from the Caspian to the Barents Sea and from the Ukraine to Siberia, which posed problems of communication and of ethnic diversity which made those of the Habsburgs seem mild by comparison. Other less obviously polygot states were far from compact and heterogeneous. The lands of the Electors of Brandenburg (later kings of Prussia) were all German-speaking, but Brandenburg was widely separated from Prussia in the East and the much smaller (but economically much more advanced) Cleves, Mark and Ravensberg, near the Rhine. Similarly much of what is now France had come under the effective control of the crown only in the fifteenth and sixteenth centuries – Brittany, Burgundy, Provence and Picardy, for example. Other provinces, such as Alsace, Franche Comté and Roussillon were added by conquest during the seventeenth century, further adding to the linguistic and institutional diversity of what might at first sight seem a geographically compact and coherent state. Of the kingdoms considered here perhaps only Sweden and England can truly be considered as integrated states – and even then there were minorities who spoke Finnish or Welsh.

Diversity, indeed, was the keynote of late medieval institutions throughout western Europe. The practice of feudalism, whereby land and authority were granted (most often by formal charters) in return for service, served to fragment and to disperse jurisdiction and political power. Many 'public' functions were in private hands: landowners dispensed justice to their peasants in their own courts; guilds and town corporations exercised a similar function within their respective jurisdictions; the church courts and the canon law regulated large areas of people's lives, including some which we would not now regard as 'spiritual' (the execution of wills, for example). With this multiplicity of jurisdictions went a multiplicity of laws, especially in those areas, mainly in the northern half of Europe, where law was based on custom. Luxemburg alone had 101 customary laws in 1600, France around 360.[5] Great magnates like the dukes of Burgundy and Brittany in theory held their lands as fiefs from their suzerain, the king of France; in practice they were independent princes – the dukes of Burgundy, indeed, held extensive non-French-speaking lands and their power at times equalled that of the king. They thus differed little from the princes and cities of the Holy Roman Empire, whose allegiance to the Emperor, if not merely nominal – the Emperor possessed considerable moral authority, backed up with the power to bestow honours and other rewards – often failed to translate itself into practical action. Within their states, these magnates developed their own administrations and institutions, which often differed markedly one from another. They too had to face the problem of dispersal of authority, which made it necessary to deal separately with towns, regions and different social and interest groups. In order to facilitate this process, and more particularly to win consent for taxation to meet the costs of government and defence, magnates created representative assemblies – estates, *états* or *stände*. In these the major orders of society usually sat separately – clergy, nobles, townsmen (rarely peasants). From the point of view of those who summoned them, the meetings of these estates often proved frustrating. Proceedings would grind to a halt because of disputes within or between the orders. Often delegates would insist on returning home for further instructions. Even so, they provided the only feasible mechanism for winning consent and helped to forge a sense of provincial – but not national – identity. Thus in fifteenth-century France while provincial estates produced at least some tangible results, attempts to create a national Estates-General broke down thanks to the insuperable divisions between the different orders and provinces. The king had to revert to bargaining separately with provinces and towns; much the same happened in seventeenth-century Castile.[6]

The monarchs of the sixteenth and seventeenth centuries thus ruled lands which were anything but compact and homogeneous; their problems were compounded by the fact that the territorial units used for fiscal, jurisdictional and ecclesiastical purposes often did not coincide. Frontiers were often uncertain, especially in mountain areas. As with those of the kings, so the lands of the great nobility were multinational: thus the princes of Orange, who drew their title as sovereigns from a tiny principality surrounded by France, held extensive estates in Germany, Franche Comté and the Netherlands. Several French magnates were sovereigns in their own right over territories outside France, such as the ducs de Bouillon and de Guise. The greatest problem facing monarchs, then, was to establish effective control over this institutional hotchpotch, to concentrate in the king the sovereignty which had been so widely scattered, to centralise decision-making and to ensure that those decisions were acted upon. Whereas late medieval kings, when not leading their people in war, had been seen primarily in a passive role, as judges and arbiters, absolutism required that the king take a much more positive, directing role. The extension of active royal power implied not only the erosion of independent jurisdictions, the subjugation of those authorities which stood between king and subject, but also the development of effective means of coercion – a bureaucracy obedient to the crown and a standing army. This process was often facilitated by a codification of the laws.

In challenging these competing authorities monarchs and their servants invoked an ideology of absolutism, which as (J. H. Burns shows) stressed the distinctive nature of monarchy and the king's duty to override particular interests in pursuit of the general good. This ideology usually included a strong religious dimension, laying stress on the supposedly divine origins of monarchy and the more-than-human attributes of kings, symbolised both in the practice of anointing at the coronation and in the belief that 'the royal touch' could cure the disease of scrofula.[7] Naturally such a view of kingship required the support of the predominant church. The Catholic church had been one of the greatest of the 'intermediate powers' between king and people; now in some states (England, Sweden) it was replaced with a new church much more closely under royal control; in others it came (though not without friction) more to reinforce than to impede royal power, especially where kings had to contend with dissident religious elements among their subjects (France, Austria). In all states the church was the most powerful force for moulding opinion and instilling values and it used its influence to inculcate a sense of duty of obedience to the crown. (This was as true of the Russian Orthodox Church as of the Catholic or Protestant churches of the West.)

In asserting that his power came from God, the king claimed an authority which transcended that of customary constitutions and local privileges. These he was prepared (as a matter of general principle) to respect, while claiming the right to override them in case of need. (This was less of a problem in the East, especially in Russia, where there was no tradition that subjects enjoyed any autonomous rights.) Domestic reorganisation, however, was not purely an end in itself. In the ruthlessly competitive world of international relations, in which the scale and cost of warfare kept growing, those states which fell behind militarily went to the wall, while others which used their resources efficiently – notably Sweden and Prussia – wielded an influence out of all proportion to their size. Concentration of resources at home was the essential prerequisite of territorial expansion and even survival.

The pattern just outlined, with its emphasis on centralisation, militarisation and the enhancement of royal authority, was found right across Europe and led to the creation in many countries of what John Brewer has called 'the fiscal-military state'.[8] Few major states escaped 'absolutism', although both England and the Dutch Republic managed, for reasons discussed later, to create a 'fiscal-military state' without sacrificing liberty at home. The experience of individual states varied widely, which (given the institutional diversity of the late middle ages) was only to be expected. Moreover, levels of economic development varied greatly, from the relatively sophisticated trading economies of the Atlantic seaboard to the overwhelmingly agrarian economies of the East. The tsar of Russia faced little opposition from articulate representative institutions or stubbornly independent towns, but had to contend with problems of distance, of marauding tribesmen and of runaway peasants escaping into wide open spaces for which there was no parallel in the West. The essays which follow consider the differing experiences of monarchs, the problems they faced and the extent to which they overcame them. First, though, we need to move from stating what happened to asking why it happened. What provided the impetus for absolutism?

Much the most comprehensive attempt at a general analysis is that of the Marxist historian, Perry Anderson, in his *Lineages of the Absolutist State*.[9] He sees absolute monarchy as the creation and defender of the landed aristocracy, which took two basic forms. In the East – above all in Russia and Prussia – it grew from a direct compact between crown and nobility: in return for serving the crown in army and bureaucracy, the nobles were granted much more extensive powers over the peasantry, notably by means of the formal establishment of serfdom. In the West the picture was more complex. With the demise of serfdom and the growth of an urban bourgeoisie outside noble control, the nobles' coercive power over the creators of wealth was reduced, but they found an effective substitute in absolute monarchy. 'Feudal coercion was displaced upwards to a centralised monarchy and the aristocracy typically had to exchange its estates representation for bureaucratic office within the renovated structures of the state.'[10] Royal armies proved well capable of suppressing popular revolts and so of protecting noble interests. Not all nobles adapted easily to this change: some failed to see where their best interests lay, clung on to their old powers and even rebelled. By the eighteenth century, however, they had adapted fully, enjoying a near-monopoly of civil and military office, confident that the monarch would protect their interests. Only in England and the Dutch Republic, both of which underwent 'bourgeois revolutions', did this not happen.

For Anderson, then, absolutism was the creation of socio-economic forces independent of human will. A second interpretation, by contrast, sees it as the product of deliberate human action, the implementation of a theory of monarchy elaborated by philosophers and divines, jurists and administrators. This view is held most consciously by historians of law and of institutions. 'The establishment of absolutism' wrote one 'is in sum the realisation in practice of the theory of monarchy which had been progressively elaborated in the fourteenth and fifteenth centuries.'[11] This theory centred on the concentration of power in a benevolent monarch, who put his kingdom's interests before his own and before those of the selfish and often myopic local and sectional groups who so often obstructed the crown. Thus Colbert tried to control the finances of town corporations, to prevent them from running up unnecessary debts and from burdening the townspeople with excessive taxes. A variant of this interpretation sees monarchs and ministers setting out to extend royal power for its own sake, because absolutism was up-to-date.[12] The style of Louis XIV had many imitators: even Charles II of England planned his own mini-Versailles at Winchester.

A third interpretation sees the key to the rise of absolutism in war, more particularly the so-called 'military revolution'. From the late fifteenth century a complex of related developments hugely increased the scale and cost of war: the French army was fairly typical in growing from 50,000 men in the 1550s to 400,000 in the 1700s.[13] Faced with the need to mobilise more and more men and money, kings became impatient of the obstruction and parochialism of estates and taxpayers. Some estates ceased to meet, others were browbeaten into voting automatically what the king demanded: the Estates of Languedoc, for example, came to appreciate that compliance with the royal will was a lesser evil than having unpaid soldiers quartered on the province. The army could also be used against recalcitrant taxpayers and to suppress revolts.[14] New officials were appointed to ensure that the army's needs were supplied and to accelerate tax collection. If war thus provided the major stimulus for the creation of a fiscal-military state, its impact was not confined to taxation and the armed forces. Monarchs sought to increase the taxable wealth of their states by promoting trade and industry, by standardising weights, measures and the coinage and by eliminating internal customs barriers. Thus the needs of war affected all areas of the economy and of government.

These three interpretations are not mutually incompatible. Anderson devotes considerable attention to the importance of war and sees the need to respond to Swedish aggression as a major stimulus to the emergence of absolutism in Russia, Prussia and Austria.[15] Similarly, whether or not kings and officials were motivated by an ideology of absolutism they invoked it frequently in their efforts to overcome the obstacles they faced in mobilising men and money. In the eighteenth century, in particular, the German 'cameralists' developed a theory of administration which emphasised the application of rational principles by trained administrators under the auspices of a benevolent absolute ruler.[16] In general, though, it seems improbable that kings would have gone to so much trouble merely in order to implement a theory – especially one which often (as in France) co-existed with a general respect for traditional forms and institutions. Practical considerations surely came first, although the theory both served to legitimate the conduct of kings and officials and helped to create a concept of service to the state, in place of the older view of office as private property (although the practice of selling offices ensured a continuing vitality for the latter). Justificatory ideologies can acquire a logic and momentum of their own.

Anderson's thesis requires rather fuller discussion. It goes to the opposite extreme to that taken by the proponents of ideology, in that he lays very little stress on the conscious actions of kings and ministers, at least at the level of general theory: on matters of detail he is well aware of the personal impact of (say) the Great Elector.[17] The absolutist state, he suggests, evolved to meet the needs of the landed aristocracy, serving as a mechanism of repression and a source of reward. This thesis is perhaps most credible in the East, or to be more precise in Russia and Prussia, where one finds the creation of a service nobility linked to the enserfment of the peasantry. Even there the question of causation is problematic: as Philip Longworth remarks, in Russia the growth of absolutism made necessary the extension of serfdom, not vice versa.[18] It is not entirely convincing to portray the state purely as a means whereby the aristocracy repressed the lower orders: in

France, Hungary and elsewhere, resistance to the fiscal-military state (and to attempts to establish religious uniformity) was often led by dissident nobles (and officials).[19] (In Russia, indeed, the greatest threat to the tsars came not from the peasants or even the bulk of the nobility, but from a few great court nobles and above all the palace guard.) Moreover, if it is possible (if simplistic) to see the state apparatus of Russia or Prussia as controlled by the nobility, it is far less plausible in the West. In many armies the officer corps was recruited mainly from the nobility, but the same could not be said of western bureaucracies, except in so far as office conferred nobility. Anderson has considerable problems with the sale of office (venality). He writes 'the prevalent mode of integration of the feudal nobility into the absolutist state in the west took the form of the acquisition of offices – a kind of monetarised caricature of investment in a fief'. But he then talks of 'the mercantile and manufacturing bourgeoisie' investing in these offices as well.[20] Later, following Mousnier, he argues that venality prevented the formation of 'grandee clientage systems' within the French bureaucracy, describes Spanish administrators as recruited from among the lesser gentry and ascribes the absence of venality in Prussia to 'the nullity of the towns'.[21] Sometimes he is simply factually wrong, as in the claim that 30 to 40 per cent of Charles I's income came from sales of office.[22]

These confusions arise from Anderson's attempt to reconcile the empirical fact that non-nobles bought offices with his view of the state as an organ of aristocratic power. In fact, those who bought or inherited offices were often neither members of 'the mercantile and manufacturing bourgeoisie' nor landed aristocrats (although they might be ennobled and purchase land as a result of holding office) but lawyers (as Anderson recognises in the case of Spain).[23] Once heritability of office was established, fathers sent their sons to the law faculties of universities to acquire the professional skills they would need. Administrators thus developed common habits of thinking and a sense of professionalism and corporate solidarity which derived not from membership of any particular socio-economic group but from service to the state. The state should surely be seen as possessing a dynamism of its own, not simply as a creation of social and economic forces. Indeed, the nature of those forces and of the changes which Anderson posits are open to question. Over the centuries one sees the end of personal serfdom (in the West), the growth of trade and manufactures, the growing commercialisation of agriculture – but it is extremely difficult to demonstrate when, where and how far such changes took place. Adequate statistics for even such basic (and quantifiable) matters as population are scarce before the nineteenth century. Written evidence of any sort of economic activity within a predominantly illiterate society is bound to be sparse and is rarely likely to yield *qualitative* data. It is tempting to place excessive weight on the scraps of hard evidence which survive and to generalise from what may be exceptional cases. By contrast the state had a vested interest in acquiring information and keeping records; evidence of its activities is comparatively voluminous and becomes more so with the growth of absolutism. It is tempting (as Anderson does) to produce evidence of state growth as demonstrating underlying socio-economic changes (which are assumed or asserted rather than proved) on the grounds that this state growth is exactly what he would expect to result from such changes.

This brings us to questions of motivation. At times Anderson sees kings pursuing 'institutional goals', which implies a conscious absolutist policy.[24] Elsewhere he discusses at length the contribution of war to the growth of absolutism: but what were the reasons for war? He argues that the large portion of state budgets that was spent on war 'does not correspond to a capitalist reality: it represents a swollen memory of the medieval functions of war', the traditional vocation of the nobility. 'Warfare was not the "sport" of kings, it was their fate; beyond the finite diversity of individual inclinations and characters, it beckoned them inexorably as a social necessity of their state.' War was, at bottom, about territory, although this was covered with 'claims of religious or geographical legitimacy'.[25] That at least is what he argues as a general theory; in practice, the facts often lead him to a rather different interpretation. Take his reasons for the French attack on the Dutch Republic in 1672. Colbert (he claims) urged Louis XIV to seize Dutch trade – advice which 'perfectly captures the social tone of absolutist aggression and predatory mercantilism'. But later he argues that Colbert's attempt to adopt the 'capitalist' objectives of the English and Dutch proved a fiasco.[26] (In fact Colbert opposed the war as long as he could, knowing it would ruin his plans for reform at home.[27]) Elsewhere Anderson subsides into vagueness: in 1688 the Cologne election dispute and

William III's accession in England (some time after hostilities had begun) were the 'signals' for the resumption of war; he then talks of Louis XIV's 'war aims' without saying what they were. Yet at other times he explains the development of states in terms of defensive reactions to outside attack.[28] On many occasions, sensitivity to his evidence leads him to explanations which do not fit too comfortably into his theoretical preconceptions. According to these, standing armies should have been used to hold down the exploited lower orders, conquer territory and provide employment for the nobility. But was that all? Are profit and power the only things that motivate human beings? Any reasonably objective investigation would suggest not: men (not least kings and nobles) are also influenced by pride, revenge, lust.[29] Religion, which underlay so many revolts and wars, surely cannot be dismissed as the 'contemporary ideological idiom' of geopolitical rivalries.[30] Strange though it may seem, seventeenth-century rulers were deeply concerned about honour, precedence and protocol. Louis XIV threatened to break off diplomatic relations with Spain when jostling for precedence between the French and Spanish ambassadors in London escalated into a full-blown riot. Even Charles II of England, that most informal of kings, insisted that his ambassador in Paris should receive all the honours and rights of precedence accorded to his predecessors and in 1673 was far more willing to drop claims for war reparations from the Dutch than his demand that Dutch ships should salute those of England in the North Sea.[31]

For non-Marxist historians questions of motivation lie at the heart of history. For Marxists, of course, they do not. 'The absolutist state' (writes Anderson) 'historically functioned to defend the nobility.'[32] Whether the nobility appreciated this was irrelevant: some at first did not and vigorously opposed the growth of absolutism. By the eighteenth century, however, monarch and nobles enjoyed a mutually advantageous partnership, as shown both by Catherine the Great's remark: 'Je suis une aristocrate, c'est mon métier' and Joseph II's disastrous attempt to go against the interests of the Austrian nobility.[33] In the last resort, however, whether one accepts or rejects Anderson's analysis depends on faith: on whether one believes that the (demonstrable) growth of the absolutist state was – indeed necessarily had to be – the product of the socio-economic changes that he posits. The problem is that neither the changes nor their effect on the state can be convincingly demonstrated. This in turn assumes that historical development occurs independently of human will and sees economics as the driving force of history. It may be so: Marx certainly taught historians that they cannot understand any system of government unless they first understand the economic and social bases of political power. It surely does not follow, however, that political change is *necessarily* the product of economic and social change. Indeed, political decisions and actions can have a dramatic impact on the economy: note the devastating effect of the Thirty Years War on Germany's population or that of war taxation in Louis XIV's last years, when whole villages gave up cultivating the land because they could not produce enough to satisfy the tax collector.[34]

If Anderson's thesis on the impulse towards creating the absolutist state is open to question, his analysis of its social basis has much more to commend it. Too many historians, mesmerised by the image created by Louis XIV, see absolute monarchy as divorced from society, or rather as subordinating all social groups to the crown. They contrast the brutal warlords of the Wars of Religion and the Frondes with the periwigged courtiers who danced attendance on the Sun King. But Louis was always careful to protect the interests of the highest nobility, the dukes and peers; and Roger Mettam makes clear the important role which the nobility continued to play in government. Moreover, recent research has shown the extent to which French nobles were involved in tax collecting and loans to the crown – albeit usually through intermediaries who could be disavowed if things went wrong.[35] In short, the nobility had much to gain from absolutism in terms of honours, office and profit – and the same was true of the eighteenth-century fiscal-military state in Britain. Although Anderson sees England as an exception, the English experience reinforces his general case for the aristocratic nature of absolutism. Unfortunately, Anderson is committed to the view that the old aristocratic order was overthrown by a bourgeois revolution in the 1640s. But as Lawrence Stone, whose work Anderson so much admires, remarked, the English aristocracy were once more ruling the roost in the eighteenth century, whatever their problems in the seventeenth.[36] Anderson argues that they had gone too far in a capitalist direction by 1640 to need the absolutist state, as they no longer needed to fear rural insurrection. They certainly continued to control local government, which some Marxist-oriented historians of the eighteenth century see as an instrument of social control. But the coercive powers of central government were also increased, particularly with the Riot Act and the growth of the army; and popular disorder in the eighteenth century was at least as widespread and severe as in the seventeenth. One could thus see the eighteenth-century British state as protecting aristocratic property, as well as providing opportunities for employment and for lucrative investment in government funds – a lush gravy-train on which the aristocracy had the best seats.[37]

The rewards which eighteenth-century nobles enjoyed made the loss of their former autonomy bearable – and that autonomy was less necessary now that the crown could maintain order effectively. One exception to this pattern would seem to be Sweden, where (as Professor Upton shows) the highest nobility lost heavily in the Act of Resumption as well as having their military role curtailed. On the other hand, the movement towards absolutism in Sweden received strong support from the other orders (including the lesser nobility) in the Diet. That should remind us that the effectiveness of any pre-modern regime depended at least as much on the subject's acceptance as on the monarch's powers of coercion. The profits which came from office and from government finance helped secure that acceptance, especially from the richest elements in society; so did the ideology of absolutism. Officials became more self-confident and professional; subjects of all ranks became imbued with the concept of obedience, encouraged by the church and by the observable fact that absolutism brought greater order and security: better a fair and distant king than the capricious violence of feudal warlords. For some peoples – for example, the Swedes and Prussians – discipline and obedience seem to have come naturally. Others found it harder, but learned eventually: tax revolts, common in France for much of the seventeenth century, were conspicuous by their absence in the great wars of 1688–1713, despite unprecedented fiscal burdens on all classes of society.[38]

It would seem then that the main stimulus to the establishment of absolutism was military need but that the elaboration of absolutist ideology both speeded the process and helped to secure acceptance. Existing social groups – above all the nobility – came to terms with absolutism and looked to the crown for employment and profit.[39] Let us now move on to consider the effectiveness of absolutism: did it work?

At the outset, one should stress that it was possible to mobilise resources for war, to create a fiscal-military state, without establishing absolutism. In England the Stuarts tried in vain to break out of the financial straitjacket imposed by the need to seek Parliamentary consent to taxation, but after 1688, with Parliament's active support, the armed forces and revenue grew by leaps and bounds. The officials who collected those revenues – above all the excise – became among the most technically proficient (and closely supervised) in Europe.[40] England's case shows the advantage of possessing an effective national representative institution. By contrast in the Dutch Republic each province and major town reserved the power to put its interests before those of the nation as a whole. That such a cumbersome system worked was due partly to the political skills and public spirit of the Republic's leaders, partly to the exceptional wealth of a few great towns in the province of Holland, which gave them a predominant voice in both the States of Holland and the States General; the fact that the members of these assemblies were nominated rather than elected and spoke for the interests of small, plutocratic oligarchies made for a greater measure of cohesion. But there was a danger here: often the mainly agricultural landward provinces accused Holland of putting its own interests first. On the other hand Holland's wealth enabled the Republic to mobilise far greater resources, in relation to its size, than monarchies like France or Spain. (It is also worth remarking that where taxation was levied by consent, it was usually collected more quickly and with less wastage: in Spain, Russia, even early Stuart England the king could receive as little as one-third of what the taxpayer paid.)[41] In addition, as the leading trading powers of their day, both the Republic and England developed large money markets where loans could be raised relatively cheaply. Even the Dutch, however, had their fears of absolutism. The princes of Orange traditionally held the offices of *stadhouder* (lieutenant) and captain general in the Republic's service, but sometimes wished to be more. William II died in 1650 just after launching a putsch against the city of Amsterdam. His son, William III, established (through the skilful manipulation of institutions and individuals) a position of quasi-regal power – it was said half-jokingly after 1688 that he was king in Holland and *stadhouder* in England – but made no move to press for the title of king.[42]

In both England and the Republic a fiscal-military state was established by consent, because it was widely seen as being necessary for national survival. Elsewhere, where consent could not be obtained or where there was no mechanism for obtaining it, fiscal-military states were established by kings. In general, the more effectively they imposed their will and eradicated or neutralised the opposition of those groups who stood between themselves and their subjects, the more successful they were. Sweden and Prussia were the outstanding examples of kingdoms with small populations whose resources were channelled rigorously into war. Other states of similar size, such as Bavaria or Saxony, achieved little on the international stage. As Jean Bérenger emphasises, the Austrian rulers never fully overcame the problems of integrating their territories, which were to become even more scattered and disparate with the acquisition of the southern Netherlands, Naples, Milan and Sicily after the War of the Spanish Succession. Poland, unable to agree on how to use its considerable resources, was to be carved up by its more organised neighbours. To west and east, France and Russia, while much less efficient than the Swedes or Prussians, had sufficient resources to put huge armies into the field. Spain, propelled by an odd mixture of fortuitous marriages and American silver into a precocious eminence which its backward domestic economy did not fully warrant, never overcame its regional imbalances (graphically described by I. A. A. Thompson) and fell behind as others surged forward in the seventeenth century. (Once shorn of some of the burden of empire, Spain's international fortunes revived somewhat in the eighteenth century.[43])

Success in war is perhaps the simplest indicator of the strength of a monarchy – and given that war was the *métier* of kings, perhaps the most appropriate; but what of its power at home? For some, like Prussia, war was virtually the sole priority: the king concentrated on raising men and money, leaving most other aspects of government in the hands of local landowners: much the same was true (though for very different reasons) in Spain and (later) England. Elsewhere the crown's ambitions were greater and the picture was more complex. Let us therefore look at the archetype of absolutism, France, with the aim not so much of showing how French government worked, as Roger Mettam does so deftly, but rather drawing up a crude balance sheet of success and failure.

In many respects the monarchy was much more powerful at the end of the seventeenth century than at the beginning. In 1690 the French fleet defeated the combined English and Dutch fleets off Beachy Head; in 1621 the royal fleet had been defeated by that of the great Huguenot stronghold of La Rochelle. Colbert had made a start on the codification of France's labyrinth of laws. The surviving provincial estates now docilely voted what the king demanded, although, as with the Cortes of Castile, the money was not necessarily collected in full. Open opposition from the *parlements* and other sovereign courts had ended (for the time being) and after 1675 there was no major revolt against taxation. The Huguenots, once a 'state within a state', had been driven underground or abroad. If the nobility had not been tamed of their habits of violence, these were now confined to the practice of duelling and posed no great threat to the public peace; the great supranational noble families (like the Guise) had mostly lost their power-bases outside France. It seemed that the effective power of the crown was greater than ever before.

As Roger Mettam shows, such appearances were in part deceptive – vested interests saw little reason to oppose measures which did not threaten them – and the crown was certainly not all-powerful. The king could deal brutally with dissident individuals, much as other kings could: even William III expressed surprise and displeasure that English law did not allow for judicial torture. In matters which the king regarded as important, unremitting effort and concentration of resources could bring spectacular results, but such effort could not be applied everywhere. Once the crown slackened its military pressure on the Huguenots and its surveillance of 'new converts' to Catholicism, many resumed clandestine Protestant worship. Some of the aims of government were beyond the capabilities of any seventeenth-century regime, especially those concerned with improving the economy. But there were other structural weaknesses at least as intractable as the problems imposed by distance and poor communications. First, Louis XIV never began to unravel the tangle of institutions and jurisdictions which he had inherited. He, his ministers and his *intendants* sought to manage the existing system, not to change it. There remained innumerable problems of competing jurisdictions, which the crown could exploit by setting one against another, but which also involved officials and litigants in a huge expense of time and money. Second, the more decision-making was concentrated in the king and at Versailles, the slower it became. There was simply too much business, the wheels of government ground slowly and the very thoroughness of the king and his councils made matters slower still. If an item came before a royal council, it would send to the local *intendant* or another local official for a report. Having read the report and other submissions, it would hand down a decision; but if some local interest protested against the outcome, the council would call for more information. As the piles of dossiers mounted, so decisions took longer and longer. Meanwhile, although sovereign courts and the like ceaseed to offer overt opposition to the royal will, they were adept at defending their interests through litigation and appeals to the council. The provincial estates, as they became more and more involved in tax collection and the raising of loans, became almost indistinguishable from other administrative and judicial institutions, practising much the same techniques of evasion, obstruction and manipulation.[44]

Now the fact that the council based its decisions on full information, and was willing to reconsider in the face of protest, meant that competing interests could hope for a fair hearing – and could pursue one another through the legal labyrinth. Few needed ever to resort to open opposition. But the cumbersome nature of the machinery and ever-growing volume of business reduced the possibility of direct personal control by the king or even by his ministers. Bureaucracies tend to grow and, as they grow, the bureaucrats come to enjoy greater and greater discretion. Strong-minded kings, like Frederick the Great of Prussia, established elaborate checks and spy systems within their administrations, but even Frederick was sometimes grossly misled.[45] In France, by the end of Louis XIV's reign the foreign minister needed a large secretariat to process all the reports he received and the king was able to hear only a small fraction of his ambassadors' dispatches. Those who selected what he heard could effectively limit the options open to him; similarly, the dossiers prepared by *intendants* (and the lobbying of powerful courtiers) could determine the council's decisions. By Louis XIV's death the administrative machine upon which royal absolutism depended had grown much too large for the king to control.[46]

French absolutism also suffered from two other major structural weaknesses. One was venality of office. French kings had long raised money by selling offices, a form of disguised borrowing. The official recouped his investment not only through his salary, but through the fees he charged to those he dealt with and various privileges, including tax exemptions and noble status. Sales of office thus brought ready cash, but at a heavy long-term cost in salaries, extra burdens on those who paid taxes and an increase in the number of those who did not. The more offices the crown created, the harder it was to sell them and the more extensive the fees and privileges that had to be added to make them attractive. In addition, in return for a modest annual payment, officials were allowed to pass on their offices to their heirs. The system had advantages: it made for professionalism as fathers trained their sons and created a body of officials independent of the great nobility; but they were equally independent of the king and intermarriage came to reinforce an esprit de corps which could be used to frustrate the royal will. For this reason, as H. W. Koch points out, venal office-holding was quickly eradicated in Prussia, but it became more and more deeply entrenched in France and Spain.[47]

Successive ministers were well aware of the problems created by venality, but it continued to grow. It represented an accumulated debt upon which the crown could not renege. One reason why Louis XIV won the cooperation of his nobles and officials was that he treated them fairly; there was no return to the sordid and dishonest expedients of Mazarin, extorting money from particular groups while hoping not to provoke a broadly-based opposition. The continuing growth of venality was a sign of French absolutism's second structural weakness: the incompatibility of war and domestic reform. To rationalise and streamline the administration, to redeem debts (including venal offices) and to overhaul the finances of towns peace was essential, as there would then be some spare revenue to devote to debt redemption (which in turn would reduce the cost of government in future). Marillac in 1629–30 and Colbert in 1668–70 hoped that their masters would put reform before war, but were disappointed. Every war brought a rash of new taxes and offices: existing offices were repeatedly subdivided. To Colbert's despair towns were allowed to borrow heavily to meet their tax quotas. The net result was that the crown was left with an ever more unwieldy administration and an ever greater burden of debt.

It would perhaps be misleading to conclude on too pessimistic a note. It would be naïve to expect twentieth-century standards of efficiency (whatever they are) of a seventeenth-century administration, hampered by poor communications, insufficient financial resources and a personnel limited in numbers and proficiency. To this should be added a legacy of inconsistency and diversity, a view of office as private property and a well-entrenched habit of putting local interests first. One could codify and rationalise to some extent, but to attempt too much too fast (as Joseph II was to find) could bring disaster. Absolute kingship, like any other form of politics, was the art of the possible. Moreover, if the ambitions of absolute monarchs often exceeded their capabilities, their achievements were considerable in the areas which mattered most to them: war and diplomacy. Gustav Adolf, the Great Elector and Peter the Great radically changed their respective kingdoms. Of course people got hurt and the English tut-tutted about the horrors of living under absolutism, quietly forgetting their own treatment of Catholic Irish and Jacobite Scots. They talked of the huge tax burden on the downtrodden French, blissfully unaware that by the late eighteenth century the English were paying more.[48]

Absolute monarchies helped to bring a sense of nationhood to disparate territories, to establish a measure of public order and to promote prosperity.[49] If minorities and dissidents suffered under absolutism, they suffered also (if to a lesser extent) in Britain and the Dutch Republic; as A. F. Upton reminds us, some seventeenth-century societies were stiflingly conformist. The differences between regimes in the seventeenth and eighteenth centuries were perhaps of degree rather than kind. And for many the alternative to absolutism was not English parliamentarism but the military anarchy of the French Wars of Religion or the Thirty Years War, or else the yoke of an alien conqueror, be he Dane, Tartar or Turk. As the Poles discovered in the eighteenth century, the price of liberty could be extinction. We need therefore to see absolutism in the terms of its own time, to jettison the liberal and democratic preconceptions of the twentieth century and instead think in terms of an impoverished and precarious existence, of low expectations and of submission to the will of God and to the king. In such a world the concentration of power, hitherto dispersed among competing authorities, in the hands of one (hopefully conscientious) individual could indeed seem in the best interests of the governed. If 'tyranny' was inevitable, better tyranny of one than of many.

The essays in this volume follow no set pattern. This reflects in part the differing experience of the various countries, in part the divergent views of historians. How far one chooses to stress the strength or weakness of a regime or institution is in part a matter of individual emphasis, but it is often difficult to devise criteria to measure such 'strength'. Thus the Estates of Languedoc in the eighteenth century voted the king without debate the 'free gift' of money which had still been a matter for negotiation in the 1660s. They also met for much longer, transacted far more business and played a much greater part in provincial administration, dealing not only with tax collection but also with improving communications, the movement of troops and so on. Seen in conventional political terms, the estates seem weaker: in terms of their ability to determine how Languedoc was run, they were stronger. More fundamentally, attempts to measure the 'strength' of monarchy imply an element of conflict (or at least friction) between the interests of ruler and ruled, but this may be misleading. It may be more helpful to think in terms of negotiation and mediation within a broadly accepted framework of laws and values, as in France; elsewhere, it is worth remembering that habits of obedience would be so deeply engrained as to be instinctive. Absolutism could never simply be imposed: it had to accommodate itself to the society in which it developed.

1. The Idea of Absolutism

J. H. BURNS

THE TERM 'absolutism' entered the language of politics – in French – during the decade after the Revolution in 1789. Its first appearance in English came more than a generation later, in the radical and liberal literature of the years around 1830. The system or concept to which the term referred was of course much older; and there is a sense in which its emergence may be located in the period with which this book is concerned. It was with absolute monarchy that the revolutionary and radical writers of the late eighteenth and the early nineteenth centuries were contending, seeing it as the most stubborn obstacle to the achievement of their aims. Absolute monarchy had been the preponderant political system of that *ancien régime* which was overthrown in 1789 only to reappear, it seemed, in the era of the Holy Alliance after 1815. And it had been the seventeenth century that saw the consolidation of the European states system of the *ancien régime*. The idea of absolutism does indeed have a wider political application: the sovereignty of Parliament, for instance, is, in juridical terms, an absolute sovereignty recognising, as A. V. Dicey pointed out a century ago, no legal limitations. It is, however, in its application to absolute monarchy that the term has had its greatest historical importance, and it is in this sense that the idea will be analysed here.

This is a case where it is helpful to begin at the end of the story, with an interpretation of the fully developed concept of absolute monarchy in the last quarter of the seventeenth century. The great exemplar of the concept in operation was of course the France of Louis XIV; and the interpretation to be considered is that of an eminent French divine. Bossuet's *Politics derived from Holy Scripture* was published in 1709, five years after his death. One of its concerns is to distinguish power that is merely arbitrary from power that is in the true sense absolute. The king's power, Bossuet argued, was indeed absolute, but it was at the same time sacred, paternal and 'subject to reason'.[1] These attributes will have to be considered more fully at a later stage. For the moment what matters is the crucial claim that absolute power is not, as such, arbitrary.

If we turn to another writer who died in 1704, John Locke, we find that such a distinction is totally rejected. For Locke, writing as the political conflicts and debates of seventeenth-century England reached their second great climax in the Revolution of 1688, the term 'absolute, arbitrary power' is virtually a compound which cannot be broken down into separate elements. Power that is absolute *is* by its very nature arbitrary; and such power, Locke believes, degenerates almost inevitably into actual tyranny. For a ruler to wield power of this kind is in any case at odds with the essential liberty of those who are his subjects. When Locke found Sir Robert Filmer apparently defending the arbitrary power of the king, he exclaimed that

> Slavery is so vile and miserable an Estate of Man . . . that 'tis hardly to be conceived, that an *Englishman*, much less a *Gentleman*, should plead for 't.[2]

That, in essence, is what the opponents of absolute monarchy believed they were resisting and seeking to refute. Plainly it is not what those who defended absolute monarchy thought they were upholding and advocating. To understand the idea of absolutism in a way that will be historically illuminating, we must see it in terms other than those which equate it in effect with tyranny. To this end it is useful to stay for the time being within the context of English political debate in the seventeenth century.

That debate came to be, and has often been represented as having been throughout, a contest between 'absolutism' and 'constitutionalism', between 'absolute' and 'limited' conceptions of monarchy. Matters, however, look a good deal less clear-cut when we examine the earlier stages of the controversy in Stuart England. When, in the 1750s, David Hume embarked on his great *History of England*, he was puzzled and disconcerted by some of what he found in early seventeenth-century sources. In particular he was surprised by a fairly general assumption at that period that the English monarchy was an 'absolute' one: that the king's powers were of essentially the same kind in England and in France; but, at the same time, that those powers did not include a power (in words Hume quoted from Sir Walter Raleigh) 'Turk-like to tread under his feet all their natural and fundamental laws, privileges and ancient rights'. This is, once again, Bossuet's distinction between absolute and arbitrary power. Hume rejected, albeit hesitantly, the possibility that the word 'absolute' had changed its meaning over the century and a half before he wrote.[3] Yet this was in effect what had happened, in English usage coloured by the ideological controversy reflected in Locke. It is the older meaning that needs to be recovered here, since that meaning is fundamental in the absolutist doctrines of the *ancien régime*.

If we look again at Raleigh as quoted by Hume, we find a way of distinguishing between two kinds of monarchy that may be helpful in this enquiry. The distinction is between what Raleigh calls 'entire' and 'limited' monarchies. In the former – which he explicitly exemplifies from 'the English kingdom' – he suggests that 'the whole power of ordering all state matters, both in peace and war, doth, by law and custom, appertain to the prince'; and this general power includes, among other things, the specific powers of making law, creating magistracies, contracting alliances, and declaring war. In contrast, the ruler under 'limited or restrained' monarchy 'hath no full power in all the points and matters of state'. Such a ruler may, for example, be no more than a 'military king', a leader in war with no sovereignty in time of peace: Raleigh illustrates this from 'the Polonian king'.[4] This may serve to remind us of an even sharper conceptual and linguistic distinction, which Raleigh does not use, but which was common enough in the political literature of the early modern period. In this usage the title of *king* was denied to rulers who laboured under such limits as Raleigh has in mind, even though they might in some respects be regarded as 'monarchs': the Doge of Venice was a frequently cited example. It is important to bear in mind that the absolute monarchy with which we are primarily concerned was emphatically a royal or regal monarchy: it is the absolutism of kings in the full sense of the word that is at issue.

There are other noteworthy points in the language Raleigh uses. Take first the notion of 'full power', possessed by the king in an 'entire' monarchy, but not by a 'limited' monarch. This clearly echoes one of the central concepts developed by medieval canon lawyers in their exposition and vindication of the papal monarchy in the church. *Plenitudo potestatis*, fullness of power, belonged to the pope as head – at least under the supreme headship of Christ – of the church on earth. Other ecclesiastical rulers there were, and they had their powers; but they held power only to discharge their *pars sollicitudinis*, their share in a responsibility which, in regard to the well-being and good estate of the whole church (the *status ecclesiae*), belonged ultimately to the pope. Bearing in mind the changes in ecclesiastical polity that characterised the era of the Reformation and Counter-Reformation, and especially the fragmentation into sovereign states of what had been, at least in principle, a universal *respublica Christiana*, we can see how easily the idea of 'fullness of power' could be transferred from pope to king. The pope, it is true, claimed to be 'the vicar of Christ'; but that title had been accorded to medieval temporal rulers too, long before the end of 'medieval Christendom'.[5]

This does not exhaust the lines of thought suggested by Raleigh's concept of a power that is 'entire'. Recalling the words John Donne applied to his metaphorical island, we may infer that a power 'entire of itself' is an *independent* power. This in turn points in two directions. On the one hand, when Bossuet sought to elucidate his description of royal power as 'absolute', he added the words 'by which is meant independent'. The absence of any kind of juridical or 'constitutional' dependence on any other power (saving always the power of God, 'By whom kings reign') had become an essential point of absolutist doctrine. Even more striking, however, is what we find by moving in the opposite chronological direction, back to the early sixteenth century. At that time the issue between what we would call 'constitutionalism' and 'absolutism' was still being contested in regard to the polity of the church, in the debate between papalism and conciliarism. John Mair, a leading exponent of the conciliarist case, offers a particularly interesting analysis of political power, with special reference to monarchy. His position, so far as the church is concerned, is firmly on the 'constitutionalist' side. The power of the whole church, represented in a general council, is ultimately superior to that of the pope as monarchical ruler. Even this corporate or collective power, however, is not absolute or unlimited: it is merely 'more unlimited' (*illimitatior*) than that of the ruler, who is in the last analysis the servant of the community. There *is* an absolute supreme power over the church: it is the power of Christ, which Mair describes as the 'supreme independent power' (*suprema potestas . . . independens*).[6] The issue between the upholders and the opponents of absolutism arose over the claim that, in the temporal realm, this supreme independent power belonged, and could belong only, to the king.

There is more than this to be derived from Mair's account of the kingship of Christ. In another phrase he applies to the *suprema potestas* two further epithets, calling it *fontalis* and *inabrogabilis*.[7] The latter translates readily into a term familiar in the language of 'divine-right' monarchy: the king's power is 'indefeasible', it cannot be annulled or forfeited. The word *fontalis* may be less easy to provide with an English equivalent; but the concept it expresses is equally central in the ideology of absolutism. The king's power is the *fons*, the source or origin of all other powers in the state. All such powers are derivative: they are dependent upon the one power that is *in*dependent. This applies, it must be emphasised, not only to powers of jurisdiction or administration vested in individuals or groups. It applies equally to law. The making of law, the legislative power, may not, in this early modern period, have acquired quite the central position it was to have in the fully developed modern sovereign state. It was none the less moving in that direction; and that development, like so much else, was not so much a radical innovation or new departure as the fuller realisation of what had been emerging already in medieval theory and practice. By the mid-thirteenth century, after all, Thomas Aquinas was including in his definition of law the requirement that it be 'made and promulgated by him who has care of the whole community'.[8] John Mair, conciliarist as he was and 'constitutionalist' though he may have been, saw the ideal king as, among other things, the 'good lawgiver', with power both to make law and to dispense from its provisions.[9]

This is by no means the end of the matter: there are complications only just below the surface of what has been said so far, to which we shall have to come back. For the moment, however, it can perhaps be claimed that the lineaments of absolute monarchy are emerging in recognisable forms. The ruler in such a system wields a supreme and indefeasible power, from which all other powers in the state are derived. All these powers depend upon his in a way that his power depends on no other. That power, again, is characterised by a plenitude or fullness which, by its very nature, cannot be shared with anybody else. It is a power not derived, humanly speaking, from any other source; and it is, in Raleigh's phrase, 'entire'.

Yet further scrutiny of Raleigh's account of the matter suggests that, however true these statements may be, they are not the whole truth. A number of nuances demand attention. Thus the absolute king's power is entire or full in respect of 'all state-matters'; the limited ruler does not have 'full power in all the points and matters of state'. 'Entirety' here is not the same as totality. We may suppose, and indeed can confidently assume, that 'state-matters' do not embrace all the varied concerns and interests of those who are the ruler's subjects in those matters. Again, if we look more closely even at those things that do 'appertain to the prince', we find that they do so 'by law and custom'. And in the passage in Raleigh that perplexed Hume in the 1750s, the essential distinction between such 'absolute monarchs' as those of England and France on the one hand and, on the other, the 'Turk-like' claims of Philip II of Spain lies precisely in the area of 'natural and fundamental laws, privileges and ancient rights'. All these, it seems, will be respected by an absolute king on pain of falling under the condemnation of tyranny. Moreover, still following Raleigh, we find the assertion that: 'In every just state, some part of the government is, or ought to be, imparted to the people, as in a kingdom, a voice and suffrage in making laws'. Yet in his posthumous *Prerogative of Parliaments*, Raleigh insists that even in parliament the king acts by virtue of his absolute power.[10] How is all this to be understood?

For elucidation we may turn to a work of much greater weight than Raleigh's political writings, illuminating though these are. Jean Bodin's *Six livres de la République* (1576; Latin version 1586) is one of the major pieces of political thinking produced in the sixteenth century, one of the most widely influential works in early modern political literature. Its reception was not, it is true, uniformly favourable or uncritical. It is noteworthy, however, that the most critical responses to Bodin's theory of sovereignty – the core of his thought – came from Germany. The complex structure of the Holy Roman Empire, embodying the jealously guarded privileges of free cities and princely states, could not easily accommodate a Bodinian sovereign. And since Bodin's purported to be a general theory applicable to any society entitled to claim to be a genuine state or commonwealth, it was entirely legitimate to question it on the lines adopted by his German critics. At the same time, it is equally appropriate, in the context of an enquiry into the idea of absolutism institutionalised in the typical monarchical states of the sixteenth and seventeenth centuries, to emphasise Bodin's primary concern with precisely that form of state. Writing during the French wars of religion, Bodin sought above all to vindicate the paramount authority of the French crown. In doing so he developed a theory of sovereignty which might or might not 'work' in non-monarchical or non-unitary systems, but which proved invaluable to those whose interest lay in elevating and upholding the 'absolutist' claims of divine-right monarchs. In such quarters the response was as prompt as it was positive. Within five years of the first appearance of the *République*, Adam Blackwood, a Franco-Scot defending Mary Stuart against what he took to be the radically subversive views of George Buchanan, drew on Bodin's analysis of the attributes of sovereignty to bolster the argument of his *Pro regibus Apologia* (1581). In England too Bodin's ideas gained wide currency – and not only through the medium of Richard Knollwe's 1606 translation of the text.[11] Here was a theory, it seemed, peculiarly apt for the defence of absolute kingship.

Sovereignty for Bodin is absolute, perpetual and indivisible. It is also – and perhaps above all – a power of *command*.[12] To make law by command, law that is universally binding upon all the sovereign's subjects, is in Bodin's view the most essential attribute of sovereignty: all its other attributes flow from or depend upon this. The language of sovereignty, we may say, speaks always in the imperative mood: here the earlier medieval idea that the king – and it is primarily of kings that Bodin is thinking – is 'emperor [*imperator*] in his own kingdom' acquires the full weight of its underlying notion of *imperium* – command, the right or power of commanding. Another medieval theme to find full expression here is what has been called voluntarism – an emphasis on will as the essential element in law and government. The formula, *le roy* (or *la reine*) *le veult*, is a surviving trace of what was once the heart of the lawmaking process. Command, expressing the will of the sovereign, is the essence of law. The concept of will, however, has its problematic aspect.

The problem emerges in Bodin's text when he says that: 'The evil will of a tyrant . . . urges him to an abuse of absolute power' (p. 35). The mere exercise of absolute power as such, even if that exercise takes the form of what purport to be sovereign commands, does not satisfy the requirements of the theory. There is no question here of defending tyranny or of a doctrine that might of itself makes right. This consideration leads us back to a closer inspection of Bodin's position. What we find is that law properly so called is not simply the command but the right or rightful command (*droict commandement*) of the sovereign. Its rightness, again, consists essentially in its conforming to the principles of divine and natural law (pp. 29, 43). Absolute though the king's power is and must be – independent of any other authority, not subject to any kind of challenge or appellate procedure, exercised freely and regardless of the subjects' assent or dissent – it is none the less a power to be used within bounds. Neither is the matter exhausted by referring to divine and natural law with no further specification.

For one thing, the absolute sovereignty Bodin envisages is a power operative only in and over a state or commonwealth; and he begins his analysis by defining the state in a particular way. It consists, he says, in the rightful government (*droict gouvernement*) of a number of families and of what belongs to them in common by a sovereign power (p. 1). Apart from its further invocation of the notion of rightfulness, this alerts us to the basic importance for Bodin – and for many other early modern thinkers – of the patriarchal family or household. This elementary unit of social life is (in the person of its head, the *paterfamilias*) subject to the sovereign and his laws. The internal government of the household, however, is a matter for the husband and father who rules it and not for intervention by the state except in emergencies. The full implications of this for Bodin's political theory, and therefore for the idea of absolutism, may escape notice if we do not bear in mind that the family Bodin is thinking of is an essentially important economic entity. Looking back to the definition of the state, we see that it consists, in part, of the government or administration of that which belongs in common to all the families of which it is composed. This is indeed the *res publica*, the *chose publique*, the common wealth. It is distinct from the properties on which and by which the several families live. Thus the sovereign has no vested right to interfere with the enjoyment of these private properties or with their administration by each *paterfamilias*. If the state cannot be fully sustained from the public domain which is the essential element in the *res publica*, the sovereign can draw upon private wealth and revenues with the consent of the citizens who, as 'free subjects' in Bodin's definition of citizenship (p. 19), control those resources. It is true that Bodin's theory of taxation – for that is what we are now considering – is not entirely without ambiguity; but one strand at least in his thinking on the subject involves an essential relationship between taxation and consent and between consent and representation.[13]

This is part – and an important part – of what is to be understood by one of Bodin's most crucial distinctions. True or legitimate or 'royal' monarchy must, according to Bodin, be distinguished from despotic monarchy; and perhaps the most important differential feature lies precisely in the matter of the ruler's power over his subjects' property. Under despotism – the result, characteristically, of conquest – that property is at the absolute disposal of the monarch. Even so, Bodin insists, despotism is not the same as tyranny; for a despot need not be committed to the merely selfish exploitation of his subjects which characterises the tyrant. Neither, however, is despotic rule to be confused with the legitimate sovereignty of a royal monarch, a true king (pp. 56–69).

Such a king will respect the laws of God and of nature in his government. Specifically, he will refrain from arbitrary interference with the *res privatae*, the property and other concerns of the families over which he rules. Even this, however, does not exhaust what Bodin has to contribute to an elucidation of the way in which absolute monarchy was to be conceived in the seventeenth century. It will be remembered that for Raleigh and those who thought like him the absolute king, unlike the Turk-like tyrant, respected not only what we might call his subjects' natural rights, but also those rights and liberties which were constituted by 'fundamental laws'. Here too seventeenth-century advocates of absolute monarchy could invoke the authority of Jean Bodin. The Bodinian sovereign, absolute though he was by juridical definition, must abide not only by the laws of God and nature but also by what Bodin calls *lois royales* or *leges imperii*. These are, in effect, constitutional norms, defining the basis and location of the sovereign power itself. They are the rules in term of which that power *is* sovereign and in accordance with which it must be exercised. Bodin, it must be acknowledged, takes for granted a good deal more than he develops explicitly in this connection. The one example he cites of such a fundamental law is the Salic law determining the succession to the French throne. There is, however, no reason to doubt that he envisaged this category of law as extending to the whole structure of the *res publica* and the protection of its integrity.[14] The realm is not at the arbitrary mercy of the king who governs it through his absolute power but who possesses that power as a legitimate sovereignty only in the matrix of a system he has not established and must not subvert.

In transmitting these ideas to his readers Bodin undoubtedly made his own distinctive contribution to the analysis of political society. At the same time, however, he was acting as a channel through which large parts of late medieval thought were passed on to later generations. The concept of absolute monarchy so far suggested here could to a considerable extent be found in fifteenth-century and earlier sources.[15] The development of the concept has not as yet been traced further than the early years of the seventeenth century; and it will be necessary in due course to consider what other versions of, or elements in, absolutist theory appeared before, during and after that period. First, however, it will be useful to go back to Bossuet's view at the very end of the century and to clarify somewhat the terms in which he depicts the power of the absolute monarch. His understanding of the term 'absolute' itself has indeed been elucidated in what has been said so far; but equally important for Bossuet – and for the ideology of absolutism – are the other elements in his picture.

The king's absolute power, then, is 'sacred'. This reminds us of something we are doubtless in little danger of forgetting: the 'divine-right' element in early modern concepts of kingship. What matters here is not, or not primarily, the basic belief that political power is 'ordained of God'. That had been orthodox doctrine from the beginning of Christian history; but in itself it said nothing about kings and kingship, or even about monarchy, as such. On the other hand, there was nothing particularly novel in the sixteenth- and seventeenth-century belief in a special divinity that hedged kings. Far back in medieval thinking about government – in the Latin west at least as far as the Carolingian period – such a belief is to be found. The sacramental or quasi-sacramental efficacy ascribed to the ceremony of anointing at a king's inauguration is one manifestation of this; and the very special place that rite had in France, the focus of so much later 'divine-right' ideology, enhances its significance for the idea of absolutism in general.[16] Even without that dimension, however, the notion that the king occupied in his realm the place of God himself in the universe he created and ruled was central in the image of kingship in the age of absolutism. James VI and I was only one writer among many to seize on the point that (as was alleged) kings were called 'gods' in the Bible:

> God gives not Kings the style of Gods in vain,
> For on his throne his Sceptre do they sway.[17]

If there was any novelty, or at least a distinctively new emphasis, in what the early modern centuries made of this medieval heritage, it was perhaps in associating the 'divinity' or sacred character of kingship with hereditary succession. Medieval realms had, it is true, tended more and more to become the inheritance of particular royal families; and certainly by the fifteenth century there was a strongly developing view that hereditary monarchy was the superior and in some sense the more 'natural' form. Yet the fact remained that the two most notable monarchies of medieval Europe – the empire and the papacy – were elective and at the same time entitled in a very special way to claim to be 'sacred'. It may be worth bearing in mind that by the period most directly under consideration here the papal claim to be a genuinely universal monarchy was, at least in respect of effective jurisdiction, a dead letter, while the Holy Roman Empire had itself become effectively hereditary in the house in Habsburg.

The hereditary character of early modern kingship also accorded well with Bossuet's second suggested attribute of royal power, that it is 'paternal'. The authority of the *paterfamilias* was, within its domestic sphere, at once absolute and benevolent. It was, so the argument ran, an authority exercised not for the benefit or selfish advantage of the ruler, but for the moral and material good of his subjects. Some advocates of absolute monarchy – Filmer is a notable English instance – built their position very largely on the foundation of this analogy.[18] There may be different views as to how far the ideology could and did draw on the realities of patriarchal family authority in the seventeenth century.[19] What is clear at any rate is that the language of patriarchalism had roots in experience sufficiently deep for the analogy to retain its vitality for a remarkably long time.

The paternal image, in any case, had its theological as well as its sociological aspect; and it is necessary at this stage to return to that aspect of the subject. The sacred and paternal authority wielded by hereditary monarchs was conceived as resembling that of God. That this implied an ultimate supremacy over all other authorities is clear enough. Yet the political theology of absolute kingship is less straightforward than this might suggest. God's power had itself been envisaged in medieval scholasticism, and was still envisaged in seventeenth-century divinity, as having more than one aspect or mode of operation. In particular, the very notion of absolute power (*absoluta potestas*) was in that context distinguished from an 'ordinary' or 'ordained' power (*potestas ordinaria/ordinata*). The latter was the power through which God normally governed the world, operating within limits and according to laws he had himself prescribed. Divine omnipotence, however, must include a power to override those limits, to suspend those laws, when God's providential care and wisdom made this necessary for the well-being of his creatures. All of this could readily be turned to account in an exposition of human kingship in which the ruler, in exercising power, normally respects the rules he has laid down, but reserves always the *absoluta potestas* which enables him to disregard law, custom, privilege and established rights in the interest of the common good of his subjects.[20] This is evidently part of what Bossuet means by defining royal power as 'absolute'; but it is also connected with his fourth point, which states that the king's power is 'subject to reason'. This needs elucidation.

The analysis of 'absolute power' here shifts from theology to jurisprudence and political theory (though it is to be noted that Bossuet, as was natural in an ecclesiastical writer, found the 'reason' to which the king's power is subject first and foremost in the divine wisdom revealed in Scripture). As the notion of *absoluta potestas* took shape in medieval thought and practice, it acquired a characteristic vocabulary of more or less technical terms. The contribution made by canon lawyers, already mentioned in connection with the notion of *plenitudo potestatis*, is again crucial here. It was in the analysis of papal authority that much of the later language of absolute monarchy was coined and deployed. The pope is envisaged in that analysis as having the right to act, to legislate, 'of his own motion' (*motu proprio*). Whatever limits may and should be recognised in the exercise of his ordinary power can be overridden by his absolute power. His will was in itself a sufficient reason for what he did: it was here that Juvenal's phrase, *sit pro ratione voluntas* ('let will stand for reason') was pressed into service by the jurists. This did not imply that the pope acted irrationally, but rather that his will was supposed to be guided by good reasons even if these were not readily accessible to lesser mortals. One variation on this theme was the formula whereby the pope decreed 'from his certain knowledge' (*ex certa scientia*). Once again the decisive will is not conceived as acting in an arbitrary vacuum but in the light of knowledge of which the certainty is guaranteed.[21]

All this was readily transferable into the temporal realm. Much of it had in any case been inspired and supported by the analogous case of imperial power in Roman civil law (at least in some aspects of that law). After all, the source, it may be argued, of the very concept of absolute power lies in the Roman-law maxim, *Princeps legibus solutus est*, 'the prince is free from the laws'. Certainly by the fifteenth century the language of absolute monarchy was becoming firmly established in the national or quasi-national kingdoms which were effectively undermining the universalist claims of pope and emperor alike. The Spanish realms, especially Castile, and the kingdom of Naples afford striking illustrations. When Alfonso V of Aragon had established himself as Alfonso I of Naples, the documents of his Italian realm became impregnated with the terminology of absolute royal power. That language might encounter greater resistance from resolutely 'contractarian' traditions of Aragonese *pactismo*; but across the border in Castile–León the Latin phrases of absolutist jurisprudence increasingly found their way into the vernacular documents of the fifteenth, with the concept of 'certain knowledge' (*cierta ciencia*) prominent among them.[22]

It is not of course to be supposed that the ideologues of absolute monarchy, flattering though their purposes no doubt often were, seriously suggested that the king for the time being – who might well, apart from anything else, be a child under indefeasible hereditary succession – necessarily possessed in his own person the qualities and the knowledge requisite for the effective and beneficent exercise of absolute power. It was indeed important that he should have that equipment in the highest possible degree and should cultivate all his talents assiduously. For this reason the education of the prince is a central, recurrent and (be it said) intolerably repetitive part of the literature of monarchical government. Bossuet, for example, plainly expects the king he envisages to engage in hard intellectual labour.[23] However, the 'reason' to which the king's power is 'subject' is not his alone, even when that is sustained by divine wisdom: it is also, and perhaps above all, the wisdom of his counsellors.

Good counsel is an absolutely indispensable element in the system of absolute monarchy. If we look back for a moment to Bossuet's insistence on the distinction between absolute and arbitrary power, we shall do well to take note of the fact that arbitrariness goes readily with caprice. Nor need the caprices of the ruler be as insane as those of a Caligula to incur the charge of abuse of power. It is in counsel, in deliberation with those whose knowledge and experience can supplement and complement his own, that the absolute ruler finds, in large measure, the wisdom he must have in order to rule well.[24]

The time has come to ask whether what has been said so far affords, even in a summary account such as this, an adequate analysis of the main elements in the idea of absolutism. The answer has to be that it does not. The first reason for this is that the essentially Bodinian view outlined above, even when elaborated in the scriptural rhetoric of Bossuet, leaves out of account some important ways of thinking about political power which certainly contributed to the idea – or at least to some ideas – of absolutism. One of these is the political philosophy of Neostoicism expressed in particular by the Flemish writer Justus Lipsius.[25]

It is true that the doctrine of Lipsius' *Politicorum sive civilis doctrinae libri sex* (1589) was by no means wholly antithetical to that of his contemporary Bodin. Both favour what has been called 'moderate absolutism', in which power is governed by the moral principles of natural and divine law. Lipsius may indeed appear to be more profoundly concerned than Bodin with the moral dimension of his theory, advocating a firmly Stoic ethos of moderation and self-control. At the same time there are also political divergences between the two. Notably, two of Lipsius' 'Six Books' are concerned with war and military organisation; and it is arguable that his most influential contribution to the absolutism of the early modern state lies just here. The army was to become one of the principal instruments of absolute monarchy in the seventeenth and eighteenth centuries. It is no accident that the standing army became one of the *bêtes noires* of Whig and other opponents of absolutism. The army envisaged by Lipsius and his many followers was something quite different from the feudal and post-feudal armies that had hitherto prevailed; and the key to the difference lies in discipline. It might be an allowable over-simplification to say that the pervasive notion of organised discipline under an authority which commands in the sure expectation of obedience is the keynote of the 'political Neostoicism' that was to be so important in the Europe of the absolutist age. It is relevant to point out that, in his more strictly political theory, Lipsius pays particular attention to what may be seen as at least an adumbration of 'bureaucratic' structures such as were to develop under absolute monarchy and then to extend their influence throughout the political life of the modern state.

In so far as we may gauge the importance and the influence of a book by the multiplicity of its editions, we must conclude that Lipsius was a writer who carried even greater weight than Bodin. His *Politicorum . . . libri sex* rapidly and over a period of many decades ran through an astonishing number of editions. Moreover, and the point is especially important at this stage in European history, it was very soon translated into half a dozen vernacular languages and more. One area of discussion where its influence was felt must at least be mentioned here, though it cannot be even tentatively explored. This is the area of 'reason of state'. To mention this is to recall that, ambiguous and controversial though he inevitably was, the figure of Machiavelli could never be ignored in discussions of political power in the early modern centuries. Obviously the notion of a skill or science directed to the establishment and maintenance of political control was relevant beyond the confines of absolute monarchy. Yet Machiavelli's most celebrated, or notorious, book had dealt with princely government, and the exigencies of statecraft might be especially urgent for a single ruler who claimed absolute command. At all events, a literature of this kind of political prudence was to appear in considerable abundance between the last decade of the sixteenth century and the middle of the seventeenth. Giovanni Botero's *Ragion di stato* appeared coincidentally in the same year (1589) as Lipsius' political treatise, and like it was soon translated into other languages. To call the book seminal may be to imply greater originality than it actually evinces; but it was certainly an important indicator of a major new emphasis in political writing.[26]

Here again, however, we may be struck by the unwillingness of those who discussed political problems in this period to break decisively with traditional values. It was central to the notion of 'reason of state' that it should authorise departures, in the interest of political success, from the ordinary rules of human behaviour. Yet nothing could have been further from the minds of most of those who wrote in this vein than to abandon or undermine the authority of those rules. They were well aware that such a subversion of moral principle might seem to be involved in what they advocated and might indeed have been the teaching of 'murderous Machiavel'. That, however (they insisted), was a false, even a diabolical interpretation of true reason of state, which fundamentally respects and upholds the restraints of natural law and religious doctrine even while allowing for the use of desperate remedies for desperate situations. The ruler may at times have to override the usual rules, but this is not to be taken as challenging their validity or their power to bind him as well as his subjects in ordinary circumstances. In this sense the doctrine of reason of state may, for our purposes, be seen as a particularly striking aspect of the broader concept of that *absoluta potestas* whereby the king might interrupt the usual course of law in the interest of the general well-being of his subjects. That the safety of the people should be the supreme law (*salus populi suprema lex esto*) was, after all, a maxim with a long and in no sense 'Machiavellian' pedigree.

Much of what has been said so far tends to suggest that the idea of what we have come to call absolutism took shape and grew largely within the matrix of traditional kingship. At the same time, it cannot be denied that tradition was being stretched, perhaps at times strained to something near breaking-point. A firmer emphasis on legislative power exercised by the sovereign's command; an ampler development of what might be called the mystique of divinely ordained hereditary monarchy; a new stress on the importance of disciplined organisation in both military and civil matters; a sharper awareness of what the realities of the political arena may demand of one who has to survive its hazards – these are some of the ways in which that strain may be said to have manifested itself. Yet the mould had not yet been decisively broken: a clear 'break-through' in fundamental thinking had not yet taken place.

It is that kind of breaking away from the established patterns of thought that we may expect to find in philosophical thinking more fundamental (though perhaps for that very reason less immediately influential) than that which has so far been considered here. In anything like a full account of the subject, such major intellectual structures as the natural-law jurisprudence of Grotius and Pufendorf and the naturalistic philosophy of Spinoza would have to be surveyed. No excuse is needed, however, for concentrating, within the present narrower compass, on the thought of Thomas Hobbes, with particular reference to his major work in what he himself called 'civil philosophy', *Leviathan* (1651). No book in the period, it may safely be claimed, threw down a sharper challenge to the accepted orthodoxies so profoundly respected in both earlier and later absolutist ideology.

To say this is not, of course, to suggest that Hobbes's ideas lacked roots in and affinities with earlier thinking. Still less does it mean that he was isolated from contemporary currents of thought; for he was in fact very much part of intellectual circles or groups both in England and in continental Europe in which there was an active and vigorous exchange of ideas. Two rather less apparent points may be made in that rather obvious connection. In the first place, it has been plausibly suggested that Hobbes's acquaintance with the work of Lipsius began during his student days at Oxford in the early years of James I's reign. The acquaintance was no mere casual encounter; for, this is the second point, Hobbes acknowledges the influence of Lipsius on his reading of history. That acknowledgement comes in the preface to his first published work, his translation of Thucydides.[27] Now Thucydides is one of the classical writers recognised as crucially important for the exposition of 'reason of state', so that we may properly link Hobbes with that genre of political writing as well as seeing him (as we must) primarily in the context of the new philosophy of nature and of man which was developing so rapidly in the first half of the seventeenth century.

In regard to the political or 'civil' dimension of that philosophy, however, it is helpful to begin with a comparison between Hobbes's position and the view we found in Jean Bodin. It is perhaps above all in this perspective that we can see the novelty of what Hobbes is advocating. If we take in reverse order the points at which the absolute sovereignty of a Bodinian monarch proved to be limited, we have first to consider the notion of 'fundamental' or (in our terminology) constitutional law. Here Hobbes's stance is firm and unequivocal. He does not deny the appropriateness of distinguishing some laws as fundamental; but he complains that the term has not been properly – or indeed at all – defined. In his view a law that is fundamental is 'that, by which Subjects are bound to uphold whatsoever power is given to the Sovereign . . . without which the Commonwealth cannot stand'.[28] The full meaning of this can be understood only in the total context of Hobbes's theory; but it is already plain that we have moved quite away from the kind of fundamental law that Bodin – or Raleigh – had in mind.

Next, Hobbes's position must be compared with Bodin's basic concept of an autonomous patriarchal household enjoying a natural right to the property that sustains it. Hobbes has no difficulty in acknowledging the reality of what he calls 'paternal dominion'; but his view of it is very different from the traditional ones. The purely natural relationship of 'generation' might, he argues, yield a parental authority shared by father and mother alike. The effective authority of the *paterfamilias* has quite another basis: it rests on the consent of the child – 'either expresse, or by other such sufficient arguments declared'; it exists, as Hobbes's marginal note declares, '*by Contract*' (pp. 153–4). The notion of natural authority, so prominent in traditionalist theories of monarchy, is wholly alien to Hobbes's political thinking. Again, where property is concerned, Hobbes insists that the 'Rules of Propriety (or *Meum* and *Tuum*)' are, and can only be, prescribed by the sovereign's command (p. 137). Specifically, in an area crucial for the patriarchal household, the distribution of land is made by the sovereign; and 'the propriety which a subject hath in his lands', while wholly proof against interference by other subjects, cannot exclude the sovereign on whose will it depends (pp. 190–1, 250–1). The family does indeed have an essential part in Hobbes's theory of society, but it is the part of 'a regular and lawful private body' existing by allowance of the sovereign power. Hobbes does not deny that in the state of affairs supposed to subsist before the establishing of civil society 'the Father and Master' were 'absolute Sovereigns in their own Families'. What he does deny is that this affords them any kind of immunity from sovereign power once that power is in being.

It may be as well to pause at this point to consider how far we are entitled to read Hobbes's theory as a theory of absolute monarchy rather than as a theory of absolute sovereignty applicable to any form of political organisation. That it does indeed have this latter character is abundantly clear: Hobbes insists that the rights of sovereignty are the same for all forms of state, regardless of how each particular state may have come into existence. Yet it is hardly less clear that he sees a decisive balance of advantage on the side of monarchy. The central part of the nineteenth chapter of *Leviathan* is given over to a careful analysis of the points at which monarchy is superior to other systems and to a minimising of those disadvantages in it which Hobbes is obliged to admit. The greatest problem for monarchical regimes, according to Hobbes, is to settle the succession to the sovereign power; and his solution of that problem reveals yet again how far he has moved away from traditional concepts. We have seen already that he rejects any allegedly 'natural' claim to hereditary succession and that he cannot, like Bodin, accept that the matter is dealt with by some fundamental law not amenable to the sovereign's will. His general principle is that: 'There is no perfect form of Government, where the disposing of the Succession is not in the present Sovereign'. Under monarchy this can only mean that each king is fully entitled to make such dispositions as he sees fit for the succession to his throne (pp. 149–52).

There remains still the question of the moral framework, so to call it, within which, or in terms of which, this absolute monarchy is intended to operate. Throughout the early modern period, as in the preceding medieval centuries, there was a general, an all but universal assumption that divine and natural law provided that framework. And in some sense this is still true for Hobbes. He never denies – indeed, he repeatedly asserts – that the sovereign is bound by the laws of nature and the laws of God. So far as the former are concerned, chapters 14 and 15 of *Leviathan* contain as elaborate and explicit a statement of what the laws of nature are as is to be found anywhere in the literature of the subject. As for divine law, Part Two of the book, well over a third of the whole text, is devoted to a thorough discussion of the scriptural basis of 'a Christian Commonwealth'; and this is preceded by chapter 31, on 'The Kingdom of God by Nature'. Yet even a brief examination of what Hobbes says under these headings will reveal that things are not quite what they seem. In regard to divine law, Hobbes of course rejects any claim by the church to an independent law-making power: this is to 'set up a *Supremacy* against the *Sovereignty* . . . a *Ghostly Authority* against the *Civill*' (p. 253). His own position is one of extreme Erastianism, insisting that it is for the sovereign alone to determine what writings are to be received as authentic scripture and how those writings are to be interpreted. It is true that the place and authority of the church was in some degree problematic for absolutists taking a more orthodox stance than Hobbes eventually adopted; but it is also true that few would have been prepared to accept a solution as rigorous as he advocated.

The authority of natural law, on the other hand, may be said to have been somewhat problematic for Hobbes himself. There is certainly no question of his according it the kind of transcendent authority it enjoys in at least some statements of an ancient and Protean doctrine. The laws of nature are indeed, according to Hobbes, accessible to human reason: they are in fact, one may say, the precepts or maxims of rational or enlightened self-interest. Their efficacy as binding rules of conduct, however, depends either on their being recognised as one of the ways in which God's will is revealed or, and this is crucial for Hobbes's political theory, on their being promulgated by the sovereign as civil laws. In any case, the restrictive or directive force of natural law is in every instance governed by the more fundamental principle of natural *right*. This – *jus naturale* – is defined by Hobbes as 'The Liberty each man hath, to use his own power, as he will himselfe, for the preservation of his own Nature; that is to say, of his own Life' (p. 99). The full implications of this, both for Hobbes's moral theory and even for his view of sovereign power, lie beyond the scope of this essay. What can be developed here is the insight it offers into the distinctive character of Hobbes's version of absolutism, and thus into its divergence from more traditional statements of the theory.

At the root of Hobbes's political philosophy there lies a rigorous individualism. This means that Hobbes can cut through or even cut out many of the traditional structures of political society which other absolutists had to accommodate. In the last resort his theory brings us to a direct confrontation between sovereign and subject, in which the latter, however absolute the ruler may be, retains an ineradicable natural right to self-preservation – a right that can never be surrendered. The essential purpose and function of the whole political system, operating through power transferred by individuals to the sovereign, is the preservation, and to the maximum extent possible, the 'commodious living' of individual human beings. This is hardly the world of Bodin or Bossuet, of Raleigh or of the learned ruler Hobbes himself called 'our most wise King, King *James* ' (p. 152).

As always in the history of ideas, contrasts must not be sharpened so much that the point breaks off. It was possible for those closer to traditional divine-right or patriarchal absolutism to find some common ground with Hobbes. Filmer is a notable example of this.[29] Again, it remains true of Hobbes as it was of the 'Neostoic' followers of Lipsius who envisaged a distinctly pervasive and authoritarian state that their view is not that of twentieth-century 'totalitarianism'. Even if we leave aside what Hobbes calls 'the true Liberty of a Subject' (p. 166) – the ultimate right to defend one's life even against the power of the sovereign – even apart from that, there is for Hobbes an important area of liberty arising from 'the silence of the laws'. There are, that is to say, important personal and economic choices and activities which no prudent ruler will seek to regulate by law. There will thus be 'liberty to buy and sell, and otherwise contract with one another; to choose their own abode, their own diet, their own trade of life, and institute their children as they themselves think fit; & the like' (p. 163). Moreover, the reference to the ruler's 'prudence' points to another crucial factor in the argument. The sovereign for Hobbes is a rational human being, equipped – always provided that he has absorbed the sound doctrine of *Leviathan* – to make rational decisions. Hobbes is no more concerned than any other theorist of absolute monarchy to defend or justify the insensate pursuit and abuse of power. He may cynically dismiss 'tyranny' as no more than a rude name for monarchy 'misliked' (p. 142); but his ideal sovereign is no tyrant, and if he may sometimes, in respect of the basis of his power, be a despot ruling by right of conquest, he is assuredly envisaged as a benevolent, an enlightened despot.

Yet in the end the impression remains that with Hobbes's Leviathan-state we have moved, or are at least moving, towards an idea of absolutism significantly different from that which predominated in the era of absolute monarchy. When A. D. Lindsay wrote on 'Absolutism' for the inter-war *Encyclopaedia of the Social Sciences*, he concentrated above all on two thinkers: Hobbes and Hegel. There are certainly important hypotheses to be explored – though not here – as to the relationship between Hegel's theory of the nineteenth-century state and the ideology (or ideologies) of absolute monarchy that have been explored in this essay. The absolutism of the seventeenth century, however, was in no way an anticipation of Hegel's historicist 'march of God in the world'. Neither, on the other hand, was early modern absolute monarchy Hobbes's 'mortal god', the object of the state-worship or 'politiolatry' to which 'reason of state' doctrine was sometimes said to lead. That monarchy was still essentially, as the seventeenth century gave way to the eighteenth, the rule of a king whose power was – ideally at least – 'sacred, paternal, absolute, and subject to reason'.

2. France

ROGER METTAM

THE appropriateness of the term 'absolutism' as a description of the seventeenth-century French monarchy has been the subject of extensive debate among historians since the year 1945, when Roland Mousnier published his impressive thesis on the venal office-holding system under the first two Bourbons.[1] His exhaustive examination of the Norman bureaucracy revealed the extent to which these hereditary offices were distinct from the royal authority which had created them. Their holders were theoretically agents of the crown, but the right of an *officier* to designate his own successor ensured that the king had little control over the personnel of his own administration. These officials often carried out the tasks entrusted to them, not least because it was by doing so that they derived their income, but there were many occasions when they openly refused or covertly failed to implement the instructions of their sovereign and his ministers.

Subsequent researches into the Parisian and provincial elites, both social and institutional, have cast further doubt on the effectiveness of royal authority. Studies devoted to the enduring influence of princely and ducal families at court and in the provinces, of the representative estates in the *pays d'états*, of municipal councils and gilds in the towns, of *seigneurs* in the countryside, of the church throughout the kingdom, and of the financiers who kept the monarchy solvent, have demonstrated that the crown was the principal, but not the only, power in the realm.[2] It is not surprising that no Frenchman of the *ancien régime* found the need to add the word *absolutisme* to the vocabulary of politics or history. There was nothing in the government or social system as he perceived it which required such a label.

Once the term had been given a political meaning, and a pejorative one, towards the end of the revolutionary decade 1789–99, it soon found favour with many historians of France. It was a useful over-simplication to characterise the kind of government which had perished in the Revolution. For some it was convenient for denigrating a political system which had deserved to be overthrown. Others used it to describe a desirable regime whose policies, had they not been undermined by the reactionary forces of privilege, would have led to a brighter future. Within this second group were writers who linked absolutism to the rise of the bourgeoisie and the assertion of bourgeois values, hailing Louis XIV and Louis XV as champions of the middle classes against a selfish aristocracy which was wedded to an outdated chivalrous ethic. This neologism soon became commonplace among the pamphleteers of the turbulent nineteenth century as they sought to set in an historical context their support for, or hostility to, a series of monarchical, imperial and republican regimes.

Ironically it was those same governments which authorised the editing and publication of immense documentary collections, in order to make the archives of *ancien régime* France more accessible to the reading public. A close scrutiny of these weighty volumes would have given little support to the inventors of absolutism, but they were not deterred and selected only those passages which could be made to fit their hypothesis. They also ignored the works of fine scholarship which were being published, in the form of books and articles, by learned academies in the provinces. Their authors painstakingly recreated the history of their region in pre-revolutionary days, and exposed a society of powerful elites in which the authority of the crown was frequently ineffective. These writers did not use the word 'absolutism', not even to attack it, because it clearly had no relevance to the provincial world they were chronicling. They dismissed the 'nationalist' historians, whether republican or royalist, as members of that self-congratulatory Parisian establishment which had always sought to impose its views on the rest of France – as if their city was generally accepted as the focal point of French life and culture. The revolutionaries of the 1790s might have replaced the old provincial names and territories with the new *départements*, but they had done little to change provincial attitudes except perhaps to create even greater suspicion of everything which had its origins in Paris. Thus 'absolutism' was espoused by some historians and ignored by others in the nineteenth century, neither group having any inclination to engage the other in debate.

Only since 1945 had a serious argument begun, and by that date the 'age of absolutism' had become an established cliché in the mind of anyone who knew a little about the *ancien régime*, and about the reign of Louis XIV in particular. Indeed many literary and art historians still use it unquestioningly, as they mistakenly describe a monarchy which allegedly exercised a tyranny over cultural fashions throughout the kingdom. Orthodox Marxist historians also continue to favour it, adding it to their idiosyncratic concepts of 'feudalism', 'capitalism' and 'class'. Among empirical scholars, there has been a variety of reactions to the problem. Many have recognised that the generally accepted meaning of 'absolutism', with its overtones of tyranny and despotism, is unhelpful when applied to early modern France, and some have accordingly proposed an additional definition in order that it can be employed safely in this historical context. As not all readers will know of this subtle change, it might have been more prudent to abandon its use altogether. Others have preferred to adopt an alternative term – 'absolute monarchy' – which at least has the merit of being found in seventeenth-century political writings. Yet it had many different shades of meaning, and was not a description of the royal government as it was currently constituted. Royalists hoped that the king might become an absolute monarch, and their opponents insisted that he should not. It is therefore not a helpful term for modern historians to use when characterising the reality of royal power under Louis XIV.

A few writers have refused to abandon the stereotype of Bourbon absolutism. They still seek to prove, by diligent research, that the crown was strong, that ministers and *intendants* exercised great power, and that major administrative reforms were successfully introduced. They persist in using emotive terms, as they describe the victory of a reforming, progressive, modern government over the reactionary forces of privilege. Another school of historians, much influenced by the writings of Mousnier, have created an alternative concept, the 'administrative monarchy', in which power resided with both king and bureaucracy, although this model has the disadvantage of excluding as many powerful groups as it encompasses. Lastly there is a growing body of scholars who have accepted that there was a hierarchy of powers in France, and that various elites combined with others in a changing pattern of alliances. They might make common cause against local rivals on specific, often short-term, issues, and they would support or oppose the royal government according to which course of action would better serve their own interests.[3]

If this last interpretation might seem at first glance greatly to diminish the independent power of the sovereign, it has led to a fruitful re-examination of the mechanisms by which the king sought to implement his wishes. Where the absolutist historians identified the rise of the 'modern state', and the adherents of 'administrative monarchy' charted the evolution of the formal institutional structure, these scholars have stressed the continuing informality of the administrative machinery, based as it was on a network of personal contacts. In an age when aristocratic ideals predominated, among bureaucrats as much as among old noble families, the king was the principal fount of patronage, having in his gift many of the most desirable military, ecclesiastical, administrative and ceremonial positions. He could enhance the rank, status, privileges and influence of an individual, although he had to avoid offending others lest they become disaffected. He was not the sole patron, because great aristocrats had their own clienteles whose membership might include middle-ranking nobles, judges and administrators. Some leading noble houses so dominated a province that they could fill lesser offices without consulting the ministers and could virtually guarantee that their nominees for higher posts would be accepted by the king. Such prestigious families could be vital to the crown if they chose to use their local influence to further its policies, but they could be extremely dangerous if they chose to rouse their province in opposition to ministerial initiatives. Fortunately these great aristocrats were themselves suitors for the highest posts and honours in the royal gift, and it therefore was usually in the best interests of both king and great nobles to cooperate. A wise king, like Louis XIV, took care to ensure that these men received their fair share of his beneficence, so that none could complain that he had been neglected or his rivals excessively favoured. Louis XV was less resolute, and bowed to the pressure first of one faction, then of another. Even the royal council became a battleground for these rival groups, each of them advocating policies which might gain them supporters. The best interests of the realm as a whole were forgotten. Worse still were the periods when a king was a child or had no direct heir. Then the factions turned their attention to the regent and ministers, or to likely candidates for the throne. They might conspire against them, or strike a hard bargain in return for agreeing to support them.

If different schools of historians can disagree so sharply about the power structures of seventeenth-century France, there is no likelihood of a consensus when they discuss the political theory of the period. Nowhere has the identification of *ancien régime* monarchy with 'absolutism' been more misleading than in this aspect of early modern French history. Once historians had created this extreme interpretation of Bourbon monarchical power, it was logical for them to assume that royalist pamphleteers were approving, justifying and defending just such an unbridled kind of arbitrary authority. Having been selective in their choice of historical documents, they cast an equally biased eye over the writings of the political theorists, taking passages out of context and attributing anachronistic meanings to words and phrases.[4] The result has been the division of the major writers into two distinct camps, separated by a wide gulf. A royalist like Bossuet has been assigned to a group which was allegedly in favour of the most extreme form of divine-right absolutism, while the Huguenot publicists have been allocated to an equally aggressive band of resistance theorists who advocated popular sovereignty and tyrannicide. Such caricatures might have had a role in a land where absolutism held sway, but as that too is a fiction it is essential to examine the precise context in which the political theorists were writing, and the exact meaning they gave to the terms they used.

Most of these theorists were neither philosophers nor theologians. They were jurists, who were commissioned by a variety of social groups and institutions to devise theoretical justifications for rights and privileges which were frequently the subject of litigation.[5] They had a difficult task, because their patrons might be at odds with many different opponents over the years, some of whom might be allies on a subsequent occasion. A royal publicist could find himself defending the king against the pretensions of the *parlements*, in which case the great nobles would support the crown; or against the great nobles, when the *parlementaires* would join the royalist cause; or against the pope, when both nobles and judges would rally to their sovereign. The same dilemma faced writers engaged by the nobles, the law courts and the provincial elites. They therefore concentrated on defending their patrons, rather than on attacking opponents who might become allies. Moreover such arguments surfaced only at times of tension between two or more groups. The theoretical debates did not develop steadily and coherently over the years. Every jurist had an armoury of weapons and used only those which were relevant to a particular confrontation, often presenting them in the form of slogans and shibboleths rather than extended and well-argued theories. Yet each elite had a core of fundamental principles to which it resorted in most moments of crisis. Often two opposing camps would use the same evidence but interpret it differently, showing that the disputants had much in common or were, in the long term, dependent on each other. For example the *parlementaires* knew that their supremacy rested on the fact that they were senior royal judges, and the king was aware that he could not hope to maintain the rule of law without the cooperation of his *parlements*. Therefore, when the judges and the crown were at odds about jurisdictional matters, both made general statements about their own judicial powers. In this kind of legal wrangle, the king would not inform the courts that he was an absolute ruler or held his authority by divine right. Instead he would remind them that he was the fount of all justice, and they would reply that they were carrying out their task as guardians of that justice as earlier kings had required them to do. Neither side denied the claim of the other, nor tried to define the precise legal implications of these two conflicting assertions. Each party had declared the legality of its position in clear but general terms, and it was now the turn of the officers to negotiate a compromise on the detailed issues which had provoked the crisis.[6]

As most of the disputes between the crown and the elites, or among the elites themselves, turned on points of law, it is essential to identify precisely the legal rights which each group claimed for itself.[7] The historians of 'absolutism' have erroneously maintained that the right to legislate was a cornerstone of monarchical power in the early modern period. It is true that the king could issue new laws, but his ability to do so did not feature among the arguments of even the most ardent royalist pamphleteers. They would all have agreed that the role of the monarch as the fount of justice was a principal attribute of his sovereignty, but they stressed that this was the ruler acting, not as law-giver, but as supreme mediator. He was the greatest judge in the realm, and it was the manner in which he exercised this function which occasioned most of the disputes between the crown and the social or institutional elites. It was generally accepted that the king might have to add to the corpus of laws in order to solve new and unforeseen problems, but on the reform of the legal system and on the promulgation of major legislation he was expected to consult his leading subjects, usually the *parlements* or sometimes the *états-généraux*. Most royal *ordonnances* were evolved through such a process of consultation. Even under Louis XIV, when an *ad hoc* council of legal experts was created to advise on the great ordinances of 1667, 1669, 1670 and 1673, the members of that body took care to seek the opinions of the sovereign courts on every detail of the proposals. Moreover these *ordonnances*, like many of those which preceded them, were attempts to systematise legal procedures, not to codify or amend the laws themselves. There were many different kinds of law in France, from the customary tradition of the north to the written codes of the south, and there were many local variants as well. The crown normally deemed it imprudent to intervene in such sensitive matters involving provincial pride. It preferred to concentrate on stamping out corrupt practices and inefficiency in the administration of justice, further evidence that the king saw himself as the giver of good justice rather than as a legislator. The historians of 'absolutism' have also claimed that the Bourbons bolstered their authority by espousing many principles of ancient Roman imperial law, but here too propaganda has been taken as reality. Royal jurists sometimes cited Roman examples, but the hostility of the judges to such alien concepts ensured that they were never incorporated into French law. Even the propaganda was double-edged. If the crown quoted the view of Justinian that the will of the emperor was law, its opponents would point out that this authority had been accorded to the emperor by a free vote of the Roman citizenry.

In the seventeenth-century French debate about the power of monarchy, the most ardent royalists never advocated unbridled sovereign authority. For the writers who used the term absolute monarchy with approval, it was to be the antithesis of tyranny or despotism. They, like the kings and their ministers, did not describe the whole system of government as a '*monarchie absolue*', because they knew that the crown did not have a monopoly of power throughout the realm. Instead they applied it to the actions of the ruler. If these were designed to promote the best interests of the people, he was '*absolu*', if not he was '*arbitraire*', although these writers acknowledged that, in the varied and separatist provinces which made up the kingdom, the decisions of a well-intentioned king might meet with suspicion or hostility. Yet they insisted that all subjects should obey their sovereign, whatever their opinion of his policies, because dissent was the first step towards anarchy. It was to be hoped that the truly virtuous monarch would not provoke widespread disaffection, because the royal publicists were not suggesting that he should encroach upon the privileges and rights of the elites. Equally those groups should not seek to undermine the authority of the crown, and the absolute king was within his rights to punish such infringements most severely.

The monarchical theorists therefore balanced the duty of the subject to obey against the obligation of the sovereign to act morally. As the ruler could not be forced to behave in this way, they couched their exhortations to him in the strongest and most emotive language. He was the supreme mediator, and therefore no human agency could judge him, but he should never forget that the judgement of God awaited him. Apart from his duty to his people, he should remember that his own salvation was at stake. Even Jacques-Bénigne Bossuet, often cited as the panegyrist of divine-right absolutism, tempered his enthusiasm for powerful monarchy with some severe moral strictures. This duality is clearly to be seen in his discussion of '*majesté*', a concept to be associated only with kings. It was that quality which placed the monarch on a plane far above his most illustrious princely and aristocratic subjects, but its presence depended on the moral conduct of the sovereign. 'Majesty', said Bossuet, 'is not the pomp which surrounds monarchs, nor the brilliance which dazzles the common people. That is the reflection of majesty, but not majesty itself. Majesty is the image of the greatness of God in the prince. God is infinite, God is all'. Thus he maintained that, while it was proper to regard a truly majestic king with the reverence appropriate to a divinity, the ruler had to behave as the untarnished image of God if he were to remain worthy of such devotion and obedience.[8]

Among those who were not prepared to laud royal power in these extravagant phrases, there was a wide variety of reservations about the wisdom of giving the monarch total freedom to exercise his authority. Yet hardly a voice was raised against monarchy as a system of government in seventeenth-century France – not least because there was no obvious alternative to it. Some writers made a distinction between the crown, as an institution which they admired, and certain individual kings, who lacked the qualities which every ruler needed to possess. Others wished to establish some mechanism for restraining the sovereign who issued an illegal command, legality still being emphasised as the criterion of good government. Only a very few wanted sovereignty to reside anywhere other than with the crown. Among this minority were the advocates of a social contract, who claimed that civil power had originally resided with the people. They had contracted with a ruler that he should exercise that authority on their behalf, and they were prepared to allow him to do so in a largely unfettered way. Only if he seriously and persistently breached their trust would they deem the contract to have been broken, resume their power and search for a new monarch. There was no school of theorists which suggested that a social group or institution should share in the royal right to make decisions, although some proposed that he should be required to consult the great nobles before he made up his mind, others that he should submit his orders to the magistrature for scrutiny, or even seek the approval of the kingdom by summoning and consulting the *états-généraux*.

Most of these remedies for arbitrary power were voiced only in times of crisis, and then it was often clearly stated that these were criticisms, not of the king, but of evil ministers and favourites who were misadvising him. The so-called 'religious wars' of the sixteenth century, the revolts, against Richelieu and Mazarin, culminating in the Frondes of 1648–53, and the later, though less frequent, provincial risings against Louis XIV, all prompted pamphleteers to write highly critical tracts, but few were directed against the person of the king and almost none against the crown. During the Frondes polemicists called upon the young Louis XIV to take personal charge of government, save his realm from the tyranny of wicked ministers, and emulate his grandfather, Henri IV, in ending civil war. These aggrieved subjects usually proposed the same solution to the problems afflicting the populace. If the ministers were to cease their illegal innovations and return to traditional ways of governing, all would be well. There their unanimity ended, because they did not agree on the strengths and weaknesses of the traditional system. Some were champions of the *parlements* or of the venal bureaucracy in general; others supported the nobility, regarding the ministers and the office-holders with equal distaste; a third group praised the provincial institutions, and disliked any increase in interference from the centre. Nevertheless, their demands always included the general statement that legally established rights and privileges should be respected, and that ministers should be compelled to obey the law.

Some of these crises were caused by genuine religious disagreements, but most resulted from the impoverishment of the royal treasury in time of war when the crown often had to attempt urgent remedies for which it could not find a convincing legal justification. Thus, during the Frondes, the financial difficulties of Mazarin may not all have been of his own making, but the dominant opinion at the time was that the minister was acting arbitrarily and often illegally, while his opponents had legality, privilege, tradition and numerous historical precedents to justify their stand against him. Even in less turbulent years, the royal publicists seeking to justify ministerial initiatives were hard pressed to find arguments half as convincing as the legal objections of which their opponents had a seemingly inexhaustible supply. The crown therefore adopted some new ideas, drawn from the philosophical rationalism which was much in vogue among intellectuals.[9] Ignoring the different customs, traditions and languages of the provinces, royalist writers assumed the kingdom to be a logical unity, its oneness symbolised by the single monarch who was the 'living law', that is to say a rational code of natural law whose validity could be perceived by all right-thinking men. Economic theorists developed this theme, demanding that the resources of the kingdom be rationalised, provincial barriers be abolished so that a single French customs union could be created, and local weights and measures be replaced by a common system which was to be observed throughout the realm.[10] Such abstract reasoning did not convince the defenders of the provincial heritage. Neither were these rationalist arguments of much use when the crown and its opponents confronted each other, occasionally in armed conflict but more usually in the law courts. In those tribunals the dispute revolved around precise points of law, not the fundamental principles of the Cartesian universe.

With the exception of the seigneurial courts of the nobility and certain muncipal jurisdictions, all justice was dispensed by royal judges, chief of whom was the king himself. Yet it was before those judicial agents of the crown that opponents of unbridled royal authority had to bring cases which challenged the legality of governmental actions. Most judges preferred to give the litigants a fair judgement, and risk the displeasure of ministers. As they could always justify their decision, often by referring to the circumstances of the particular case, it was difficult for the government to challenge the result. It could evoke the whole matter to a higher court for a retrial, but usually the original judgement would be confirmed, not surprisingly given that the ministers had often overstepped the bounds of legality. Most dangerous for both the crown and the judge was a confrontation at the highest level of the judicial hierarchy – between the king and the *parlement* of Paris. Both sides began their theoretical justification of their position by agreeing that the sovereign was the supreme mediator. The king went on to say that he was currently exercising that function, either personally or through the royal council. The *parlementaires* took a longer term view. Their institution had been entrusted with substantial powers by past sovereigns, and it alone had the right to exercise them. Unless kings respected the decisions of their predecessors, the whole basis of law would be undermined.

If the crisis deepened, the *parlement* would remind the monarch that it was the sole guardian of the '*lois fondamentales*' of the realm, laws so fundamental that not even he could change them. This was not a coherent legal doctrine which was developed over the years. It remained a series of vague, and largely unenforceable, precepts which could be paraded when necessary. Not all of them were equally relevant in every crisis, but two were of particular importance. The first was the Salic Law, which determined the order of succession to the throne and insisted that it pass only through the male line. The *parlement* reminded the king that, had not this law been strictly observed over the centuries, he would not now be sitting upon the throne. He could obviously not deny the validity of the rules which had governed his own accession. Secondly he could not alienate parts of the kingdom, because it was not his to dispose of. The patrimony of the crown antedated his own reign, and he was obliged to leave the realm as he found it. The royal publicists ignored, rather than tried to refute, these bold claims, advancing other arguments to justify the supremacy of the monarch. In these squabbles, as in disputes involving other courts and elites, historians and jurists raked through the legacy of the past in search of supporting arguments. Not only legal precedents, but evidence about the origins of the monarchy, the establishment of the nobility and the creation of the *parlements* were cited. The interpretations of these events were tailored to suit each party. They were therefore unlikely to convince the opposing side or to facilitate the resolution of a dispute, but they did permit each group to claim that it had right, tradition and history working on its behalf.

Equally important, and less theoretical than the '*lois fondamentales*', was the power of the sovereign courts to register royal edicts and to remonstrate against their provisions before doing so. This procedure had been instituted by the monarchy in the distant past, and it was so well established by the seventeenth century that for a king to abolish it would have been very provocative. Even Louis XIV, when he tried to speed the registration of his edicts, was careful not to challenge the right of remonstrance itself. In the 1667 Civil Ordinance he insisted that the sovereign courts should have only a limited time to voice their objections, after which the edict would be deemed to have been registered. In 1673 he added that, when he sent his instructions to the courts in the form of letters patent, they should be registered at once, and remonstrances submitted afterwards. He took care to explain that these changes in procedure were necessitated only by the demands of war and were to be regarded as temporary. In fact they were not reversed until after his death but that was largely because, for most of his later reign, there were no open confrontations between the king and his sovereign courts.

The monarch could always suspend the entire process of remonstrating against edicts by attending the courts in person. As he entered the chamber and took his seat on the *lit de justice*, the powers of the judges were returned to the sovereign from whom they originated. This impressive assertion of the royal judicial power was fraught with dangers. At moments of crisis, the judges openly flouted the authority of the crown by continuing to discuss, and even by remonstrating against, edicts which had been registered at a *lit de justice*. They also had the practical remedy of allowing appeals against their provisions when cases were brought before them. As it was in the best interests of neither side for the king to be at odds with his own judges, an accommodation was usually reached, often through a retreat by the crown because it had been the innovator and the judges had ample legal evidence to justify their objections. Usually, therefore, the *lit de justice* was used as a ceremonial means of reminding the *parlementaires* that they held their powers at the royal pleasure, and the edicts chosen for registration on those occasions were of the uncontroversial kind which would have been registered without demur had the king not been present.

When the *parlement* of Paris, as the senior court of appeal, was likely to give a judgement which would be unpleasing to the king, he could evoke the case to himself in person or to a branch of the royal council, usually the *conseil privé*. These *evocations* usually caused uproar in the *parlement* which strongly denied the right of the council to intervene in its jurisdiction. Sometimes a case might then proceed in both tribunals, each refusing to give way to the other, and once again an accommodation would have to be reached through informal channels before the dispute could be resolved, often by abandoning the hearing altogether. The council also evoked cases from the lower courts, sometimes retaining cognisance of them but on many occasions handing them to the Paris *parlement*. As there was such a confused hierarchy of judicial tribunals in France, each of them frequently disputing the jurisdictional powers of others, it was not uncommon when two were locked in legal combat for one to appeal to the *parlement*, the other to the council. Neither the Parisian judges nor the royal councillors wished to be on opposite sides in these local wrangles, or indeed to become involved at all in most of them. After private discussions, they would agree which of them would take responsibility for the appeal, and an investigation of the case would begin. Often the outcome would be a declaration that there was insufficiently conclusive evidence for the hearing to proceed in either their own or the lower courts.

Historians who have concentrated on periods of crisis have given the impression that the crown was regularly at odds with the *parlements*, and the 'absolutists' among them have erroneously portrayed the king as the ultimate victor in these confrontations. During the Fronde of 1648–9, when the entire judiciary was briefly united in opposition to Mazarin, it was the minister who had to give way and concede most of its demands. Moreover at that time the king was a child, and the dispute was not between the sovereign and his own judges. It was an attempt by the 'guardians of the fundamental laws' to restrain an 'evil' minister who was behaving illegally. Both sides claimed to be defending the power of the monarchy. In more normal times the king and the judges tried to maintain amicable relations, because each had much to gain from the support of the other. The crown welcomed the additional legitimacy which the *parlements* gave to royal edicts through the process of registration, especially over controversial extensions of monarchical authority at the expense of Rome and the church. In such cases, Louis XIV sometimes specifically stated that approval of his edicts by the sovereign courts signified the endorsement of his actions by the entire kingdom. Unlike Mazarin, he took care not to antagonise the *parlementaires* by the *évocation* of proceedings to his council. During his personal rule this practice virtually ceased, and he was more likely to tell appellants to the *conseil privé* that they should address themselves to the *parlement* instead. Albert Hamscher has recently shown that the two bodies worked closely together in their attempts to give good justice.[11] Judges and councillors were deeply concerned at the expense and the delays caused by the confusion of overlapping jurisdictions at the lower levels of the judicial hierarchy, and both groups warmly supported the attempts of Colbert – largely unsuccessful as they proved to be – to simplify the legal system.

On those occasions when the *parlements* were locked in conflict with the king or his ministers, the judges took great care to act with the utmost legality as their profession required that they should. This gave them the moral advantage when they questioned the legality of new financial measures taken by the government in an attempt to solve the desperate problems of the royal treasury. At such times the ministers often accused the *parlements* of meddling in affairs of state, because the refusal of the courts to register fiscal edicts had serious implications for the financing of the army and for the conduct of war. They were even charged with giving comfort to the enemy. The *parlementaires* vigorously rejected such accusations. They expressed their wholehearted recognition of the tradition that foreign policy, the making of war and peace, the maintenance of an army and the defence of the realm were exclusively matters for royal prerogative action. They insisted that they had never sought to advise the king on these matters, and they deplored the activities of some great aristocrats who demanded a voice in international affairs and were even prepared to negotiate directly with the agents of foreign powers. The judges stressed that they had confined themselves entirely to considering the legality of the fiscal measures proposed by the crown and, if their refusal to register them had implications for the solvency of the government in time of war, that was not a consideration which could be allowed to influence their decisions which were made on purely legal grounds. Although there were rival family groups jockeying for position within the sovereign courts, the judges collectively were fiercely proud of their own professionalism, their expertise, their thorough apprenticeship in the law and their scrupulous fulfilment of their judicial responsibilities.

If there were therefore disputes about the precise legal limitations on monarchical authority and if relations between the king and his judges were usually amicable, the power to enforce the law was at the disposal neither of the sovereign nor of his courts. The policing of the kingdom was in the hands of numerous local bodies, whose attitude to each other was far from harmonious and whose response to directives from the crown or from the sovereign courts was often not one of subservience. In the many disputes between the centre and the provinces about the raising of taxes and the implementation of new edicts, the local police forces were often on the side of the provincial elites in resisting these innovations of a distant central government and its Parisian judges. Nor could the army be used as an alternative force for law and order. The worst confrontations about new taxes occurred in wartime, when the royal treasury was under the greatest strain. Then, either troops could not be spared from the battlefront or they were so seriously in arrears with their pay that they were more likely to loot than to police. Also the aristocratic officers objected on principle to their regiments being used as policemen, while in practice they often sympathised with the provincial resistance to arbitrary or excessive taxation. So the king and the *parlements* had to accept that they did not have the means to ensure the implementation of duly registered edicts in all parts of the realm. This applied not only to their decisions on fiscal and legal matters, but even more so to their combined efforts to carry out a fundamental reform of the judicial system. Even in Paris, where both the crown and the judges were normally on good terms with the municipal authorities, the task of law enforcement was not easy, because most of the Left Bank fell under the jurisdictions of the university and the abbey of Saint-Germain-des-Prés, two large religious enclaves into whose territory the civil police of the capital could not enter.

The First Estate of clergy and the Second Estate of nobility had considerable powers which co-existed, and sometimes conflicted, with the authority of the monarchy. They, like the secular judiciary and the bureaucracy, might use their influence to support or restrain the royal government. As their rights and privileges were firmly founded in law, their attempts to defend them usually took place in the courts. They adopted similar tactics to those of the crown and the *parlements*, making ringing declarations of general principle as well as debating the specific issues involved in each dispute. During the seventeenth century teams of pamphleteers, jurists, historians and even playwrights were commissioned to defend the status, rank, honour and liberties of the nobility, but most of these writings were not directed against the crown. The burning preoccupation of the *noblesse d'épée*, an hereditary caste whose origins lay in chivalrous valour and whose current concern was to preserve its social pre-eminence as the sole military order in the realm, was to resist the rise of a rival nobility, the *noblesse de robe*.[12] This too was an hereditary elite, being composed of bureaucrats who had purchased ennobling offices and had the right to pass them on to their heirs. Yet these men possessed none of the traditional military qualifications which were deemed to be essential for ennoblement. They had adopted the superficial trappings of an aristocratic life-style, purchasing country estates and building fine town houses, but their families were bourgeois in origin and as bureaucrats they worked for their living in a manner that no true noble would have thought proper. Although the *nobles d'épée* directed most of their venom against these parvenus, they also criticised the sovereign who had instituted this new social order. They insisted that he did not have the power to confer titles of nobility on such socially unworthy men, and they therefore refused to acknowledge these office-holders as nobles.

Some other legal concerns of the military nobility were more directly focused on the authority of the monarch. One issue which aroused passionate feelings was the right to duel. Again this was largely a question of principle because the crown could not have eradicated duelling throughout the kingdom, although stern action was taken against duellists who fought within the confines or environs of the royal court where loyal guards could be dispatched to apprehend them, no matter how prestigious their aristocratic rank. In the provinces the forces of law and order might well be on the side of the combatants, if they were pillars of local society, and refuse to arrest them. Kings issued a number of edicts prohibiting duelling during the seventeenth century, and a fierce debate accompanied each one. The insistence of the noble that he be able to defend his own honour with his own sword clearly challenged the claim of the king to be the supreme judge, who either exercised his powers in person or delegated them to others. The judiciary staunchly supported the crown, demanding that the nobles should always seek redress through the royal courts, an assertion which implied that the judges of the *noblesse de robe* were in no way inferior to the military aristocracy. The right of the noble to hold his own seigneurial court was less controversial, although kings and *parlements* stressed that those tribunals should take cognisance only of matters which involved the tenants and estates of the seigneur. If any outsider was implicated or interested in a case, then it was to come to a royal court. There was some opportunity for pamphleteering on this issue, because the noble publicists could stress that the seigneur had acquired the power to administer justice by right of birth or by his possession of certain fiefs, while the royalists would argue that it was the king, of his own royal volition, who had permitted and continued to permit such a practice. The debate was never very heated, because the crown did not seek to undermine seigneurial jurisdictions as such, confining itself to regulating the relationship between them and the royal courts.

The very greatest nobles posed more of a threat to the authority of the crown, and their publicists engaged in fierce arguments with the proponents of '*la monarchie absolue*'. They also produced diatribes against the hereditary venal office-holders, suspending these attacks only during the brief moments of crisis, like the Frondes, when the two groups had to make common cause against the royal government. Usually therefore the judges supported the crown in rejecting the claims of the high aristocracy. The most serious challenge came from the *princes étrangers*, members of families which had been sovereign princes in their own right or still exercised sovereignty in other parts of Europe. Houses like the Guise, Bouillon and Rohan were truly international, with relatives and lands in more than one kingdom or principality. Those branches of these dynasties which were based in France acknowledged the suzerainty of the French king, and in return were given precedence in the hierarchy immediately after princes of the blood royal and cardinals, and above the entire native nobility. Yet there was much disagreement about the extent to which they had submitted to the authority of the king. He insisted that their subservience was total, but they maintained that they could not blindly obey a royal order which threatened the best interests of their relatives in another country, as when war broke out between the two rulers. In an age when all political action was planned for the greater good of the extended family, these international houses had to put the well-being of their kin above their obedience to any one sovereign. Accordingly they were the only group in France which sought to influence the foreign policy of the crown, an aspect of government which was regarded by other Frenchmen as falling entirely within the royal prerogative. By doing so, the *princes étrangers* hoped to lead the king away from confrontations with certain other sovereigns so that their own families would never be put in the position of having members spread across two warring states. The French monarchs strongly resented these attempts to interfere with their monopoly of foreign affairs, while lesser nobles and *parlements* accused these princes of putting family interests above the good of the realm. Some *princes étrangers* had to enlist the support of their family, even on occasion inviting them to invade the kingdom. Such treacherous behaviour was vigorously condemned by the king, his judges and the majority of the nobles. Yet the *princes étrangers* could not abandon their relatives, and so the problem of their divided loyalties could be solved only by a prolonged period of international peace, and for that the princely subjects of the Bourbons had to wait until 1713.

The church also posed an international threat to the authority of the French crown. As in the disputes between king and *parlement*, there were few consistent arguments about the respective powers of monarch and pope because there were instances when different, and often conflicting, elements in the ecclesiastical hierarchy joined the royalist or the papal side. The regular orders of monks and friars usually stressed that their prime allegiance was to Rome, although the Society of Jesus might be 'gallican' or ultramontane as the issue of the moment demanded. That most austerely moral sect, the Jansenists, would almost always join the opposite camp to their hated enemies, the Jesuits, and therefore they too might find themselves supporting or opposing the pontiff. The bishops tried to be on good terms with both king and pope but that was not always possible, and there were occasions when their ranks were divided in their response to royal and papal initiatives. The lower clergy included an increasingly vocal group of priests who were calling for the moral reform of the church, a reduction in the power and wealth of the episcopate, and a greater voice for the humble *curés* – and even for their parishioners – in ecclesiastical affairs. At times these *curés* enlisted the support of the *parlements*, at other times of the pope, although both Rome and the French judges feared the possible long-term consequences of their more revolutionary demands.[13] The influential theological faculty of the University of Paris also sought aid, as the issues changed, from the pope, the crown, the *parlements* and the bishops. All these allies were, on other occasions, opponents of the Sorbonne doctors, although those theologians never found themselves totally without some powerful friends. These ever-changing alliances were responses to a number of religious issues, many of which had implications for the theory and practice of kingly rule in France because they raised the question of the extent to which the sovereign was master of the church in his realm.

A convenient starting point for the early modern historian is the Concordat of Bologna of 1516, when François Ier and the pope reached a practical solution to the problems which had been souring Franco-Roman relations in the later middle ages. Most importantly it was agreed that the French king could nominate worthy men as bishops, abbots and priors, and that the pope would confirm his choice and institute the candidate unless he disagreed over his suitability for office. The Concordat was hailed as a triumph by a number of rival interests. François claimed that it was an acceptance by Rome of his right to select the holders of the great benefices within his realm. In contrast the pope cited it as proof that the authority to make such appointments undoubtedly resided with the Holy See but that he had voluntarily chosen to delegate this aspect of his power to the monarch, while reserving to himself alone the right to accept or reject the French nominees. The *parlements*, which had been asked by the king to register the concordat and had done so only after much debate and negotiation, emphasised that this procedure demonstrated the superiority of the secular judiciary over the church, because papal decisions had no validity in France unless they had signified their approval of them.[14]

The arguments about papal and monarchical powers were spasmodic during the Italian Wars of 1494–1559. There were both rapprochements and confrontations between France and Rome as a series of popes oscillated between the French and imperial camps. Then the kingdom was plunged into more than three decades of civil war in which some of the protagonists espoused religious causes with varying degrees of sincerity. Perhaps the most dangerous threat to the crown came from the house of Guise and the Catholic League, adherents of an extreme Catholicism who positively welcomed the international authority of the pope. The Valois kings preferred a more moderate and tolerant attitude to religious matters, while the growing number of Protestants rejected any idea of papal interference in the kingdom. It was from both the ultra-Catholics and the Huguenots that some of the sharpest criticisms were soon to emerge.[15] These two groups, at opposite ends of the religious spectrum, used many of the same arguments in their attempts to impose restrictions on arbitrary royal power. Ironically, given their strong religious convictions, they borrowed and developed arguments which in the middle ages had been employed by secular powers in their attack on the authority of the church. This situation arose because some of the justifications for papal supremacy which had been devised by medieval canon lawyers had now been appropriated by royal publicists, who were stressing the divine aspect of monarchy and the belief that the king was answerable to God alone. The ultramontane and Huguenot writers took the opposite stance and asserted that monarchical authority came, not from God, but from the people. It was the citizens who had created the ruler in order that their own collective interests might be more securely protected, and they could resume their sovereignty if he failed to provide that protection. For both these groups, it was the religious policy of the crown which had moved them to demand the right to dethrone their king, and their means of justifying their right to practise their own religion was to postulate a secular origin for the authority of the monarch. They made no attempt to formulate a theologically-based theory to counter the concept of kingship by divine right.

These writings were produced by desperate men in the chaos of a civil war. The Huguenots blamed the crown for the massacre of some members of their faith on St Bartholomew's Eve in 1572, while the ultra-Catholics believed that the king might ultimately agree to tolerate the presence of these Protestant heretics within the kingdom. Although many of the warring groups in this internecine struggle had social and political motives as well, it was the religious struggle with which the theorists were preoccupied. Even so, their theories of resistance were not as extreme as historians of 'absolutism' have maintained. Some of the religious polemicists did mention tyrannicide as a last resort, but the main thrust of their writings was that extremes of royal policy should be prevented by the traditional regulating mechanisms, usually the authority of the magistrates and of the *parlements* in particular. They accepted monarchy as the form of government, and concentrated on defining its powers and limitations. When they talked of popular sovereignty, they were not advocating political action by individual citizens. They were envisaging a collective response to royal excesses, expressed by the social, and especially the judicial, elites on behalf of those below them but without directly consulting them. Yet it was not suggested that any of these elites should participate on a daily basis in the exercise of the powers traditionally associated with the crown. The essence of this contract theory was that it was a long-term agreement between the collective citizens and the ruler, in which they entrusted to him the task of governing them, and could remind him through the magistrature that his first priority should be to further their interests and even that he was failing to do so. Only as a final resort would they abrogate the contract and therefore be faced with the problem of finding another ruler.

The tone of these arguments reveals a great deal about the way in which sixteenth-century France was governed. Most routine administration was under the control of local institutions and elites. The crown affected the daily lives of its subjects only through its religious and foreign policies, the latter because it might give rise to higher taxes, the conscription or billeting of troops, and for the peripheral provinces the danger of enemy armies, the disruptive presence of native regiments and the interruption of local trade across the frontiers. The fact that the theorists placed the duty of resisting arbitrary royal power on the shoulders of the magistrature is a reminder that no effective representative institutions existed which could have fulfilled this role. The irregular meetings of the *états-généraux* were occasions for presenting local grievances to the king but not for serious political discussion, although the deputies were sometimes asked to endorse a royal decision. The judges welcomed the suggestion that they, and not the *états-généraux*, were the legitimate defenders of the people, although they never liked religious dissenters, whether Protestant or ultramontane. Nevertheless the resistance theorists were supporting their own belief that it was sound justice, not representative institutions, which made for a well-run kingdom. Even the most distinguished royalist thinker of the civil war period, Jean Bodin, stressed the duty of the magistrature to influence and restrain the sovereign, although he did believe that the king should have the power to disregard their advice and act as he chose. A ruler should govern in the best interest of his subjects, but in order to be effective he needed to be strong. That strength, essential if he was to rule well, also gave him the ability to become tyrannical. An ineffective sovereign was no sovereign at all. Bodin had to accept that judicial and moral appeals might not sway an evilly inclined monarch, but he believed that this situation would not often arise. He also reminded rulers in the plainest terms of the divine judgement which awaited them when their earthly reign was over.[16]

The controversy about royal and papal power was to recur many times under the Bourbons. When the 'religious' wars were finally ended by the general acceptance of Henri IV as king in 1593, the pope took care to welcome the new monarch who had brought peace to his realm. Henri had reconverted to the Catholicism of his youth and seemed determined, despite his politically expedient Edict of Nantes of 1598 which granted toleration to the Huguenots, to achieve the ultimate conversion of these dissenters to the Roman rite. Yet papal and royal publicists continued to defend the authority of their respective masters, at the same time as these public courtesies were being exchanged. That mood changed when an ultra-Catholic fanatic assassinated Henri IV in 1610. There was an outcry in France against ultramontanism and against all theories which envisaged tyrannicide as the last resort. Pamphlets praising monarchy as the greatest force for stability poured from the presses during the regency for the new child king. In the subsequent confrontations between the adult Louis XIII and the Huguenots, the leaders of the reformed religion were careful not to disinter the resistance theory which they had espoused during the 1570s and 1580s.

One term which was often used in the religious and political conflicts of the seventeenth century was *'l'église gallicane'*. The historians of 'absolutism' took these words and invented another neologism – 'gallicanism'. Their use of it erroneously implied a systematic body of doctrine and political theory. In fact gallican ideas were more like slogans, and their definition varied according to which group was using them. Kings, *parlements*, bishops, parish clergy, Jesuits and Sorbonne doctors all had differing interpretations of the term 'gallican church'. Royal publicists denied the right of the pope to intervene in the internal affairs of the kingdom, and sought to bring the regular orders under the control of the bishops – who were, of course, royal nominees. The *parlements* insisted that any papal initiative had to be turned into a royal edict which was to be submitted to them for registration, although their gallican ideas were devised primarily for use in their ceaseless battle against ecclesiastical jurisdictions in Paris and the provinces. The bishops tried to distance themselves somewhat from papal authority but had no intention of being totally subservient to the king and to his *parlements*. The Jansenists and the *curés*, both hostile to the laxity and secularism of the hierarchy, turned at times to the pope who might endorse their rigorism and welcome their support against excessively royalist bishops. On other occasions the parish priests and the Jansenists appealed to the *parlements*, who were consistently hostile to the episcopate but did not always want to become embroiled in a religious quarrel. The Jesuits always remembered their prime obligation to the pontiff, but at times of tension between Rome and Versailles might prefer to support the king, especially when their Jansenist enemies were seeking papal help against royal and episcopal oppressors. The Sorbonne doctors, who claimed that they alone had the right to pronounce on matters of faith in France, had a series of disputes with popes who were trying to force their decisions upon the kingdom and the university alike. The faculty also clashed frequently with the *parlements*, because both jurisdictions claimed the monopoly of censorship, and many of the most controversial books found favour with either the doctors or the judges. The Sorbonne did seek papal support in this quarrel, and in their resistance to the civil authorities which were always ready to attack the immunities and privileges of the university. Thus various groups might ally in different ways according to the issue of the moment. Most disputes involving the church had implications for the authority of the crown and its secular courts. Moreover the majority of them turned upon jurisdictional, not theological, differences.

During the personal rule of Louis XIV, most of the royal plans for reducing papal interference in the internal affairs of the realm were ultimately unsuccessful. Attempts to divert papal revenues into the treasury; the aggressively royalist Gallican Articles of 1682; the assertion of French diplomatic immunities in Rome; the seizure of the papal territory of Avignon – all these provocations had to be abandoned. Instead Louis found himself outwitted by the pope in foreign policy, and subsequently had to beg Rome to help him solve the Jansenist problem, his own efforts at a solution having failed. When the pope condemned the sect in his Bull *Unigenitus* of 1713, his action divided French opinion. The king, the Jesuits, the Sorbonne and most bishops supported him, many after voicing considerable reservations about such direct action by Rome. The Jansenists, a few bishops, many parish priests and the *parlements* protested vigorously. Louis had also failed in his labours first to convert and then to repress the Huguenots. Many of these useful citizens, along with foreign Protestants who had resided in France and performed valuable functions, now left the kingdom. Others remained as an embittered underground force, awaiting its opportunity for revenge. Moreover many Catholics, including hitherto staunch royalists, condemned this persecution as '*arbitraire*', a tyrannical act which had none of the beneficence expected of a truly 'absolute monarch'.

After the attack on the Huguenots in the early 1680s, criticism of Louis XIV mounted.[17] His wars were denounced as largely self-inflicted, excessively protracted, costly in money and lives, harmful to his subjects and achieving nothing. Yet only a few extreme Huguenot publicists suggested the overthrow of the monarchy, and the establishment of a republican regime like that of the Dutch. For most French critics the survival of the monarchy seemed inevitable because there was no alternative, and therefore fundamental constitutional arguments did not feature in their writings. Attention was focused on the inadequacies of this particular king, and much time was spent on planning a better education for his successor. Self-seeking ministers were to be removed from office, and the aristocratic critics suggested a drastic reduction in the powers and the personnel of the hereditary bureaucracy – although they could suggest no alternative to the *parlements* as the supreme courts of law. A revived and reformed *états-généraux* and a network of local assemblies were to be consulted on policy and to have considerable freedom in implementing it. Yet at the centre the final power of decision would rest with the king. He would be resisted if he tried to act illegally and encroached on privileges, but on those matters where he had the right to decide, and in his judicial role as the supreme mediator, he would still have the unfettered authority to pronounce. It was fervently to be hoped that, with wiser counsel and after widespread consultation, his decisions would be better than those of Louis XIV – but it remained a hope rather than a certainty.

3. Castile

I. A. A. THOMPSON

I

ENGLISHMEN in the early seventeenth century were prone to contrast the traditional liberties of England with what we would now call the absolutism of her continental neighbours. Although it was France that had customarily been the model of the *dominium regale*, in the seventeenth century many of that generation reared under the influence of William of Orange's *Apology* and the Armada and Gunpowder scares were coming to see the Spanish 'Pharaoh' as the epitome of the political tyranny they feared was developing in their own country. Their fears were intensified by Spain's overwhelming military preponderance and presumed fanatical, Catholic irredentism which were seen as threatening the liberties of the whole of Protestant Europe. In an anonymous treatise of the middle years of James I, Philopolites, one of the discussants, summed up what he regarded as the essential difference between the regimes:

> The government of England is not perfectly imperial and monarchical, that is, the prince's pleasure is not the rule and law of his subjects' lives and liberties such as the Emperour and Spaniards, and some other (in some sort) are, whose government is built on this main maxim, 'Quod principi placuit legis habet vigorem'; for then might he also change the laws of the realm, and charge the commons with tax and tallage without their consent. But it is politique and mixtly regal, that is such as is the dominion of the head over the body natural, raised out of the embrion.[1]

When such commentators referred to Spain, they were really thinking about Castile. The seventeenth-century Spanish monarchy was composed of an aggregate of separate territories, in the Iberian peninsula, in Italy, in the Low Countries, in America and the Far East, ruled by a single king whose power varied from kingdom to kingdom, depending on their different constitutions and on the nature of the governmental apparatus that existed in each. Even Spain itself, consisting of the three crowns of Aragon, Castile and Portugal, contained three different currencies, half a dozen languages, at least ten representative institutions, and something like a score of royal titles. Of all these kingdoms, however, Castile was the dominant – in size, in population, in its financial contribution, in its political role. The king was born in Castile, resided in Castile, maintained his court and councils in Castile, and seemed to most of his subjects to be nothing but a Castilian. Castile too was commonly regarded as the most subservient of the king's dominions. That belief was deep-rooted. Even in the fourteenth century a king of Aragon had contrasted the liberty of the Aragonese with the subjection of Castile,[2] and the notion of an historic conflict between the centralising statism of Castile and an Aragonese 'constitutionalism' has been an enduring topic in Spanish political historiography. If the concept of absolutism has any meaning in seventeenth-century Spain, therefore, it is in Castile that it has to be sought.

In recent years, connected no doubt with the process of regionalisation in Spain, a revulsion against the politics of authoritarian centralism, and a desire among Castilians to provide their history with a similar libertarian tradition to that of their compatriots in the regions, there has been a tendency for historians, to reexamine Castilian history from the inside rather than in terms of its relationship with the monarchy. This has led them to deny the reality of absolutism and to lay emphasis instead on the pluralist nature of power in seventeenth-century Castile, the 'judicialist' nature of the monarchy, its progressive decentralisation, or its permanent weakness as an effective power structure. The starting point of this revisionism has been the laying aside of *a priori* categorisations and the attempt to see how the early modern political system actually worked. To this end we first need to know what powers contemporaries commonly attributed to their kings, what sort of constitutional structures existed in Castile, and how far the authority of the crown was translatable into effective power.

II

The irony is that the image of the English constitution held by Philopolites is all but identical to that which most Castilians held of their own government. Even the rhetoric was the same, the all-pervasive analogy of the head and the body united in the *corpus mysticum* and bound by reciprocal duties for their mutual support. The idea that the mere pleasure of the prince was the rule and law of his subjects, or that the prince could tax at will and without consent, was as remote from the mainstream of Castilian political thinking as it was from the English. The great philosopher-diplomat, Saavedra Fajardo, even speaks of the Castilian monarchy as '*mixto*'.[3]

And yet there was a paradox, as the Swiss traveller, Thomas Platter, noted in 1599: '"Todos somos reyes", say the Spaniards, but this has not prevented Philip from being the most absolute monarch in the world.'[4]

The view that the king was 'absolute' was hardly to be challenged in seventeenth-century Castile. The term *absoluto* was regularly used of the prince in the seventeenth century. Indeed, the concept of 'absolute royal power' (*poderío real absoluto*) had been current in official documents for some 200 years, and unequivocal assertions of royal '*soberanía*' are to be found in the law codes of Alfonso the Wise dating from the second half of the thirteenth century. The question is, what was understood by *absoluto*?

Its starting point is sovereignty, the assertion of independence from all other princes, 'recognising no temporal superior', as the formula of the royal pragmatics maintained. Nobody would have denied that in Castile the king had no superior in temporal affairs, was the source of all authority within his kingdom, exercised supreme jurisdiction, made and unmade the laws, and was the fount of all civil honours and offices. In the words of Diego de Covarrubias y Leyva, President of Castile in the reign of Philip II and the greatest legist of his age: 'In the Castilian state the entire jurisdiction and civil power are deposited solely with the king, and it is from him that they derive to others.'[5]

That did not mean that the power of the prince was unbounded. In saying the king was 'absolute', the jurists were making a statement about the law. The absolute prince was the coping-stone of the legal system, the supreme element of the law, but he was part of that system, not above, or outside it. Although, by virtue of his office, the king could not be subject to the 'coercive' power of the law, in so far as laws and customs were just and necessary and because it was proper that he set an example of respect for the law, he was subject to their 'directive' force, in Aquinas's celebrated distinction, and subject both to the laws he himself had made and to his own private contracts.

All power was of God and was subject to God's purposes as revealed in his Divine Law and in the Law of Nature, whose light was Reason. But, in the consensus of early seventeenth-century Spanish political thought, implicitly rejecting any strict theory of Divine Right, the residence of that power and the form of government under which it was exercised were a decision of the people. In a mutually binding compact the people had entrusted to a king the totality of their powers in order that they might be maintained in peace, justice and liberty, and in the full enjoyment of their lives and property. They, in their turn, owed the king trust, obedience, aid and sustenance. Reciprocity is the very marrow of the relationship between king and kingdom.

Kings were created by the people; they were, therefore, ministers of the people, 'our mercenary', as the Cortes (the Castilian Parliament) told Charles V in 1523. The notion of the king, not as master or proprietor of his kingdom and of the lives and goods of his subjects, but as a steward or administrator *for* the people, was a commonplace. 'You kings are but labourers', wrote Quevedo (†1645), 'as you work so are you paid.'[6] 'A country is not made for its king', insisted Luis de Molina (1535–1600), 'but the king for his country – to defend, administer and direct, not for his own whims, vanities and convenience, but for the common good.'[7]

It was the common good that was the absolute measure of the legitimacy of a prince's actions, as it was of the justice of the laws themselves. Indeed, one might more properly talk of the absolutism of the common good than of the absolutism of princes. If the prince could dispense with the law, by-pass ordinary channels of government, break his contracts, override property rights, and do injury to individuals, he was justified in doing so only by necessity and the common good. The absolute priority given to the common good is one of the key differences between the political cultures of Castile and England in the seventeenth century. There is no sense in Castile that the common good might be inseparable from the private good of every individual. 'Truly, for the common good private individuals may, and must suffer, even guiltlessly', declared Dr Alvaro de Villegas in the Royal Council.[8] As it was in the common good that the king's majesty and estate be maintained, and as what was in the common good was for the king to determine, the supremacy of the common good was in practice a powerful support of monarchical authority.

It was a support, however, not to the king as a man, but to kingship as an institution. The depersonalisation of kingship, the separation of king and crown, was a crucial element in the authority of seventeenth-century Castilian monarchy. The formality of the court, its clockwork routine, the privacy of the royal person, the public impassivity of the king – Philip IV was described by foreign visitors as like a statue – were part of a propaganda of monarchy as an institution in which the office was greater than the man. The comportment of Philip IV was no different in this respect, despite their contrasting personalities, from that of his grandfather, Philip II. Whereas in England and France ritual and iconography were designed to make the prince seem more than human, in Castile they made him seem less than human.[9] Princely power did not imply the servitude of man to man, but the common subordination of king and subject to the crown.

The 'absolute' power of the king, therefore, was something that operated within the limits of reason and the law, on behalf of the common good. The king could be absolute only so long as he was just. Wilful rule, in the personal interest of the prince, was nothing more than tyranny. All that was, of course, part of the common coin of Thomist political theory. If there was anything distinctive about the Spanish neo-Scholasticism of the later sixteenth century, it was its rejection of the extremer, absolutising propensities of some of the fourteenth- and fifteenth-century glossators, a much more explicit emphasis on the contractual nature of the relationship between the prince and his subjects, and a much stronger tendency to retain a residuum of inherent rights in the people which could not be infringed without consent.

The obligation to obey the just command of a legitimate ruler was binding in conscience and theorists not uncommonly indulged in the language of the sacred, the image of the king as the vicar of God, 'God on earth' (that is, the 'imitator' of God), to assimilate disobedience to sacrilege. What is striking about the reality of seventeenth-century Castilian monarchy, however, is its almost total lack of the sacral dimension. To talk, as some do, of the 'divinisation' of monarchy in the seventeenth century is to misrepresent the common perception of royal authority. The monarchy in Castile was Catholic and it was religious, but it was not 'divine'. It was in this respect a very much more mundane and temporal monarchy than either France or England. The king of Castile was not crowned, or anointed, did not have thaumaturgical powers, did not rule by 'Divine Right' and did not demand obedience as God's vicegerent. By the seventeenth century the sacral formulae that are found in fifteenth-century royal pragmatics have disappeared, and the medieval belief in the king's power to cure the possessed had all but died out. Even the lemma SCCR (Sacra Católica Real Majestad) was abandoned in the 1580s and replaced by the simple address, *Senor*. The unpretentiousness of the Spanish monarchy was commented upon by the Welsh royalist traveller, Sir James Howell, who visited Madrid with Prince Charles in 1623: 'Here it is not the stile to claw and compliment with the King, or idolise him by *Sacred Sovereign*, and *Most Excellent Majesty*; but the Spaniard when he petitions to his King, gives him no other character but *Sir*, and so relating his business, at the end doth ask and demand justice of him.'[10] The preambles of the official propositions the crown put to the cities and the Cortes for their consent, emphasise not the king's divinity, but his religion, his piety and his Catholicism. They are appealing for obedience not to the mystique of kingship, but to something rather more immediate, the deserving goodness of the king as the real guarantee of the justice of his commands.

The key to political obedience in Castile rested with the score or so of great cities which were represented in the Cortes and which, as the hubs of the fiscal and administrative system, dominated the Castilian countryside. We have in the debates of those city councils an exceptional source for the ideas current at that intermediate level of practical, political discourse which determined the reality of compliance or non-compliance with the royal will. Those debates reveal an extensive local awareness of theological and *ius commune* principles and of history and legislation. The formal treatises of the great neo-Scholastic and civil law theorists of the sixteenth century were not, therefore, of merely academic importance, for they formed part of the political education of both prince and people, their precepts purveyed by the lawyers in the royal councils and in local government, and by theologians and spiritual advisers in the pulpit and the confessional, often briefed by the crown in anticipation of their consultation by municipal councillors, or members of the Cortes.[11]

But there is also revealed in the cities a parallel political culture, with ways of thinking different from those of the canon and civil lawyers. Here obedience was seen not so much as an obligation in law and in conscience (though it was both of those), but as the expression of a personal relationship between the 'vassal' and his 'king and natural lord' (*rey y señor natural*). Both the language and the obligation are, therefore, somewhat different from the formulations of the jurists and theologians. For the *buen vasallo*, the good vassal, obedience to a loving lord was a primary duty. It was the essence of vassallage to give his lord loyalty, trust, love and service, to support his estate, and to come to his aid in need. To serve one's king was thus an opportunity to show 'fidelity and love' (*fidelidad y amor*). Not to obey the legitimate demands of the king was 'not the action of gentlemen' (*azion ajena de Cavalleros*).[12] This was a much more affective view of obligation than that of the lawyers, one in which the king by his 'paternal benignity', sacrificing his own well-being and putting his life at risk in the defence of his vassals, could expect in return their loving and grateful obedience. In this regard, the references in the city councils to the presence of Philip IV at the front in the war against France show how valuable a propaganda weapon were the king's personal journeys to Aragon between 1642 and 1646.

This set of ideas, which reflected the 'hidalgo' ethos of the dominant *caballero*, or gentry, oligarchies, helps us understand the repetitious and almost universal expressions of pride in a tradition of family and corporate service to the king voiced by the gentry of the cities, and why among the most insistent arguments of the *corregidores*, the royal governors in the cities, was that their city should not fail in the honour of always being the first in the king's service. The loyalty and obedience of the Castilian to his king was proverbial in the seventeenth century. It was part of the political calculus. That did not mean that Castilians complied with the law, but they obeyed the king. One can easily fail to appreciate the moral intensity of the king's command. In 1597, the *corregidor* of

Jaén wrote asking the king to change the terms of a demand for money from 'charge' (*encargo*) to 'command' (*mando*) because the city councillors were saying the tax was unjust, otherwise the king would have commanded and not just requested it, and 'if His Majesty commanded it, they would do it'.[13]

III

It is frequently argued in favour of the concept of 'absolute' monarchy that whatever 'moral restraints' there may have been lacked the institutional forms without which they were but hot air. That is at best a half-truth. Each of those moral restraints, justice, reason, the common good, religion, had an institutional expression which in some way determined the forms of royal action, even if they were not always – though not never – able to determine its substance.

The first of these was the law. Law in seventeenth-century Castile was royal law. The reception of the Roman civil law from the mid thirteenth and fourteenth centuries, with its presumption that all law was royal unless there was concrete proof to the contrary, weakened the force of custom and prescription, and of any rights not emanating from some royal act of grace or compact. Gradually the old prescriptions, *fueros*, were transformed into royal codes and ordinances. Yet codification amounted to a reification of the law. By the seventeenth century, the *Siete Partidas* of Alfonso X and the great collection of laws published by Philip II in 1567, known as the *Nueva Recopilación*, had come to acquire something of the standing of a written constitution, to which the crown no less than the subject appealed repeatedly as authoritative *leyes del Reino* (laws of the Kingdom).

It was a crucial element in the power of the crown in seventeenth-century Castile that neither the consent nor the participation of the kingdom, or its representative body, the Cortes, was necessary for the making of law, as it was in England. Legislation was the prerogative of the king alone. The question was not whether the king alone could make laws, but what laws he could lawfully make, and whether whatever laws he might make were to be observed. The answers to those questions were sufficiently well-articulated in the law codes and the manuals of legal practice which interpreted them, like Jerónimo Castillo de Bovadilla's *Política para corregidores y señores de vasallos* (1597), or Juan Hevía Bolaños's *Curia Philipica* (1603), both with numerous subsequent editions, for it to be possible to argue that there were formal legal restraints in Castile. Those restraints may not have been enforceable against the king, but neither were they in England, except by revolution.

There were, in fact, strict canons which determined the legitimate form and substance of royal decrees and how they were to be received. The *Partidas* and the *Recopilación* laid down that royal commands contrary to Divine and Natural Law, against conscience, the Church, or the faith, or uttered in anger or fury, were of no force. Commands contrary to established law and legal principles, contrary to privileges, contrary to the common good, or contrary to specific laws, unless expressly excepted, were not to be obeyed until confirmed. Commands prejudicial to any individual not cited or heard in law were invalid, even with express clauses of derogation. The conventional recognition of the right, indeed the duty, of supplication to the king and his Royal Council in such cases was embodied in the famous formula, *Obedézcase, pero no se cumpla* (to be obeyed, but not put into effect).[14] This was not a legal myth, but actual practice to which the recipients of royal orders resorted over and over again. The supplication did not nullify the royal order, it merely imposed a temporary suspension of its operation until the reasons for the supplication had been heard and the order rescinded, or reiterated, in which case it had to be complied with, but it did maintain the principle that legality was to be defended even against the intervention of the king himself, and that the king's orders were to be weighed against external standards of justice and public policy.[15] This was true most of all in the realm of private law, where the public interest was not involved, and when the prince himself was subject to the judgement of the courts. In purely private matters there was no ground for royal intervention allowed by the law, and the royal 'grace' could modify private dispositions, the terms of wills and endowments, for example, only in so far as such modification was not expressly excluded.

The appeal against unacceptable royal commands was made to the king in his Council. The Royal Council, or Council of Castile, as the highest judicial tribunal in the kingdom, was inclined to see itself as having a responsibility to the law that was independent of the king. Some even held that the Council was the vestige of the popular origin of royal power and in that sense 'represented' the people. It certainly had pretensions to being an 'intermediary' between king and people, the guarantor of the legitimacy and respectability of royal resolutions, and claimed a right of remonstrance (*replicar*), reminiscent of that of the French *parlements*. The Council of Castile stood for legalism and due process against arbitrariness, and for a 'judicialist' as against an 'administrative', or 'executive' mode of government.[16] It was the Council and its sister body, the Cámara, which were, for example, the most consistent defenders of the rights of the Cortes and the inviolability of the contractual obligations the king had undertaken with them.[17] The new, non-feudal class of university-educated *letrados*, so often portrayed as the chief proponents of absolutism in both theory and practice,[18] thus had another and very different constitutional role.

Furthermore, the general process of bureaucratisation within the conciliar organisation created a structural resistance to arbitrariness from within the administrative system itself, as principles of hierarchy, division of function, professional expertise, the concept of the career, with graduated promotion by experience and seniority and security of tenure, came to be established. It was argued that councillors had primary obligations imposed by their oaths, their professional integrity, and the ordinances of their councils.

The councils, therefore, and the Councils of Castile and the Cámara in particular, were active opponents of the politicisation of government, resisting by protest and obstruction all 'extraordinary' and irregular procedures, like the establishment of *ad hoc* committees for special areas of business, the summary jurisdiction of commissaries, the appointment of councillors without appropriate qualifications, or their removal without just and proven cause.

The Royal Council and, indeed, the entire system of councils which were usually thought to have emanated from it, were the institutional expressions of the requirement that the king must take counsel and heed reason. They were not, however, merely advisory bodies. Each of the twelve principal councils in Madrid represented a particular jurisdiction, or franchise, a form of procedure, and a separate institutional interest. No royal order that was not in the proper form was legally valid, and that proper form required not only the '*Yo el rey*' of the king, but the countersignature of a royal secretary.[19] A royal decree was the outcome of a recommendation from a council (the *consulta*) and a decision of the king, promulgated by the despatch of that council's secretary. The decree was not, therefore, solely an order of the king; it was also the expression of a council's competence in a particular area of business. The systemic conflicts of jurisdiction among the councils at the centre were then echoed in the field by the denial of the validity of royal decrees by recipients who belonged to a competing jurisdiction. The Captain General of Oran even refused to comply with an edict issued by the naval secretariat of the Council of War, 'his office depending on the army secretariat'.[20] These conflicts were most acute where they involved demarcations of competence between civilian and military, or between secular and ecclesiastical jurisdiction. They expressed fundamental differences of professional formation and political mentality, between legist and lay councils, law and prerogative, due process and pragmatism. Administratively they were a serious nuisance. Politically they provided a way for local resistance to tax demands or military levies, for example, to plug into the opposition of the civil justice of the Council of Castile to the legal exemptions and arbitrary procedures of the Councils of Finance and War, and by playing off the competing jurisdictions of the central tribunals against each other, to find legitimate means to thwart the execution of royal policies. The conciliar system itself therefore served as a sort of official, internal opposition, a channel for the expression of grievances, and a protection for individual and corporate rights, as well as a buffer deflecting any legal challenge away from the king's authority and against the council which was implementing it.[21]

The belief held by many contemporaries, like Philopolites' author, and later historians that the king of Spain could tax the commons without their consent and that the kingdom, as represented in the Cortes (*el Reino junto en Cortes*), had no role in the government of Castile is also wrong. The need for the consent of the kingdom to new taxation was laid down in the *Nueva Recopilación*,[22] and although there was some argument as to the nature of that consent and the form it should take, neither in principle nor in practice was that need ever repudiated. Indeed, during the course of the seventeenth century, as the collapse of its existing revenues, in the wake of economic decline, obliged the crown to turn to the Cortes for extraordinary grants, consent was sought for a wider range of measures than ever before, and even for many that had hitherto always been regarded as independent regalian rights.

The Cortes of Castile have been generally written off by historians as an institutional check on absolute monarchy after the failure of the Comunero Revolt in 1521 seemingly put an end to the power of the cities to resist royal authority. A small body of twenty-six (rising in Philip IV's reign to forty) deputies, representing only eighteen (rising to twenty-two) cities, the Cortes in the sixteenth century had not succeeded in vindicating their claim to be consulted over legislation, preventing the king from increasing his customs revenues without consent, or getting prompt replies to their petitions of grievances. The relative fiscal independence of the crown in this period did not derive primarily from the king's more spectacular sources of wealth in the New World, as is so often believed – royal imports of gold and silver never amounted to more than about one-quarter of total revenues – but from a prolonged period of economic growth. From the 1590s, however, economic downturn and the enormous costs of war made the crown increasingly dependent on the 'services' of the Cortes. In the 1560s Cortes grants made up only about 25 per cent of royal revenues; by 1601 they reached 50 per cent, and during the reign of Philip IV they exceeded 60 per cent. The financial crisis enabled the Cortes and the cities they represented to insist that the new services they granted, known as the Millones, were to be conditional on their having full administration of the grant, determining the purposes to which it was to be applied, and on the promulgation of a series of measures considered to be for the common good of the kingdom. Those conditions were written into a formal contract with the king which stated unambiguously, 'this service is granted by the Reino for as long as the conditions of this contract are observed, and if any of them are broken it shall *ipso facto* cease, and the Reino will have no obligation to continue with it.' That contract was renegotiated and reissued with every renewal of the Millones or new grant of 'services' until the Cortes ceased to be summoned in the 1660s. From 1601, therefore, the relationship between the crown and the Cortes was put on to an explicitly contractualist basis. In the words of the formula with which the king customarily ratified and accepted the legal instruments drawn up by the Cortes: 'It is my wish that it have the force of contract, mutual, reciprocal, and binding, made and exchanged between parties.'

By the end of the reign of Philip III (1598–1621), the Cortes and the Cortes cities had secured a formidable position in the government of Castile, such as they had not had since the end of the fourteenth century. It was acknowledged that there could be no new services without the vote of the Cortes, and that there could be no vote of the Cortes without the prior consent of the cities. The possibility of independent revenue increases was drastically curtailed by the state of the economy, and the conditions of the Millones limited the scope for the usual exploitation of expedients by the crown. After 1600, the king's prerogative was more constricted by his formal, signed, contractual obligations to the Cortes than in any other monarchy outside Poland. The intervention of the Cortes in financial administration was denounced by ministers as a usurpation of the functions of the royal councils and offensive to the *soberana regalía* of the king, and the conditions demanded for the renewal of the Millones were variously described as 'harsh', 'improper', 'unbridled' and 'outrageous'.

It was against the powerful position that the Reino (in the Cortes and in the cities) had acquired between 1590 and 1620 that the government of Philip IV's authoritarian chief-minister, the Count-Duke of Olivares, set itself after the king's accession in 1621. By the end of the 1630s it had succeeded in establishing its authority over the administration of the Millones, evading the inhibitions on royal action imposed by the conditions of the contracts, and breaking the dependence of the Cortes on their cities. What the crown never felt able to do was to dispense with the Cortes entirely, or with the need for their consent for taxation. That was not because the Cortes were totally submissive. On the contrary, the dilatoriness, the obstructiveness and the expense of the Cortes induced ministers on a number of occasions to recommend that the king avoid calling them altogether. Not only was such a course of action rejected, but whereas Parliament in England met for only a few weeks at a time and not at all between 1629 and 1640, the Cortes of Castile were in session for three-quarters of the reign of Philip IV. If they eventually granted the king most of what he wanted, that was no more than Parliament gave James I and Charles I. It means only that they did not see their primary role to be to refuse the king money, that, given the military situation of the monarchy, there was no alternative, that they were well paid for it, and that they were able to buy off, or block proposals which they regarded as inimical to the best interests of the country and of the urban gentry they represented.

It was not in their relationship with the crown, which was, at bottom, transactional, that the weakness of the Cortes lay, but in the lack of support they received from the country and from the cities they formally represented, once Philip IV had succeeded in breaking their dependence on their cities in 1632. Consequently, it was the cities which emerged as the alternative to the Cortes and as a more satisfactory forum for seeking the consent and support of the kingdom. Sporadically from 1643, and conclusively from 1667, it was directly to the Cortes cities that the crown applied for consent to taxation and to dispensations from the conditions of the Millones contracts. The Cortes of Castile met for the last time in the seventeenth century in 1664. Thereafter, their functions were taken over by the capitals of the twenty provinces of whose representatives they had previously been composed, and their two permanent standing committees, the *Diputación* and the *Comisión de Millones*. The ending of the Cortes was thus a victory for a particularist, or federal concept of the kingdom, over the national principle of representation embodied in the Cortes and promoted by the crown. It had as a consequence the effect of freezing taxation in the forms and at the levels of 1664. To that extent it marked not a victory of royal absolutism over a dualistic concept of the state as *Rey y Reino*, King and Kingdom, but the recognition by Charles II's government of the crown's inability to change the fundamental balance of the constitution.[23]

For Protestant Englishmen it was more than anything the association with Catholicism and the Inquisition which demonstrated the tyrannical nature of the Spanish regime. Yet, ironically, the most effective restraint on the authority of the Catholic king came from the Catholic Church. Attention is frequently drawn to the control the crown had over the Spanish Church. The king of Spain had unique rights of patronage, his Royal Council could evoke temporal cases from the ecclesiastical courts, and the Inquisition, also a royal council, in effect nationalised the supreme jurisdiction of the Church in religious affairs. Papal bulls were allowed currency in Spain only with royal approval, and the Council authorised church synods, intervened in matters of ecclesiastical discipline, and censured bishops for temporal transgressions. In addition, the Spanish Church contributed so substantially to the royal coffers that it claimed it was being bled white.

And yet, the king of Spain, sovereign and without superior as he might be in things temporal, could not make any episcopal appointment, tax the clergy, dispose of church lands, or alter the jurisdiction of the Inquisition without the approval of the pope in Rome. Whereas the king of England, holding both royal and papal authority, could dispose of the Church at his pleasure, in Spain, as Philip III himself somewhat wryly observed, 'the King here tooke to himself Authoritie Royall only, and submitted all Jurisdiction Spiritual to the Pope, whom under Penalty of Excommunication he was bound to obey.'[24]

The great wealth of the Church, which made it the most powerful estate in the realm, was built not only on its immunity from lay taxation and secular justice but, perhaps more importantly, on the fear and devotion of a deep popular respect. Elements of both lay and religious anti-clericalism never spilled over into any spontaneous attack on the immunities of the ecclesiastical estate. The grants of taxes by the Cortes and the cities were always carefully and explicitly non-committal in neither burdening nor exempting the clergy from the 'service'.

Without papal approval in a formal Brief, the king of Spain was unable, in theory or in practice, to get his clergy to accede to taxation. If the Papal Brief was late, or in improper form, the clergy simply refused to pay. Even when a Brief had been issued, ecclesiastical contributions had to be renegotiated – and always downwards – by the representative assembly of the clergy, the *Congregación del Clero de Castilla y León*. Conflict with the clergy was endemic, and more often than not the clergy won.[25] It was clerics who generally spearheaded resistance to taxation in the seventeenth century by preaching, agitation and the liberal use of spiritual sanctions to defend their immunity and the large-scale fraud and tax evasion which it cloaked. 'The loss Your Majesty's revenues suffer on account of the religious exceeds anything that can be imagined', complained the Council in 1677.[26] Faced with censures, interdicts and excommunications, the laity, not excluding the royal *corregidores*, refused to enforce registration or collection against the clergy, and even the king was reluctant to face the scandal of 'His Catholic Majesty' appearing publicly to be persecuting his bishops, priors and deans.

Ecclesiastical immunity was not only a fiscal problem, it was a problem also of law and order. The Inquisition, rather than an instrument of royal absolutism, which it was only rarely, acted more often in a quasi-autonomous pursuit of its own policies and interests, defending its jurisidiction *à outrance* against all comers and instituting proceedings against the king's crypto-Jewish financiers in conscious disregard of government policy. The Royal Council repeatedly condemned abuses of sanctuary, unwarranted extensions of ecclesiastical authority over the laity, and usurpations of crown jurisdiction, which were hindering 'the normal course of government', leaving malefactors unpunished and encouraging criminality. But the Council could see no solution other than to get the ambassador in Rome to bring the matter up with the pope. In addition, papal jurisdiction in Spain, exercised by the Nuncio, and the granting of pensions, exemptions and indults were, it was said, draining away two million ducats a year to Rome.[27]

Undoubtedly, the king had ways of getting money out of the Church without having to go begging to the pope, by means of pensions against episcopal revenues, donatives, levies of troops and provender, but the imposition of general contributions on the clergy (*subsidios, excusado, decimas*, Millones) always involved, as well as the acceptance of ecclesiastical immunity, the public recognition of papal, rather than royal, supremacy over the Spanish Church. The regalist counter-attack launched during the reign of Philip IV, asserting the crown's independent authority over the Church, never penetrated very deep, and the government of his weaker successor, Charles II, was unable to prevent the clergy's abuse of its fiscal and judicial immunities reaching new heights. Backed as it was by an external authority over which the king had little leverage, and in the seventeenth century, often divergent political interests, 'the clergy', their most knowledgeable historian has written, 'represented an enormous power, invaluable as a support, terrible in opposition'.[28]

IV

The crown was thus not without formal, legal and institutional restraints. And yet the law allowed the king enormous discretion in the execution of his duties. He could alter judicial procedures, retain cases, suspend sentences and remit punishments. He appointed ministers of his choosing, and could remove them with or without cause. He was free to accept or reject the advice of his councils and to ignore their legal scruples. He could legislate to control the economy, morals, ideas, modes of dress, or modes of address. He could requisition property, demand personal services for war, and exploit a wide, and imprecisely defined, range of regalian rights over money, trade, land, offices, status and honours. The municipalities were controlled by royal ordinances, and seigniorial government and justice were subject to supervision and review by the king's courts. The towns were unable to raise local taxes or mortgage their communal properties without specific authorisation, and the nobility could not borrow against their entails without royal licence. The grandees even needed permission to marry. The royal prerogative of 'grace' was an instrument of exceptional influence in a polity in which privilege was power, and power could only be achieved through a privilege that no one but the king could grant. Political crimes, like *laesa majestas*, defined not by statute but by legal doctrine, were extraordinarily flexible in their application, permitting even the titled aristocracy to be put to the torture.

As in England, during the course of the seventeenth century royal authority, both with respect to its ideological pretensions and its practical exercise, was pushed well beyond the conventional limits of the sixteenth century. Although the chronology of this process has not yet received the careful study that it needs, there does seem to have been a perceptible change of tone in seventeenth-century attitudes.[29] In the new, centralised, court culture of the 1620s and 1630s, the propaganda of art and architecture and the eulogies of the court hacks are promoting a more elevated and triumphalist image of the prince, 'the Planet King', 'Felipe el Grande'. Even the pitiable boy king, Charles II, is portrayed by Sebastián de Herrera carrying hat and baton, but with a crown and sceptre held above him by a cherub. In the cities, extremist assertions of royal authority are becoming more common: 'the command of the prince is law' (1655); 'His Majesty is absolute master and may so order, without excuse or delay permitted' (1660); or, more egregiously, 'it will be necessary to obey by serving him as the absolute and despotic lord of our persons and property that he is' (1697).[30] Consent to taxation is being transformed from a right into a 'grace', an expression of the king's benignity. Ministers are arguing the contingency of all privileges and exemptions. Under Philip IV, during the Olivares regime, the crown is adopting a noticeably harsher tone in the voicing of its commands and a consciously intimidatory attitude towards individual and corporate opposition, the *mal estilo* that the jurist, Solórzano Pereira, deplored as demeaning to the royal authority. Olivares is even said to have threatened the total expropriation of private property, justifying the infringement of liberties and privileges and the more general use of prerogative power on the grounds of financial and military 'necessity', the imperatives of war and defence, and the need for prompt obedience. As the Cámara argued in February 1642, 'the unavoidable commitments that face Your Majesty do not permit new privileges or exemptions, nor even that old ones be observed, for according to the law everyone has an equal obligation to come to his aid, even in less pressing circumstances.'[31]

The more authoritarian behaviour of the government in the seventeenth century was not based on any new theory of power, but on the more vigorous utilisation and a more elastic interpretation of the *poder absoluto* it already had, '*according to the law*'. The ability of the crown throughout the seventeenth century – and no less during the minority and reign of the limp Charles II than during the tough ministry of Olivares – to overcome the contractual limitations of the conditions of the Millones, or to get the Cortes and the cities to consent to services and donatives, did not depend primarily on arbitrary breaches of those conditions, although there were a number of those, or on a denial that consent was necessary. The king was almost always able to get that legitimising consent, if not by agreement, by command. The issue was the obligation to obey the legitimate command of the king, and whether the king's command to consent to a just demand was itself a legitimate command. In the 1590s the answer was more likely to be, no!; by the 1640s it was more likely to be, yes![32] If the politics of accommodation that Philip II had preferred proved unavailing, Philip IV was prepared to enforce obedience to that command by insisting on the coercive measures, black-lists, fines, imprisonment, that Philip II's *corregidores* had wanted to employ in their cities but which the king had usually repudiated. That was itself part of the climate of the seventeenth century, a greater cynicism about men's motives and about the methods needed to govern them.

V

Absolutism is not only about theory and the constitution, it is also about politics. That is to say, it is a description of the decision- and policy-making process. Once the constitutional question between king and kingdom had been resolved, the politics of the monarchy took place within the court. It took place at two levels, a political level which was primarily a conflict between ministers and courtiers, or court aristocracy, the latter usually operating through the Council of State, and a constitutional level, which was in essence a conflict between prerogative and law, protagonised by the Council of State, on the one hand, and the Council of Castile, on the other. The issue was, as contemporaries perceived, whether government was to be monarchical or 'republican', ministerial or conciliar, executive or judicial.

What distinguishes the seventeenth-century reigns from that of Philip II is that it had ceased to be clear who was ruling and whose voice the command of the king represented. After the repression of aristocratic faction at court by Philip II and the atrophy of the councils in the 1580s and 1590s, the seventeenth century is a struggle for 'voice'. Despite all the modifications that can be made to the proposition, it is broadly true that the premiership of the duke of Lerma in the reign of Philip II was a manifestation of the recovery of political influence by the great aristocracy, or a section of them, and the councils, the Council of State in particular. 'What is surprising in Spain', wrote a Polish visitor in 1611, 'is that, although their government is absolute, their kings do nothing without the councils, they sign nothing without them, and even the most minor questions of public policy they do not resolve alone.'[33]

It was one of the principal objectives of Olivares after 1621 to re-establish the belief that it was the king, and not the court and the councils, who was making the decisions. He succeeded only in convincing everybody that the decisions were his, and in uniting aristocracy and bureaucracy against ministerial tyranny. With his fall ended any serious prospect of absolutism at court. Despite the sporadic attempts of Philip IV to rule alone, or those of the Queen Regent to rule independently of the grandees and the councils, for the rest of the Habsburg period policy-making was essentially 'republican', in that it emerged out of a political balance involving the king, the chief minister, or ministers, the councils and the grandee factions at court. Observers were all but unanimous that the king was incapable of decision, or incapable of imposing his decision on government.[34] One after the other the ambassadors resident in Madrid during the later part of Philip IV's reign and that of Charles II report that, in the words of the Luccan envoy, Guinigi, in 1649: 'One could say that at no time have the ministers and councillors held more unlimited and more absolute authority.'[35] The succession of *validos* (favourites) and ministers after the death of Philip IV demonstrates the ability of the grandees to drive out unacceptable royal favourites and to impose alternative ministers on the king. To contemporary observers the Spanish court had the appearance more of an aristocratic republic than an absolutist monarchy. 'Thus, this seems to me to be more of an Aristocracy than a Monarchy', wrote Guidi, the Modenese envoy, after Olivares' fall in 1643. 'The government has come to be and continues more in the manner of a Republic than a Monarchy', reported Cenami, the Luccan ambassador, in 1674. 'I have written to my king', Sir William Godolphin undiplomatically told Charles II's chief minister, Medinaceli, in 1677, 'that although in England there is a Parliament which is wont to have the king march to the dictate of the law, he should console himself that it is worse in Spain, where every lord is a Parliament who imposes laws on the king.' The Marquis de Villars described it in 1681 as 'a government in which everyone was sovereign'. 'Though this be a great monarchy', Godolphin's successor, Stanhope, repeated in 1691, 'yet it has at present much aristocracy in it, where every Grandee is a sort of prince.'[36]

Of course, as Henry Kamen has so rightly observed, the idea of a 'strong' or 'weak' government in Madrid was largely irrelevant to what happened in the regions.[37] If the language of absolutism is not appropriate to the politics of the court, it is in almost inverse relation to the effective power of royal government outside it. Indeed, it might well be that the public assertion of royal authority in the seventeenth century was essentially defensive, an ideological counter to administrative collapse and the breakdown of effective central control over the government of the country.

VI

The sense of a total breakdown of government and law and order pervading the documents of the seventeenth century is overwhelming. In looking back to the reign of Philip II as a golden age of justice, contemporaries were, of course, mythologising both the past and the present. Even before 1600 there are indications of a relaxation of the rigour and equity of the law. By the mid-seventeenth century, banditry was widespread, even in the heart of Castile, and there were enormous crime waves in both the countryside and the cities.[38] In the 'dark corners of the land', on the Valencian frontier and in Asturias, in the north, gang warfare and clan faction were the rule. Even in the capital, Madrid, it was impossible to go out at night except in large numbers and armed to the teeth. Whereas in the sixteenth century the complaints had in the main come from the consumers of justice, in the seventeenth they come increasingly from its purveyors. In every decade, the councils, as well as reformers and foreign observers, are saying the same things: 'justice is in confusion and is without authority' (Council of Castile, 1654); 'the administration of justice is today totally discredited' (Council of State, 1664); 'justice is in the greatest disrespect in the world; day and night they rob and murder, and there is not the slightest indication of punishment or remedy' (Duke of Montalto, 1685).[39] For all of them the causes were the same, the laxity, corruption and venality of the magistrates, the debilitating conflicts of jurisdiction – there were reputedly 82 different judicial competences in Spain – and the multitude of local immunities and exemptions from the ordinary jurisdiction of the crown, so many, claimed the Council of Castile, 'that the voice of justice has been reduced to a babel of jurisdictional tongues'. Already in 1618 a *junta* was warning that royal jurisdiction was so curtailed by the large number of lay lords (*señores de vasallos*) and by the Church, the Inquisition, the Military Orders and the Cruzada that if they were allowed to usurp more authority royal jurisdiction would be on the point of extinction.[40] During the course of the seventeenth century royal justice was becoming even more remote from the king's subjects. Between the last quarter of the sixteenth century and the last quarter of the seventeenth, the number of cases coming in appeal from inferior jurisdictions to the high courts of Valladolid and Granada fell by three-quarters.[41]

It is the history of the revenues, always the real barometer of the strength of the state, which exposes most starkly the gulf between the theoretical authority and the effective power of royal government in seventeenth-century Castile. On the one hand there is a string of, seemingly arbitrary, fiscal exactions imposed in Castile from the 1630s to the 1660s, involuntary donatives, compulsory purchases of *juros* (a kind of bond on crown rents), retentions of interest on *juros*, resumptions of offices and rents, monopolies, currency manipulations, and so on, many of which were formally prohibited by the conditions of the Millones, and all of which bit hard, not least into the wealthier elements in society. In effect, the crown was successfully depriving the privileged of their fiscal immunity. On the other hand, there was much that the crown was not able to do. In the first place, the most important fiscal policies of the government, a series of projects for the fundamental reform of the financial system, the rural banks scheme of 1622, the single flour tax, the general taxation of rents, and the 'medio grande universal' of 1655, all proved impossible to implement; the salt tax, introduced in 1631 by regalian right in order to free the king from dependence on the Cortes and the pope, had to be withdrawn after a year. In the second place, although the king was able to raise taxes, he was unable to increase revenue. If there is one single measure of the failure of government in seventeenth-century Castile, it is the enormous gap which opened up between expectation and receipt in the reign of Philip IV. According to one calculation in the mid 1650s, new taxes granted the crown since the accession of Philip II totalled a nominal 14.5 million ducats a year, of which the king actually received only 5.5 and after deducting debt obligations, only 1.7 million. By 1649 it was claimed that Castile as a whole owed over 36 million ducats in tax arrears.[42]

The decline of population, production and trade undoubtedly played a major part in this shortfall, but the failure of the revenues was primarily a failure of control. Nobody had any doubt that the country was actually paying far more, perhaps three, four, or five times more, than the king was receiving, and that the rest was being diverted into the pockets of an army of administrators, collectors, receivers, treasurers, notaries, bailiffs and enforcers, all of them venal office-holders, recouping their investments, and of the lords, squires (*señores*), *regidores* (aldermen) and 'bosses' in the localities, who controlled, manipulated and exploited the fiscal system in their own interests.

At the root of this loss of control were the fiscal policies to which the crown had been driven since the reign of Charles V. With the collapse of all other resources, the crown was forced to sell its authority – jurisdiction, lands, rents, offices. The consequence was the extension and the reinforcement of the seigniorial regime. During Philip IV's reign alone, some 55,000 families were sold into seigniorial jurisdiction, about 5 per cent of the total population, 10–12 per cent of royal vassals, and at least 169 new *señoríos* (jurisdictional lordships) created, each with primary jurisdiction and the right to appoint village magistrates and officials. Lords were enabled to buy extensions of their jurisdictions and patronage, crown lands with rights of justice, and the sales taxes (*alcabalas*) and other royal rents of their villages. By 1637, in excess of 3600 places were paying their *alcabalas* to their lords (one-third or more of the population), and the alienations were continuing apace.[43]

A second consequence was the commercialisation and patrimonialisation of local government through the sale of office. Of particular importance was the renewed sale of *regimientos*, voting offices in the city councils. Philip III had enabled the already venal *regidores* to make their offices legally hereditary, and the repeated sales of new *regimientos* by Philip IV confirmed the oligarchic character of an inflated and overblown municipal government, profiteering from its control of the local market, municipal taxation and the exploitation of communal rents and properties. Furthermore, by selling immunities and pardons, even for murder, the crown was undermining the judicial and institutional sanctions against such misgovernment. In 1639, for example, the local magistrates and other officials of the 44 towns of the province of Seville bought exemption from judicial review by the city. They were offered the same privilege again in 1652, by which time they had gone twelve years without visitation.[44]

The selling of jurisdictions, offices and indemnities, as pure acts of the royal grace, was itself the very mark of absolutism, not least because the alienation of the royal domain was a clear breach of the king's oath sworn to his kingdom on his accession. These alienations in no way diminished the king's sovereign jurisdiction, his *majoría*, which was in its very essence inalienable, but they contributed to a serious diminution of royal *power* in the localities and a major shift in the balance of local power to local 'bosses', the *poderosos* as contemporaries called them. The effect of the fiscal expedients to which the crown had to resort was that immediate control over the king's subjects was being passed to those who were willing to pay for it, and increasingly it was through their brokerage of power that royal policy had to be implemented.

The lack of articulation between central and local government was the crucial weakness in the structure of authority in Castile. The key links in the chain of command were the 80 or so *corregidores*, who presided over the town councils and acted as chief magistrates and executives in their districts. There are, however, many indications that the *corregidores* were too often less than reliable instruments of royal authority in the localities. They were not, in general, career bureaucrats, but most often aldermen (*regidores*) of other cities, appointed as a reward for their services and, therefore, men of the same social background and political and economic interests as the *regidores* they were sent to manage, as likely to be thinking of the short-term benefits of their term of office as of their long-term career prospects. Not surprisingly, there is a good deal of evidence of collusion between the *corregidor* and the *regidores*, widespread complaints of their lack of vigour in pursuing malfeasance, and of venality and favouritism in the appointment of their legal assistants and ancillary officials. Olivares, and others, had proposals for reforming the office and making it part of a graduated administrative career, but nothing was done. On the contrary, the increasing use of the appointment as a reward for complaisant deputies of the Cortes magnified the very weaknesses that needed reforming.

Moreover, in at least half the country where primary jurisdiction belonged to lay lords, or the church, there were no royal *corregidores*. As new areas of permanent business of a general incidence were created in the seventeenth century attempts were made to forge new links in the chain of command and to unify administrative space in each area of competence, with the appointment of officials who operated throughout their districts regardless of jurisdiction or exemption (*administradores generales de Millones*, provincial *superintendentes, sargentos mayores de milicias*) and *jueces de comisión*, judges of the councils or appeal courts sent out to the localities on specific missions, recruiting, disciplinary investigations, negotiating donatives, sales of lands, or offices. Not much is known about these offices, but they seem not to have been entirely successful. Militia service was subject to the same abuses as taxation, and the *administradores generales* generated not only considerable extra expense, but endless conflicts with other agents of the fiscal system. The *jueces de comisión* were not ineffective as occasional, high-level trouble-shooters, but they could not operate as an alternative body of permanent administrators. They are illustrative of the more general proposition that in the localities the crown was able to exercise effective control only extraordinarily and erratically. Madrid lacked the local information to check evasion and abuse, its bailiffs were unable to prevail over local resistance, and its own officials frequently blocked administrative changes which threatened their own competence. The forces of coercion at the crown's disposal, the *alcaldes*, or justices, of the royal courts and their constables, and the aristocratically commanded, mounted Guards of Castile, nominally some 1000 strong, were sufficient to bring individuals, even the greatest, to justice, but not to discipline the whole country on a continuous basis. The royal armies, on the Portuguese front in Galicia and Extremadura, equally aristocratically led and officered by the local gentry, were powerful engines of financial and material oppression, but they operated essentially in the interests of their own sustenance, rather than as coercive agents of royal control. Order in the cities, and the suppression of popular disturbance, largely depended on the armed forces mustered by the local nobility and gentry and their clients and servants, whose inventories reveal a disproportionate share of the offensive weaponry in private hands and a near monopoly of armour and horses. Royal authority was simply not transferable, on a regular basis, to the local level without the informal machinery of affinity and clientage which linked the court aristocracy and the higher bureaucracy with the local elites. It was with the *poderosos*, therefore, that power in the country rested. Everywhere local power, as a general rule, prevailed over central authority, the *regidores* and *poderosos* operating through a series of alliances, with the *corregidores*, with the law courts, with one tax administrator against another, playing off jurisdictions, manipulating appeals procedures, challenging the competence of inspectors and bailiffs, and not flinching from violence. Olivares' frustration, even after fifteen years of vigorous, and sometimes brutal, reforming zeal, is comment enough on the limits of the effective power of royal government: 'Sire, no town councillor in Spain, no constable, no notary, no lord, no grandee, no squire, nobody who owns the sales-tax of a village, nobody who has a *juro* on it, nobody who has any property, nor any man of influence in the place he lives, pays taxes, and when I say nobody, I mean nobody.'[45] Two decades later there had been no improvement. The councils in the last years of the reign are condemning the 'usurpations' of the powerful in very much the same terms. Indeed, throughout the century the litany was endless and uninterrupted.

It is no doubt true as some argue, that seventeenth-century Castile was a 'much governed' country – the contemporary estimates of the number of government officials, however fantastic, reflect a sense of administrative overpopulation which had much basis in reality – but it was not a country governed by the king. At the heart of the problem was the inability to translate command into compliance. 'Everywhere there is a general carelessness in the execution of my decisions', complained Philip IV in 1635. 'The lack of compliance and obedience which is shown by everybody has everything in turmoil and without any kind of respect', warned the Council of State in 1664. 'The situation demands a remedy, its being of the utmost importance that this seed be dug out and proper respect established for Your Majesty's orders.' 'This country is in a most miserable condition', wrote the English resident, Alexander Stanhope, at the end of the century, 'no head to govern, and every man in office does what he pleases, without fear of being called to account.'[46] Castile may have been subject to arbitrary, even tyrannical rule, but it was not the rule of an 'absolute monarch'. The popular demand, as expressed in the mass of satirical pamphlets of the seventeenth century, was not for less, but for more and stronger royal government. What was needed was a revolution from above. That is what Olivares had attempted. His failure demonstrated that it was something of which the government of the so-called, 'lesser Habsburgs' was not capable. As the French envoy, the Count of Rebenac, observed in 1689:

> If one looks closely at the government of this monarchy, one will find in it an excessive disorder, but in the state it is in, it is scarcely possible to bring about change without exposing it to dangers more to be feared that the evil itself. A total revolution would be necessary before perfect order could be established in this state.[47]

VII

How then are we to categorise the Castilian polity in the seventeenth century? If we are talking about the authority of the crown, 'absolutism' is not entirely inappropriate, but it was an absolutism according to and within the law, which both constrained and justified it. There was, therefore, no development in the seventeenth century of a special doctrine of reserve, or *extra*ordinary powers. Those powers were already recognised as part of the king's legitimate prerogative. As Covarrubias y Leyva insisted: 'We should refrain completely from calling power "absolute". What the prince is permitted to do by natural, divine and human law, even if it is the derogation of human laws, is his ordinary power . . . for the law allows nothing absolute to anyone, however powerful a prince he may be.'[48] The apparently arbitrary fiscal measures imposed on all social orders, the ability to make the grandees levy soldiers, to enforce consent to the granting of services and to dispensations from the conditions of the Millones show us a monarchy that was able to get its way not by insisting on some innate charisma, but by extending and exploiting its accepted, customary and common-law, regalian rights in the cause of the public weal, in despite of contractual restrictions, legal quibbles, or local resistance, and to do so when necessary by peremptory and coercive methods. What was different about absolutism in the seventeenth century was largely a question of the style and manner of government, an authoritarian impatience with conventional compromises and the extraction of the maximum advantage from the letter of the law.

In Castile, however, we have the paradox, common in early

modern states, yet here perhaps in an exaggerated form, of absolute *authority* and limited *power*, or in specifically Castilian terms, absolute obedience and limited compliance. There is a marked dissonance between the assertiveness of royal authority and the lack of effective power reported by ministers and councillors and manifest in the administration of justice, finance and war. This ambiguity makes it difficult to categorise simply the polity of seventeenth-century Castile. For some historians the period is part of a steady, though not yet completed, advance of monarchical absolutism, a phase of what has been called 'contested absolutism'.[49] For others, the key to the period, from the 1580s onwards, is not 'absolutism', but the reverse, the fragmentation of state power, a 'regression towards the bases of the feudal and regional system', the disaggregation of authority, government and community at both central and local level.[50]

One's assessment of seventeenth-century Castilian monarchy depends very much on one's field of view. Historians of ideas and of law tend to come up with rather different judgements from historians of government and administrative practice. The latter are more likely than the former to regard the processes of localisation and privatisation, whether they call them 'devolution' or 'decentralisation', 'seigniorialisation' or 'refeudalisation', as incompatible with the practice of 'absolutism'. From the legal point of view, however, these processes not only did not diminish the king's supreme jurisdiction, his *mayoría*, but indeed depended for their force on that very authority. This has led a number of historians to argue that to see absolutism in terms of a necessary unification of authority and power, or a conflict between the centralisation and the localisation of government, is to misunderstand the nature of the early modern state. Localisation and seigniorialisation are seen not as a weakening of the state but as one of its modes of operation, an 'integration' of local forces into its service, but under its control.[51] In its turn, however, the crown had to lend its weight to support the existing social order and uphold the authority of its noble and *poderoso* allies in the localities, and it had to reward them for their cooperation by recycling tax revenues to them in the form of pensions, offices, grants, and the financial and economic benefits of administration. From this perspective the early modern state is perceived not as an independent force of unification and centralisation, but as a 'monarcho-seigniorial' regime, the political expression of the prevailing, aristocratic social order during a phase in which 'feudal' relations of production were being transformed. Absolutism thus appears as a 'redeployed apparatus of feudal domination', a centralised form of feudal extraction.[52] Such a characterisation has seemed particularly appropriate to an early modern Spain in which the bourgeoisie is generally thought to have been too weak to give the alternative notion of the absolutist state as the independent arbiter of the class struggle much credibility.

Both 'absolutism' and 'devolution' are rejected by those for whom the Castilian monarchy was never absolute, never had a fullness of power unlimited by the law, or by other parallel, power centres.[53] The seventeenth century is, in this respect, no different from the sixteenth. As there never had been an effective machinery of state control to fall apart, there could consequently be no 'devolution'. Absolutism, as a system of government involving a centralisation of power, a uniformity of law, and executive rather than judicialist principles of administration, was not to be achieved, or indeed consciously pursued, until the Bourbons in the eighteenth century were able to impose the necessary revolution in government by conquest.[54]

We are still a very long way from the resolution of these differences. One problem is that, given the subjective and generally interested nature of the grievance literature which provides us with so much of our material, it is not at all easy to establish firm measures of the variations in the effectiveness of government in different periods. How much of the evidence for governmental breakdown is more than conciliar jeremiad, and how many of the denunciations of administrative abuse are more than the easy excuses of ministers for their own failures? The statistical evidence of tax returns, court cases and military recruiting suggests that there was a real deterioration in the seventeenth century; but a contrary case has been made for certain periods of the seventeenth century and for certain areas of administration, and the issue cannot yet be considered resolved.[55]

The argument that monarchical rule was not absolute, but transactional, that the compliance of the nobility and the local governing oligarchies was merely part of a collusive bargain with the crown for the exploitation of the governed, is easier to postulate than to prove. Too often a crude materialist definition of interests precludes serious consideration of interests of other kinds, whether loyalist or paternalist. On the other hand, the evidence for royal intervention to control the seigniorial regime, through the revision by the king's courts of the judicial visitations of seigniorial officials, for example,[56] begs the question of the effectiveness of that intervention and, given that there are no records of non-intervention, of its statistical significance. In specific cases, royal supervision over both the seigniorial regime and the municipal councils has been shown to have been of very uncertain effect.[57] The problem of the relationship of the monarchy to the social order requires, among other things, a knowledge of that area of royal policy and of the dynamics of social change which we do not at present possess in sufficient breadth. Within the general framework of an ordered and orderly society, as good a case can be made for a radical as for a conservative interpretation of the social function of 'absolute monarchy'.

Perhaps one thing can be said with reasonable confidence, and that is that the assertion of monarchical absolutism is by no means the same thing as an increase in the power, or effectiveness of the state; nor, indeed, may it have much to do with the personal role of the prince in the government of his realms. In this respect the 'absolutism' of seventeenth-century Castile, where there was no concurrence of a strong monarchy and a strong state, is peculiarly revealing. The gap between the hyperboles of political language and the realities of political life in the Spain of Charles II exposes in an extreme form what was a fundamental contradiction of absolute monarchy everywhere in Europe, the maximum concentration of authority at the summit, and the minimal extension of power to the base.[58]

4. Sweden

A. F. UPTON

I

THE royal absolutism that was consolidated in Sweden in the last two decades of the seventeenth century had peculiarities which distinguish it from other contemporary absolutisms. It was funded by a massive resumption of crown lands, which involved a radical attack on the landed property of the nobility: in a small, poor, underdeveloped country it created what was probably the most efficient military-bureaucratic machine in Europe: and did this without any gross breach of legal norms, without physical force and apparently with the consent of the great majority in society. For the Diet of four estates, which was Sweden's representative institution, endorsed the measures taken and survived with a much reduced, but still recognised role in public affairs. This was possible because although early modern absolutism was a system of coercion which imposed rigid constraints on the subject it was quite different from modern totalitarian dictatorship. That is imposed on societies that are ideologically and culturally pluralist. But in spite of the Reformation, most societies in early modern Europe were consensus societies whose members subscribed to one common set of values, prescribing what the ends of society were and how they should be pursued. There was no provision for lawful deviation from the accepted norms; individuals or groups who did deviate were seen everywhere as heretical and subversive and rightly open to ruthless repression. Their motives must be either diabolically inspired, or self-seeking at the expense of the community as a whole. Such societies were inherently totalitarian, in denying even the possibility of alternative values, and authoritarian in accepting the moral right of society to impose its values by whatever degree of repression was necessary.

The moral right derived from their being Christian societies, the fact that Sweden retained much that had survived from the pagan past did not alter the fact that its mental world was shaped by Christian ideology. This saw history and politics as a divine drama: God had not only created the world, but placed man in it as an actor in the grand historical design that would reach its climax in the Second Coming and the transcendence of this world of sin and death. Everyone had their allotted place in the scheme, and in this life God rewarded and punished according to how well men played their role – and at the last day of judgement there would be a terrible, final accounting. The king who presided over the consolidation of Sweden's absolutism, Karl XI, exemplified this ideological position. He saw all events as providential divine judgements, to be accepted with Christian humility. As he reviewed the year 1685, in which three of his infant sons had died, he wrote in his almanac: 'God is eternally to be thanked who has left us with health, and well-being and peace and quiet in this past year.'[1] It was wholly natural for him to put soldiers on the streets on Sunday, in time of divine service, to ensure that everyone was in church. It was his plain duty to see that God was not mocked by his subjects and that so far as it lay within his power, they should behave like Christians. The king's outlook was shared by most of his subjects and expressed the repressive authoritarianism which was the basic ethos of the society.

The unifying force of Christianity in Sweden was unusually strong. It was one of a few European communities free of religious dissent. After some decades of uncertainty the Declaration of 1593 committed Sweden to the Lutheran evangelical faith, as defined in the Augsburg Confession. In one of the most successful Protestant reformations in history, Catholicism was eliminated, Calvinism excluded and even the internal Lutheran controversies which afflicted the German churches were kept out of Sweden. The country came as close to the ideal of total religious unity as any post-Reformation European society ever could, and as a consequence, through an intolerant, authoritarian but all-inclusive state Church, enjoyed comprehensive thought control. The hegemony of the Lutheran Church over Swedish minds sanctified and sustained the prevailing social order. There was no danger of dissent being cloaked in an alternative religious creed, because there was none.

This society, which religious unity underpinned, was reflected in the structure of the Diet. It was a society of estates, each with a distinct function and privileges and liberties which were appropriate to it. The estate of peasants was the lowest and its task was to supply society with its food and other basic necessities of life. All Swedish peasants were tenants, for land belonged to the crown or the nobility, the Church having been dispossessed at the Reformation. There was a numerous elite of tax peasants, virtually freeholders as long as they paid their fixed dues and taxes: the rest were tenants at will of the crown or the nobility. In addition to feeding the community, the peasants supported the crown with taxes, labour services and military conscription: they supported the nobility with rents and labour services so that the nobility in turn could serve the crown: and they supported the Church through tithes and dues. In return the Swedish peasant enjoyed privileges: he was a free man who could choose his own landlord and leave if dissatisfied: he could sue in the royal courts and protect his rights against his social superiors: in principle and to some extent in practice his burdens were fixed and could be altered only with his own consent. The Swedish peasant was a full legal member of society, and as such participated in government, by serving on juries in the crown courts, and in parish self-government, where he had a voice in the appointment and remuneration of his priest; he was represented in provincial assemblies and in the Diet, and always by fellow peasants. Thus he could take part in deciding taxation and legislation and present the grievances of his estate to the royal government.

The urban sector constituted the estate of burghers. It was very small, even by seventeenth-century standards, and largely sustained by the crown policy of concentrating trade and manufacture in the chartered towns. In return for their specialist services, the chartered towns enjoyed a monopoly over their rural hinterland. They enjoyed limited rights of self-government and the full rights of an estate in the Diet where, because of their wealth and specialist skills, they carried more weight than the peasants.

The bishops, priests, university and school teachers and parish clerks formed the estate of the clergy. They were a service class, and in return for upkeep from public funds they promoted the salvation of society by preaching the pure evangelical faith and excluding all false doctrine, hence they controlled education and censorship. They also provided society with most of its social services and, through ecclesiastical discipline, sought to raise standards of community and personal behaviour in what was still a rough and primitive society. They were the main public media, preaching obedience and conformity and offering the main channel through which the royal government communicated with the common people. The Swedish clergy were wholly professional, barred by law from holding secular office or pursuing secular employment. They were distinguished by their closeness to the common people. As a married profession they were largely self-sustaining, clergy children following the family trade, but they recruited new blood almost exclusively from the peasantry, in whose midst most of them spent their lives. Social ties and empathy between the peasants and the clergy were close, and at local level and in the Diet, the clergy enabled the disadvantaged peasants to articulate their demands and protect their rights against landlords and officials.

At the top of society was the first estate of the nobility. In Sweden, geography and climate inhibited noble landlords living off demesne farming and they had always been a service class. Originally constituted from all who could maintain a war horse they became a privileged elite, exempt from taxation and common burdens in return for military and government service. The medieval nobility had been a small relatively homogeneous class, but the Vasa kings began to enlarge and diversify it, creating a new elite of titled counts and barons, endowed with crown lands and private jurisdictions, and ennobling aliens and commoners who had risen in public service. This reinforced the service character of the Swedish nobles and developed the rule that the higher ranks of the public service were their exclusive preserve. The nobility were an estate in the Diet, and some of their number had a further position in government as members of the Council of State, which kings were required to consult, and which was associated with the king in most major political acts.

Thus Swedish society was divided between the four estates, each one autonomous in the exercise of its functions and privileges. They were meant to work together in frictionless consensus, grounded on mutual respect for rights and privileges, but in reality there were endless demarcation disputes. The potential for bruising confrontation between estates was manifested repeatedly during the seventeenth century, as in the Diet of 1650 when the three commoner estates united to demand of the nobility a general resumption of crown donations. Yet for all the extravagant polemical debate, these confrontations always ended in renewed consensus. The horizontal divisions of society were crossed by integrating forces acting on all classes. For an early modern society, Sweden had an unusually highly developed sense of community. In part it may be traced to the successful assertion of sovereignty against Denmark under Gustav Vasa, who rose to power as the leader of a war of liberation. Terms like 'fatherland' and 'honest patriot' were commonplace in Swedish public discourse. The concept of joint involvement was dramatically expressed in Gustav Adolf's farewell to the estates, before embarking for the German war in May 1630. His speech assumed that it was a community enterprise, to which each estate would make its distinctive contribution. But he also introduced a concept of common ancestry, 'the far-flung fame and immortal name of your Gothic ancestors . . . who in their day conquered almost the whole earth'.[2] Swedes displayed a highly developed sense of common involvement in a common destiny. Some of the social bitterness of the 1650s arose from the sense that all had sacrificed to sustain the war effort, but only a privileged few had benefited. It was an unusual seventeenth-century society in which it was publicly declared that peasants were entitled to reward for the extra burdens they had undergone. At the peak of the absolutism, in the Diet of 1693, Karl XI presented a full reasoned report on the work of his government. He was careful to remind them that hereditary kings were not answerable to any human agency, but clearly accepted that his subjects were entitled to know what their king had done and why. Sweden was in fact, by seventeenth-century standards an exceptionally homogeneous community where 'one faith, one king, one law' actually existed. The core political unit, Sweden-Finland, possessed geographical contiguity, unity of religion, a common language spoken by all classes, except the Finnish-speaking peasantry, and a common system of law and administration, under which all the king's subjects were legally free men entitled to the equal protection of the laws. The structure was rigidly hierarchical, but it was not a closed hierarchy, all estates were open to recruitment from below. Even the disfranchised plebeian mass of labourers, servants and common soldiers could, by diligent service or finding themselves a tenancy, enter the ranks of the estates – there were no legal barriers to stop them.

In such a society, absolutism was not an inevitable development but it was a rational and natural option. Where a wide consensus, sanctioned by religion, prevailed, it was not unreasonable to accept broad authority in a sovereign appointed by God, who could be assumed to share the consensus. If a society of estates was to function smoothly, it needed an impartial arbiter and supreme judge, who stood above all sectional interests, and could uphold justice and equity between them.

II

Sweden was distinguished among early modern states by possessing a sketchy written constitution in the fourteenth-century Land Law of Magnus Erikson. This was accepted as normative and reinforced in 1608, when Karl IX issued an official, printed text.[3] The Land Law defined kingship as limited and contractual. It was elective, and at the coronation the king and his subjects exchanged oaths, and it became customary to negotiate a coronation charter specifying how the king would discharge his duties. The Land Law ruled that the king governed his kingdom according to law and custom, with the advice of a Council of 'native born Swedish men from the nobility and gentry'. This limitation also applied to appointments to the higher public offices. For all decisions on war and peace, or changes to the laws, the king was required to consult representatives of the community. Royal government was funded from traditional taxes and the revenues from the public lands, which were an inalienable endowment of the crown. Any additional taxation required the consent of representatives of the communities. The Land Law, with its provisions for consultation, stood in the way of absolute monarchy: yet the kingship it prescribed was powerful, 'All those who live and dwell in his kingdom shall show him obedience, order themselves at his command and be at his service.' The executive power was vested solely in the person of the king: once the oaths were exchanged, 'then may he grant donation, govern his kingdom and all that has been stated above, in addition he has in his kingdom supreme jurisdiction over all judges and over all petitions of his subjects, according to law.'

The sixteenth century saw two modifications to the Land Law, both of which strengthened the monarchy. In 1543 the estates declared the crown hereditary in the family of Gustav Vasa. To contemporaries this was a qualitative change, an elective kingship was clearly contractual, but a hereditary king got his sovereignty as a gift from God and could claim that he was answerable only to God for the discharge of his office. The hereditary ruler could not do as he pleased, on the contrary he was strictly bound by God's law and would be called to a strict accounting – but never by his subjects. The second was the formal adoption of Lutheranism in 1593. Lutheranism had a clear political theory: the basic textbook used in Sweden was M. Haffenreffer's '*Compendium doctrinae coelestio* . . .' which described society as a strict, authoritarian hierarchy: the sovereign stood above all his subjects as the presiding guardian. Haffenreffer described the ruler as, 'a person established by God . . . in order to be a faithful guardian of both tables of the Decalogue, and the other good and profitable laws agreeable with it. For this reason it is usual in Holy Writ that rulers are called gods, because they exercise an office conferred by God.' The duty of the subject 'does not consist only in outward deference, but in addition acknowledges internally that the ruler is ordained of God, loves him rightfully, is humble, prays for him . . .'[4] Generations of Swedish Lutheran clergy had these ideas drilled into them, and purveyed them in turn to their congregations, most of whom had no access to any alternative view. It is easy to understand how most seventeenth-century Swedes were predisposed to accept that royal absolutism was ordained by God.

However, it would be wrong to explain the development of Swedish absolutism solely in terms of Lutheran indoctrination. Gustav Vasa died in 1561 the master of his kingdom, and had practised a strong authoritarian style of kingship. In the 50 years after his death dynastic misfortune and disharmony threatened to undo his work. In the ensuing instability a group of leading noble families which came to dominate the Council developed a system of ideas later called 'aristocratic constitutionalism'. They sought to give effect to the limitations on monarchy in the Land Law by claiming that the Council was a fifth estate of the realm and an arbiter between the king and his subjects. This doctrine appeared to triumph in 1611, when the Council magnates, led by Axel Oxenstierna, imposed a strict coronation charter on the new king Gustav Adolf. In addition to confirming all the privileges of the nobility the king swore that in all major matters of state he would rule with 'the knowledge and advice of the Council of State and the consent of those who are concerned'.[5] This could have launched a power struggle between a vigorous young king and the magnate chancellor, who dominated the Council, but instead produced the remarkable partnership of Gustav Adolf and Axel Oxenstierna which carried through a radical political reconstruction.

They launched Sweden on a course of predatory, imperialist warfare as the basis for a renewed internal consensus. The precondition was military success, and Gustav Adolf provided this up to his death in 1632, and Oxenstierna, who survived him, contrived to sustain it up to the victorious peace of Westphalia in 1648. Foreign conquest took the strain off the internal political structure: the nobility could win military commissions and booty, and lands and appointments in the conquered territories. There were openings for commoners too and the whole community basked in the reputation of the charismatic, hero-king, and the glory he won for the Swedish name. The war was sustained by a major reconstruction of domestic government. The Council supervised five great officers of state, each of whom presided over a collegiate department, the Chancery, Treasury, Justice, War and Admiralty. These were ministries, working by prescribed remits and regulations and staffed by professional, salaried public servants. They gave Sweden the most advanced and efficient national administration in seventeenth-century Europe. Local administration was provided by dividing the kingdom into prefectures, each headed by a royal governor, who was also a salaried crown servant, and the law courts regularised into a hierarchy under a central supreme court. Finally public finance was reconstructed. The traditional base was crown land, but the yield from this was inelastic and mostly rendered in produce. Oxenstierna grasped the need to change to a cash system, and began to disperse crown lands for money, or to settle obligations and seek compensatory revenues from indirect taxation, mainly customs and excise. This was boosted by revenues from Sweden's mining industry, which was modernised and expanded by offering concessions to foreign investors.

The death of Gustav Adolf in 1632 necessitated a long regency for his only daughter Kristina, and created a classic opening for the nobility to extend its power at the expense of the crown. This did not happen: instead, in 1634, Oxenstierna put before the Diet a draft constitution, the Form of Government of 1634.[6] This prescribed 'an orderly government, whereby the supremacy of the king, the authority of the Council and the due rights and liberties of the estates shall be preserved'. The personal nature of the kingship was stressed, 'the king has the right to rule and govern his castles and lands and all that is the right of the crown and himself, as the law says'. This was emphasised by the rules for a regency, which was provisional and restricted. The king could review and annul anything the regency had done when he assumed power. The Form of Government confirmed that strong, personal kingship was the basis of Swedish government. The Council was 'next to the king's Majesty, the highest dignity in the realm'. It was assigned a mediatorial role, for its remit was 'to put the king in mind of the law of the realm, to advise him what is profitable for himself and the realm . . . to urge the estates and common people to fidelity and compliance'. The council's position as the coordinating agency for the state bureaucracy was established by the five officers being *ex officio* members and by its appointing assessors to the governing board of each college. The Council magnates had the central government machine firmly in their own hands. The Diet was assigned a limited role, for full meetings were envisaged only in exceptional circumstances. But when it did meet it was sovereign, 'the joint meetings and resolutions shall be observed and taken as a lawful, general Diet, against which no-one may object, since king and kingdom are to submit with obedience and loyalty'. The Form of Government of 1634 confirmed the authority of an adult ruler, but set real restrictions on the exercise of the royal sovereignty – the king was supreme, but not absolute. On the other hand the constitutional status of the Form of Government was unclear, for although approved in the Diet of 1634, this was under a regency, and it was never given the formal confirmation of an adult ruler, which would have made it a constitutional law.

The peace of 1648, in one sense, crowned the policies of Gustav Adolf and Oxenstierna with success, but in another threatened to test the system to destruction and led to the repeated crises which were the main and proximate cause of the establishment of absolutism in Sweden. Peace ended the foreign subsidies and profits of war which had sustained the expanded bureaucratic and military establishments. There were the conquered provinces to be exploited, but they had been acquired by force from resentful neighbours and required costly, permanent defence. The burdens this placed on Sweden's domestic resources demanded painful sacrifices and threatened the consensus which had been built up. The social conflicts that threatened to destabilise Sweden in mid century had two distinct, but interrelated, basic components. One was the perception of the commoners that although all estates had sacrificed for the war, the nobility had monopolised the benefits. They had had the war booty, and in addition were the beneficiaries of the dispersal of crown lands. This had the further effect of subjecting former tenants of the crown to private, noble landlords. The joint petition of the commoner estates in the Diet of 1650 alleged: 'Your Majesty is well aware what pains we have endured. . . . But what honour, what glory has your Majesty by the subjection of foreign lands, when some few only are allowed to possess them, and on top of that they diminish the crown's ancient patrimony and property in the fatherland? Or what have we gained beyond the seas if we lose our liberty at home?'[7] Modern research has shown that the commoners' allegation that a predatory nobility had stripped the crown of its assets and was reducing Swedish peasants to 'Livonian servitude' was a considerable exaggeration, but it was what they believed. Their solution was a general resumption of crown lands, an end to extraordinary taxation and opening of public office to all 'that no estate may claim a monopoly of the service of the state, but every native Swede may by law participate therein'. These solutions would be wholly at the expense of the nobility.

The second component was the divisions within the nobility which prevented them opposing a united resistance to the commoner demands. These divisions had been institutionalised by the ordinance for the House of the Nobility in the Diet of 1627. Then there were 127 noble families, but by 1650 wartime expansion had raised this to 350, with about 1000 adult males. The ordinance divided the nobility into three classes, the titled nobility, families of conciliar rank, and the much more numerous class of esquires. Land and appointments had not been spread evenly among the nobility, but the bulk went to the first two classes, and among them the Oxenstierna clan in 1650 held four of the five great offices of state, dominated the Council and had become immensely rich. In consequence the nobles of the third class, who had surrendered their immunity from taxation, but got very little of the crown lands or the better paid employments, mirrored the attitude of the commoners to the nobility as a whole and in a confrontation, many would support the commoners.

Although the internal conflicts threatened the stability of society they were also the crown's opportunity, for the contestants all recognised the crown as the neutral arbiter. Kristina used this in 1650, exploiting the pressure of the commoners on the nobility to secure confirmation of the hereditary monarchy. Being unmarried herself, she secured from the Diet unconditional acceptance of Karl Gustav of the Palatinate as her successor, averting the danger of a return to elective kingship. But Kristina worsened the underlying crisis in her last years by further lavish distributions of lands, titles and jobs. It was left to Karl X, when he succeeded in 1654, to find solutions. The new king was an ambitious soldier and an able manipulative politician. He had all the potential of royal populism and in the Diet of 1655 used commoner pressure on the nobility to force the latter to concede a partial resumption of approximately one-quarter of their donations. This both increased crown resources and gave the king a weapon, in that the severity of the resumption depended on how the king chose to implement it. But Karl X's central policy was to resume the imperialist expansion, and from 1655 he was continuously at war. Since on balance he was victorious and won new territories from Denmark, his own prestige and authority increased. While the king was absent on campaign, routine administration had to be left to the Council in Stockholm. But the tendency was to draw more power into the king's hands: major decisions were not referred to the whole Council, but to select groups of councillors. Full meetings of the Diet were avoided, when in 1658 a 'Committee of Estates' was called to Gothenberg to endorse the war, and taxation and conscription were negotiated at separate, provincial meetings of estates. This could all be justified as dictated by the necessities of wartime administration, but the effect was to undermine the constraints on the unfettered exercise of royal authority. How far the process would have gone is obscured by the king's early death in 1660. He had not overtly infringed the Land Law, and while he was victorious no group in Sweden showed any desire to contest his growing authority. But Karl X was demonstrating the potential for absolutism built in to Swedish society, and also the inescapable link between absolutism and the demands of war.

Karl X left a five-year-old son, Karl XI, and the prospect of another long regency. In his Testament, the king sought to avoid the dominance of the Council magnates by adding his widow and brother to the regency of the five great officers, and posthumously appointing a devoted servant, Herman Fleming, to the vacant post of treasurer. In the two Diets of 1660 the magnates frustrated this attempted dynastic coup by insisting on the Form of Government and asserting that the late king's Testament exceeded his lawful authority. But because the commoner estates and many of the lesser nobility were reluctant to reinstate magnate power, there had to be a compromise. An amended Form of Government of 1660 declared explicitly that it was provisional, for the duration of the minority, and not a fundamental, constitutional law. This secured the long-term interest of the crown, which was reinforced by adding the queen-mother to the regency government. Other amendments declared the regency government answerable both to the king, when he attained his majority, and to the Diet. The Diet was to meet every three years and would itself fill any vacancies in the regency government. In consequence, between 1660 and 1672 Sweden experienced an apparent development of parliamentarism. Diets subjected the policies and personnel of the government to outspoken criticism, exercised their rights of appointment, controlled public finance and withheld supply if they were not satisfied. But this apparently mature constitutionalism was wholly deceptive and there was no solid support for it as a permanent system in Swedish society. It arose because Karl XI's regency lacked the unifying force given to its predecessor by the ascendancy of Oxenstierna. The immensely wealthy and powerful chancellor, Magnus Gabriel De la Gardie, never attained the authority of Oxenstierna, and his power was contested from within the Council by men like Sten Bielke, Claes Rålamb and Johan Gyllenstierna. In typical early modern fashion, these factional divisions spilled over into the Diets. The pragmatism and opportunism of political attitudes was revealed by the role reversals that took place after 1672. Under the regency De la Gardie championed strong government, while Gyllenstierna asserted the controlling powers of the Diets. After 1672 De la Gardie moved into opposition to absolutism, while Gyllenstierna became its principal organiser.

Partly in consequence of its divisions, the regency of 1660 could not successfully handle the problems it faced, basically those of 1648, how to maintain Sweden's position without the proceeds of imperialist war. The regency could not take the advice of the commoner estates – strict retrenchment and general resumption of crown lands – for this would have struck at the roots of their own power in society. But neither could they resume predatory warfare in the new post-1660 Europe. Eventually, in 1672, De la Gardie found the apparent solution: in the Europe of Louis XIV, with its developing power blocs, Sweden could sell her support for substantial foreign subsidies. So a French alliance was concluded: in return for subsidies Sweden would garrison her German provinces, and use the pressure this would create in the Empire on Louis XIV's behalf. It was not supposed to lead to war – in 1672 Louis did not think he needed active armed intervention – but if it should, the subsidies would increase. The Swedish leaders thought they could stabilise the budget, and strengthen Sweden's defences at the expense of the foreigner. What they failed to grasp was that in this arrangement Sweden was not an independent partner, but the hired lackey of France, and this led directly into the disasters from which absolute monarchy in Sweden finally emerged.

III

It had been agreed that Karl XI would take up the government when he passed his seventeenth birthday in 1672. There was no reason to expect political changes since he seemed to have no views of his own and De la Gardie remained in power. The king had shown little aptitude for learning or intellectual pursuits, his passion being the outdoor life, hunting, rough games and all things military, and his personal entourage consisted of young noblemen of similar tastes. When introduced to Council meetings in 1671 he sat silent and if compelled to intervene looked to his mother for advice. But the signs were that a potential for royal populism was still there, should the king wish to develop it. At the accession Diet of 1672, the magnates canvassed imposing a restrictive accession charter, requiring the king to confirm the Form of Government as a constitutional law. The proposal was firmly rejected by all the commoner estates and Class III of the nobility. This underlined that the constitutionalism of the regency period had been purely pragmatic and that there was no desire to apply comparable restrictions on an adult king. Karl XI therefore issued the same accession charter as his father in 1654. Its final clause stated, 'we shall uphold Sweden's laws for the estates, collectively and separately, and so each and everyone's legitimate rights, privileges and property . . . and where anything in the kingdom needs to be changed . . . all such shall happen and be executed with the advice of the Council, and the knowledge and consent of the estates.'[8] But it was apparent that the clear commitment to government by consent was undermined by the divisions among the estates. The commoners in 1672 refused to consider fresh taxation until resumption was extended; the clergy declared, 'let the resumption take precedence'. The nobility, meanwhile, were locked in fierce precedence disputes, which produced a resolution, accepted by the king, that in appointments to public office merit should take precedence over rank. These signalled that if Karl XI wished to extend royal power at the expense of the higher nobility, he would find popular support in all estates.

Absolutism was in the air in the Europe of the 1670s, and certainly freely discussed in Sweden. Leibniz, an informed observer, wrote in 1673, 'all the power of the kingdom has been put into his hands . . . the king has become absolute master of affairs'.[9] But Leibniz was wrong in believing that this represented change, since that was the position of a Swedish king under the Land Law. Swedes themselves were not too concerned about theory, they tended to judge systems by results. In 1671 De la Gardie had discussed absolutism in Denmark in the presence of Karl XI: 'the king of Denmark has now become an absolute ruler . . . and by this Denmark has become more formidable than before . . . but whether this will, in the long run, be to the advantage or disadvantage of that king we cannot yet say for certain.'[10] The probability is that Karl XI believed he was already as absolute as he needed to be. In 1676 Sweden's enemies published an intercepted letter from Louis XIV, recommending the establishment of absolutism in Sweden. The Council expressed concern and Karl XI wrote to define his position, which was that as an hereditary king he was absolute already, 'since We are answerable to God alone, by whose grace We inherit the government of the kingdom . . . yet We hold the most secure and safest sovereignty to consist in the faith and obedience with which Our subjects assist us, and that law and justice be maintained and thereby each and everyone . . . be upheld and protected inviolate.'[11] It was war that created formal absolutism. Karl XI went to war in 1675 an optimistic adolescent: he dreamed of emulating the father he had never known but intensely admired. He found Sweden's military resources entirely inadequate, his navy was crushed, his German provinces overrun by the enemy, and a Danish invasion of the homeland beaten back only after three years of heroic endeavour led by the king in person. Even then Sweden had to be rescued by Louis XIV in the peace settlement and most of the lost territory recovered. It was a humiliation Karl XI never forgave and he hated his French benefactor steadily for the rest of his life. He blamed the regency government for the unpreparedness and was determined it should never happen again. The war of 1675–9 matured Karl XI and made him a popular hero: he had been compelled to take charge of the government, which for three years was run from his field headquarters. The Council in Stockholm was marginalised, bureaucratic routines set aside, and he discovered in Gyllenstierna a minister who was a tireless and able administrator. The king wrote of him, 'he is a hero in war as in peace and is competent at everything'.[12] Finally the king was reminded of the popular support he could look to. The Diet of 1675 set up a commission to review the work of the regency, with a view of fixing blame on it, and the Diet of 1678 renewed the call for general resumption as the only foundation for financial reform, and showed that there was support for it within the nobility. Posse, speaking for the Class III nobility, said, 'it is essential we get to retain our privileges and throw off taxation: as long as the crown lands are dispersed, neither of these is possible', and he went on, 'then it would be possible to pay our salaries, which we have been deprived of so many years.'[13]

During the winter of 1679–80, the king, Gyllenstierna and a select group of military and financial advisers participated in a series of planning meetings at Ljungby, the site of field headquarters. It can only be surmised, since the hard evidence is sparse, that a programme was sketched out to rebuild Sweden's international position and military strength and to finance this through the Diet by a penal prosecution of the regency governments, to make their members disgorge their alleged illegal profits, and a general resumption of the crown lands.

IV

Gyllenstierna died suddenly in June 1680 but the Diet met in October. The proposal to act on the report on the regency government and exact financial reparation from the guilty touched only a small and unpopular clique of noble families, had been approved in principle by earlier Diets and caused no major problems. But when the three commoner estates, nominally led by the peasants, recommended a general resumption, the nobility treated it as an attack on their privileges and proposed to remonstrate, since most of them would be affected. In the crucial debate in the House of the Nobility on 29 October 1680, the royal spokesman, Wachtmeister, broke the united front by suggesting the king would exempt small donations of 600 dalers or less, which would let out many of the lesser nobles. This left the magnates in Class I isolated and their continued protests were overruled by Classes II and III. The crown now had what it wanted, but the arguments had been between the nobility and the commoners, and between the greater and lesser nobility. The crown was not a party and the king figured as the neutral arbiter. When the Council protested that the proceedings had been irregular and the policies ill-advised, the king could reply: 'It is only with astonishment that I perceive the Council wishes to advise me on that which the estates have approved . . . how should it be safe for me to do anything contrary to what the four estates have advised?'[14] The Council yielded, but at the end of the Diet realised it was planned to indict the Council collectively as a participant in the regency government. The Council claimed immunity since 'the Council is a distinct estate like the other estates of the realm'.[15] If conceded, this claim would enable the Council to obstruct the king's proceedings, and he responded by putting three constitutional questions to the Diet. Was the king bound by the Form of Government of 1634? Was the Council an estate of the realm and a mediator between king and people? Did the Land Law oblige the king to follow the advice of the Council? These questions were freely debated by all four estates and they easily reached an agreed response. An adult king was in no way bound by the Form of Government; the Council was not an estate and had no mediatorial position; and the king sought the advice of the Council as he saw fit and was in no way bound by it. The formal response, published as the 'Answer and opinion of the estates', added a justification. It was 'because your royal Majesty, as an adult king who rules the kingdom according to law and lawful custom, as your own hereditary kingdom granted by God, is solely responsible to God for your actions.'[16] With this the Diet of 1680 had taken decisive steps towards formal acceptance of royal absolutism. Karl XI was recognised as possessing full personal authority to govern, the Council had been constitutionally downgraded and its members made open to prosecution and the resumption promised the financial resources for a major restructuring of the state. The downfall of the Council was consolidated in 1682, when unacceptable members were required to resign, and the title changed from 'Council of the Realm' to 'the king's council'.

The Diet of 1682–3 advanced the public recognition of royal absolutism by three further measures. Firstly, the king had proposed a change in the system for recruiting the armed forces, which had been based on levies that had to be approved by the Diet. It was now proposed to establish a standing army on a permanent basis: the king would negotiate directly with the peasants of each province, who would club together to maintain in perpetuity a stipulated number of men. This would eliminate a major function of the Diet, and also cut out the participation of the nobility in selecting men for service, one of their disciplinary sanctions over their tenants. The estate of peasants was naturally in favour, the nobility opposed but faced a united front of the commoner estates: the king's declared preference for the reform was then decisive and the nobility gave way. The second measure apparently arose by accident when, in a debate in the House of the Nobility, Anders Lilliehöök challenged the right of the crown officials to issue binding administrative orders. He declared, 'if it is a law, it must be accepted with the approval of the estates, or it is no law'. Karl XI responded with a demand to know if the nobility agreed with Lilliehöök, 'who sought to criticise his Majesty's actions and to prescribe to his Majesty how he should instruct his servants'. Not a single voice was raised to defend Lilliehöök, on the contrary, all four estates united in a 'Declaration of the king and the estates'. This acknowledged that the king had an unlimited power of legislation and that no subject had any right to challenge the legality of anything the king had resolved. The estates expressed only the hope that, in the case of a general law, 'your Majesty, of your royal grace, will be pleased to communicate the matter to your estates . . . that they may thus have an opportunity . . . in all submission, to put forward their humble thoughts'. Without any public dissent, the estates had explicitly surrendered their right to participate in legislation.[17] Thirdly, the king indicated that his financial necessities required that the exemptions from the resumption, granted to the nobility in the Diet of 1680, should be withdrawn. The nobility argued that a valid resolution of the Diet was a binding law, but the king countered by asserting that the Land Law gave him absolute power to make and recall donations, so that the resolution purporting to limit this power was void. The commoner estates were strong in support of the king's position and the nobility gave way – the Diet resolved that the king had unlimited powers of disposal over the crown lands. Thus the king, with the enthusiastic support of the commoners, crushed the last effort of aristocratic, constitutional opposition to assert that there could be legal constraints on the king's absolute authority.

In the Diet of 1686 an opposition group did try to argue against the king's proposal to repudiate part of the public debt on the basis of sanctity of contract. The Marshal of the Nobility explained why no law could bind the king.[18] 'In hard times . . . his Majesty can interpret the law . . . there is in addition public necessity, which is the most powerful and surest law', and this 'makes that just and right, which in itself would be unjust'. But it was the Diet of 1693, which was largely a public relations exercise to glorify the king's achievements, which issued the most striking public recognition of the fullness of royal authority. After the estates had heard a complete and detailed exposition of what had been achieved, and had been gratified with the announcement that because of the success of the financial reconstruction, the king had no need to ask for any extraordinary taxation, they responded with a formal resolution of the Diet which declared: 'by God, Nature and his high hereditary right . . . he and all his heirs . . . have been set to rule over us as absolute sovereign kings, whose will is binding on us all and who were responsible for their actions to no man on earth, but have power and authority to govern and rule their realm, as Christian kings, at their own pleasure.'[19] This and the preceding constitutional definitions had not resulted from confrontations between the king and the estates. The royal influence had certainly been exerted, though usually indirectly, but the arguments had mainly been between the commoner estates and the nobility, or within the nobility between the different classes of noblemen. Formally, the king had largely preserved the appearance of being the impartial umpire, which was precisely what an absolute king was supposed to be. This suggests that for most people in seventeenth-century Sweden absolutism was a natural and acceptable form of government. When Karl XI and his officials defined the fullness of the royal powers, they were not imposing absolutism on a recalcitrant society, but articulating what the majority in that society believed and accepted. The Swedes were proud to be the subjects of a powerful, absolute ruler, and looked down on those, such as the Poles or the English, who had limited monarchs. Theirs was a polity ruled as God's word ordained and they could expect appropriate blessings to follow from this.

But the strength of an absolutist system could not be sustained by theoretical declarations alone, it needed to demonstrate a capacity to deliver an acceptable set of policies. The Diet resolution of 1693 recognised that the regime had done this and declared: 'since the whole administration is now established upon a just and solid ground and since the welfare of the realm depends (next the help of almighty God) only upon preserving it in its present condition, therefore we undertake . . . we will and shall hold unshakeably to all that which has been so graciously established and well ordered by his Majesty.' Karl XI had justified his absolutism by the constructive use of his powers for the public welfare. The problems of adjusting to the end of imperialist expansion, which had defeated the regency, were effectively tackled under Karl XI. The basis was the huge increase in the resources of the state: the king personally drove through the work of the tribunal on the regency, which recovered over 4 million daler, and in the process broke the political and social hegemony of the Council magnates. But the general resumption was the key to the process: its precise financial dimensions have still not been fully researched, but as an indicator of its scope, in 1680 two-thirds of the peasants were tenants of the nobility and only one-third in 1700. A bureaucracy of nobles had loyally carried through the despoilment of their class. It is true there were new men, rising civil servants and officers, ennobled by Karl XI, who were made upwardly mobile in the process. Their rise is reflected in numbers – in the Diet of 1680, 350 noblemen attended and in 1693, 556, half of whom owed their promotion to Karl XI. Most of the noble families of 1680 lost someothing, but the resumption was not inflexibly applied, families could consolidate property round their principal residence, satisfying crown claims with outlying properties, and most had some compensation from the increasingly full and regular payment of official salaries. It has been shown in many individual cases that the financial loss was moderate on balance, and that the process was as much a redistribution as a confiscation.

The resources thus recovered were subjected to strict control. One of Karl XI's most enduring monuments was the State Budget Office, set up in 1680. The order establishing it specified: 'the king's Majesty entrusts and commissions the Treasurer and the Budget Office alone with the disposition and assignment of all the king's Majesty's and the kingdom's resources . . . without exception . . . the king's Majesty will annually have a budget established and make a firm allocation of all the kingdom's resources.'[20] In a process still incomplete in 1697, each regular source of revenue was identified, and each stem of expenditure set against an appropriate source, leaving a small surplus annually, which the king, characteristically, hoarded in cash in a special vault under the palace. Most of the revenue was assigned to the armed forces on the allotment system. The armed forces were organised on a territorial basis, the officers living on farms allocated for their upkeep, the rankers in cottages provided and maintained by groupings of peasant families charged with their maintenance. It was a system which allowed a standing army to live off the land in peacetime, without damaging the rural economy, and yet allowed a high level of professional training and readiness. The military allotment system was Karl XI's greatest achievement, and he supervised it intensively, tirelessly checking the financial provisions, endlessly riding round the kingdom to inspect the troops and check their equipment and letting off terrifying blasts of royal displeasure when he detected slackness or evasion. It was a model of rational adaptation to the problem of defending Sweden's empire within her means. All absolutist systems were militarist, but Karl XI's was distinguished by being inherently defensive and linked to an appropriate foreign policy. After 1679 the king sought to avoid war if he could: together with his chancellor, Bengt Oxenstierna, he had grasped the potential of collaboration with the maritime powers, the United Provinces and Britain, who wanted peace in the Baltic so that naval stores and grain would flow without interruption. They supported the status quo, as did Sweden, and were prepared to discourage Sweden's neighbours from thoughts of wars of revenge. Karl XI, after 1679, gave his subjects twenty years of peace, something they had not known for a century, and it was appreciated. The Diet resolution of 1693 declared: 'we call to mind the happiness that we still enjoy in the preservation of the blessed state of peace . . . we can ascribe this happy state of affairs (under God) only to your Majesty, whose pacific temper and love of his subjects has always ruled and guided his councils.'

There were two further major examples of how the absolute monarchy produced decisive action after decades of inconclusive debate. Since the beginning of the century the estate of the clergy had been discussing a definitive church ordinance. In 1682 the king ordered them to produce a draft, which they did, naturally stressing the independence of their order. This was sent to a committee of royal officials who saw it as derogating from the royal sovereignty and rewrote it, stressing at each point the absolute authority of the king and the royal courts over all but purely spiritual matters. It was then issued as a law on the king's personal authority and when the clergy assembled in the Diet of 1686 they faced an accomplished fact. Although some parts of the new Church Ordinance of 1686, another enduring monument to Karl XI's activity, were distasteful to several of the clergy, they could hardly protest since they had consistently preached the duty of unquestioning obedience to the decrees of the Lord's annointed. This was particularly the case with such a paragon of Christian piety as Karl XI who, as bishop Spegel put it, 'because of his great and numerous virtues was as like almighty God as any mortal can be'.[21]

A parallel example was the plan to codify and revise the Land Law, which had also been under discussion for decades. The Diet of 1686 had petitioned the king 'to order that the law may be generally approved and brought into good order'.[22] The same method was used and a committee of royal servants was to produce a draft which, after consultation with legal experts, would be issued by the king as 'a general law by which all the kingdom shall be judged'.[23] Even Karl XI's restless drive could not get this project completed in his lifetime, but eventually it produced the definitive Swedish law code of 1737.

The credibility of the system was boosted by the personality of Karl XI. He was a model of Lutheran piety who shunned all frivolity, and while maintaining the royal dignity had no fondness for elaborate ceremonial and no expensive personal tastes. It was manifest that the king lived only for his duty. In 1687 the king wrote to Nils Bielke, his governor of Pomerania:

> I desire nothing more in this life than to make a good end when the time comes for me to quit this painful world: for all we do here is but vanity. And for this I daily pray to God, beseeching him that the kingdom which it has pleased him to commit to my charge may by his aid be brought to such a condition that my successors and my faithful subjects may find in it welfare and security.[24]

It was not difficult to accept such a man as the stern but benevolent father of his people. He certainly did not make Sweden an easy or comfortable society to dwell in: he could not lighten burdens overall, only redistribute them more equitably, for his whole work was an exercise in retrenchment. But after 1679 there was peace at home and abroad, and even, until the harsh 1690s, some modest economic growth and rising standards of living. The regime was authoritarian, but Sweden had never been a liberal or permissive society: from top to bottom it was regulated and repressive. Individualism was neither valued nor defended: on the contrary it was seen as the root of sin and disorder. There was endless coercion in this society, but most of it was self-administered. The royal government had to inspect and regulate, to ensure that coercion was applied steadily, but also equitably and within the rules. And as a final resort, the absolute king, God's deputy on earth, could be appealed to for a final and unbiased resolution. It is not difficult, from a seventeenth-century perspective, to see why this style of absolute kingship could be genuinely popular: in an inherently violent and insecure world it promised a measure of stability combined with equity, and under a ruler such as Karl XI seemed able to deliver what it promised.

However, it suffered from the fatal flaw built into all systems of hereditary authority, the results of the genetic lottery: royal minorities and female successions were hazards which had more than once threatened the stability of seventeenth-century Sweden. Thus in the person of Karl XI's only surviving son, Karl XII, Sweden was delivered into the hands of a charismatic psychopath who, given enough time, would have inflicted on his kingdom the kind of destruction that Adolf Hitler brought on Nazi Germany. It is sobering to observe how thoughtful Swedes slowly came to realise that their anointed king and absolute sovereign lord was unbalanced and yet were inhibited by the established mystique of absolute monarchy from effectively opposing his will. Trance-like the Swedes followed Karl XII as he systematically destroyed most of his father's achievement, and only the merciful bullet at Frederikshall in 1718 liberated them. But then the same men who had devotedly served their absolute king seized the opportunity to ensure that it could not happen again and instituted the constitutional regime of the Age of Liberty.

Royal absolutism had been a natural development in seventeenth-century Sweden. It did not have to be imposed for it possessed an inherent ideological and practical appeal. Under a king such as Karl XI it could seem to most of his subjects that it was truly capable of giving them what they appear to have wanted above all from government – basic security combined with rough justice and equity. But in the end any political system, however well grounded in theory, must continue to produce acceptable results in practice or its credibility will fade and it will fall victim to any contingency that exposes it to overthrow. So it proved in Sweden: a shrewd Danish diplomat had reported in November 1682 that, 'now the king has drawn to himself Jura Majestatis and his government is sufficiently absolute, but so long as the Diet is not completely abolished, in certain circumstances . . . a meeting of the Diet could alter everything and the estates seek once more to establish their former rights.'[25] Events were to prove him a true prophet.

5. Brandenburg-Prussia

H. W. KOCH

I

'NO PERIOD of early modern German history is so lacking unity . . . and is therefore so difficult to describe within the context of German history as is as a whole the century between the end of the Thirty Years War and the outbreak of the Seven Years War', comments Rudolf Vierhaus in his recent magisterial work.[1] What applies to the history of the Holy Roman Empire as a whole, applies equally to its constituent parts; in this case to the Electorate of Brandenburg, whose rule over and ultimate absorption of Prussia concerns a territory which in fact had never been part of the Empire.[2]

However, this difficulty does not simply apply to the *age of absolutism* – an artificial construct of which contemporaries were unaware, and which historians began to use freely only in the middle of the nineteenth century. The term is the product of liberal political and social thought, describing the negative effects of an allegedly unlimited power exercised by territorial princes and lords.[3] Making *absolutism*, especially as applied to Brandenburg-Prussia, the equivalent of outright despotism, was mainly the achievement of those German émigré historians who, after 1933, turned their attention to Prussia and who, it would seem, had received their chief historical inspiration from that eloquent populariser of Marxist thought, Franz Mehring.[4] The *New Cambridge Modern History* has been more careful in avoiding the term despotism altogether.[5]

Terminological difficulties do not end here. The relationship of *feudalism* and *absolutism* presents another crux. The early socialists used both terms without much differentiation,[6] as did Marx and Engels, and likewise Werner Sombart, who originally set out to complete Marx's social and economic analysis.[7] One might almost suppose that the great works of Ganshof, Huizinga, Pirenne, Bloch and many others on feudalism had not percolated into the thought of historians of more recent periods.[8]

Feudalism in a nutshell was a system 'in which the feudal lord had a certain portion of land, the demesne, cultivated for him by the peasants, in return for which the lord protected them and administered justice'.[9] It was a social, economic, military and administrative system, embracing all members of society from the emperor, king or prince down to the lowliest peasant. It was contractual in character, any violation of the contract being tantamount to its termination. King Gustav Adolf of Sweden as late as the 1620s still regarded the contractual relationship as governing society, even at a time when the preconditions for this relationship, such as the pre-eminence of land as the basis for material wealth, were rapidly disappearing. He frequently quoted, in German:

> Treu Herr – Treu Knecht.
> *Obligatio reciproca*[10]

In essence the state was a patrimonial institution, headed by the sovereign as the greatest landed proprietor, on which basis, at a time in which the economy was almost exclusively agrarian, he established his secular power. The history of the medieval *feud*, originally a perfectly admissable means of judicial self-help, its gradual restriction and absorption by the sovereign and the law, shows clearly how by various stages the monopoly of force was acquired by the sovereign and thus concentrated in the state.[11] But the feudal state, with its rights, duties and privileges enjoyed by individuals as well as by groups was one thing; the state of the *absolute* monarch, with a centralised administration and codified law – on the European mainland at least – was quite another.

The feudal state had its own concept of loyalty, though the true nature of that, of *Treue*, is to this day a controversial subject among scholars.[12] But there is a consensus that it was not unconditional. It was part and parcel of that feudal contractual relationship binding its participants: *Treue um Treue*, loyalty in return for loyalty, with a legal character, though this relationship was not specifically Germanic. Under the Caroliginians in the ninth century this relationship had already found a new definition, one which no longer distinguished between loyalty and obedience.[13]

The notion of a specifically Germanic concept of loyalty emerged around the turn of the fifteenth and sixteenth centuries among German humanists in the region of the upper Rhine. Thanks to the printing press it gained wide popularity, especially among the rebellious German peasantry, who in their pamphlets argued that the law was divinely ordained, and that man could not *make* law; at best he could discover it or set out to *find* it. This law, of which the contractual relationship of *Treue* was an essential ingredient, was in essence static and indestructible; it was natural law. A thousand years of 'un-law' could not invalidate eternally existing natural law, divinely ordained and framed in the spirit of liberty. Law stands above states, kings and princes. They could not make new law, but merely apply existing law, to which they were as much subject as was the humblest peasant.[14]

However, a breach of *Treue*, and thus the law, had taken place when formerly independent free peasants were subjected to become unfree serfs. This was the belief firmly held among the peasants who rebelled against their lords. It was a revolt that had been going on since the end of the fourteenth century against the emerging territorial state whose aim was to maximise efficiency by a direct centralised administration, and a common legal code. For this process old Germanic law seemed singularly unsuited, not least because of its regional diversity. The alternative offered itself in the adoption of codified Roman law, which had existed for 1000 years. Once it was introduced, the entire territory would then have one law book, systematically structured and unified.[15]

But for the peasants this new law was 'un-law', written in a language they did not understand, and they rose on behalf of the old-established law. Far from being lawbreakers, they saw themselves as the defenders of the true law against their territorial lords. In a pamphlet addressed to the Emperor they appealed to him and indicted their lords as having broken loyalty, *die Treu gebrochen*, and appealed to him to restore the law as they had known it since time immemorial.[16]

Thus the feudal state was already in the process of disintegration, being replaced by a territorial entity, at a time which we still describe as the High Middle Ages. The heritable monarchy established by the greatest of the Hohenstaufen Emperors,

Frederick II (1212–50), had been, in Jacob Burckhardt's words, preceded 'by the complete destruction of the state based on fiefdoms'. What happened in Southern Italy 'aimed at the complete destruction of the feudal State, at the transformation of the people into a multitude destitute of will and of the means of resistance, but profitable in the utmost degree to the exchequer'.[17] Frederick's work was not to last, but the cities of Italy, in which feudalism had never had roots as deep as in Europe north of the Alps, could by recourse to the political principles of antiquity realise within their own narrow confines the principles upon which the modern state was built. Feudal remnants disappeared to give way to a corporate political community, entrusting power to the hands of magistrates, councils or even tyrants, and thus establishing the supremacy of the *polis*.

Another point frequently overlooked, but which Burckhardt emphasises time and again, is the strong oriental influence deriving especially from the administrative institutions and practices of the Saracens. Frederick II had adopted these on a large scale,[18] and they were taken over by that late-comer among the ranks of the knightly orders of the crusaders, the Teutonic Order, which was to transplant them to Europe's north-eastern corner – to Prussia. The rules governing the Order and its activities, whether secular or lay, were strictly hierarchic. Consent as the result of deliberations among equals gave way to authority and unquestioning obedience.[19] On the one hand this obedience and earlier contractual relationships were mutually exclusive; on the other, sooner or later, it was bound to bring the order into conflict with the burghers of their cities among whom former principles were still very much alive.

Much the same development, though more indirectly and in a convoluted fashion, took place throughout Europe. But the details differed widely with correspondingly differing results. It is surprising that not only students but also 'experts' again and again ignore Gooch's dictum that 'geography is the mother of history'.[20] Many historical debates and controversies would never have taken place if their protagonists had in the first place looked at a relief-map of the territory concerned.

Given the question of 'increasingly monoglot students' (Zara Steiner)[21] and, one might add, of similarly handicapped historians, only passing reference can be made to Franz Schnabel's important work, in which, by contrasting the Seine basin with the complex and highly diverse geography east of the Rhine, he provides the foundations for a geographical explanation of the different historical development on either side of that river. In the west nature favoured the natural growth of the consolidated territorial state, ultimately to become the French nation state, while to the east of it geography dictated a plurality of state-units, inhabited by a people of one nation but separated and divided into a multitude of territorial principalities which only through the influence of such factors as the industrial and technological revolutions, as well as a psychological one, could overcome nature's physical handicaps and achieve short-lived national unity.[22] Yet that handicap did not prevent considerable achievement in other spheres.

> The sheer inexhaustible fecundity of the Germans throughout the Middle Ages resulted in a continuous migration to the East, first of knights and monks, then of peasants and merchants. They retrieved the lands beyond the Elbe and Saale from the Slavs, founded cities and territories and spread themselves across the lands of the Baltic region and that of the lower Danube: the colonisation of the East represents the greatest achievement of the German people during the Middle Ages. But already at an early stage the geographic handicap exercised its full effect on German soil.[23]

Eastern colonisation, beginning with Charlemagne and in the main completed before the Reformation was a process from which, among many other states, first Brandenburg, then Prussia, and finally Brandenburg-Prussia emerged.

II

Absolutely nothing destined Brandenburg-Prussia for the role it was to play in German and European history. On a map of Germany at the beginning of the seventeenth century the Eastern March, the Mark of Brandenburg, looks more impressive and important than it really was. Consisting of territories and principalities, either minute or at best medium-sized, between the Elbe and Oder rivers, with the *Altmark* to the west and the *Neumark* in the east beyond them, Brandenburg was one of the Empire's seven electorates, that is, territories whose princes formally elected the Emperor. Thus within the Holy Roman Empire Brandenburg occupied a recognised constitutional position. But in political terms it was weak. Brandenburg at no point touched the sea, commerce on its rivers was impeded by a host of tolls raised by each territorial lord whose land they traversed and these lords were frequently at odds with their neighbours. There were no minerals, or industries of any significance. Whatever economic influence its cities had once possessed was now in the hands of the nobility, not in those of the burghers. The decline of Germany's once flourishing cities, a result of the change in the trade routes since the discovery of the new world, affected Brandenburg especially badly, since at the very outset it had been blessed only with a modest prosperity. Once Augsburg, Nuremberg and Rothenburg-ob-der-Tauber – to mention but three once important cities – had become economic backwaters, the same fate overtook the lands between Elbe and Oder, a territory offering little to the aspiring merchant or artisan. Agriculture was badly underdeveloped, since much of the land was suitable only for grazing or for conifers, which sustained a very modest timber trade. The country was underpopulated, and such peasantry as there was lived in dependence on the landlords, neither side being really prosperous.[24] Brandenburg had its legal system, but the Elector, devoid of financial resources with which to build up a counterweight to the nobility, could do very little to enforce it, especially against his nobility. Signs of a more positive development came during the second decade of the seventeenth century, when by inheritance Brandenburg acquired the duchy of Cleves and the counties of Mark and Ravensberg, while not long thereafter Prussia, the territory of the Teutonic Order, which for the two preceding centuries had been in the hands of Poland, was added; it was held as a fief from the Polish crown, thus making the Elector a vassal of the Polish king. But initially these additions were a liability. For one thing they lay far apart, involving Brandenburg in the politics of Germany's territorial extremities in the north-west and north-east. In addition they were structurally different from each other, and from Brandenburg.

Cleves, on both sides of the Rhine, had close connections with its neighbour the Dutch Republic; it was very prosperous, with burghers of substance and an independence of mind no longer to be found in Brandenburg. In the county of Mark, in the Ruhr valley, efforts were well under way to mine coal and to produce iron.[25] Prussia, too, possessed inherent wealth; it was Europe's bread basket, farmed not on a basis of medium and small holdings, as in most of central and southern Germany, but on the demesne system, the large-scale *Gutsherrenschaft*, a form of early agrarian capitalist enterprise. This was the legacy of the Teutonic Order, which had introduced it and in the course of time had enserfed once-free farmers from Germany and the Netherlands, who had been part of the eastern colonisation movement.[26] However, it would be incorrect, at least for the seventeenth and eighteenth centuries, to lump the *Junkers* of Brandenburg and Prussia together: the economic bases of the two regions were quite distinct.[27] Even the use of the term *Junker* is questionable in spite of its popularity among scholars.[28]

Königsberg, Prussia's capital, provided an outlet to the Baltic. It was a city of considerable wealth, a trading centre the like of which could not be found in Brandenburg. Nevertheless after having made these acquisitions, it was by no means certain that Brandenburg was in a position to hold on to them, let alone consolidate and expand its power within them. This is the point to which we shall have to return in due course, which 'the problem-orientated structural historian'[29] believes to have consigned to the oblivion of 'old-fashioned' historiography – namely the fact that it is man who makes history. Structures of whatever kind may no doubt influence him, widen or narrow his choices, but ultimately he *has* a range of choices. Rulers other than the Great Elector, Friedrich Wilhelm I, and Frederick the Great might well have chosen differently, in which case history would probably have taken another course. Brandenburg at the beginning of the seventeenth century was much weaker than its immediate neighbours Saxony and Hanover or Brunswick and no one would have thought that within little more than a century and a half it would be Brandenburg-Prussia which would dominate northern Germany, its dynasty being second only to the House of Habsburg among the German lands.

The Thirty Years War, despite Elector Georg Wilhelm's attempt to stay out of it, brought Brandenburg very near to the point of extinction. It was quite incapable of raising a force equal to those of the Catholic Empire or the Protestant League; it could not even raise a force strong enough to maintain armed neutrality, and thus it received the worst of both worlds.

At the end of that war, territories such as Mecklenburg, Pomerania, Hesse and Württemberg had lost about 70 per cent of their population, more fortunate areas such as Bavaria, Alsace and Thuringia and Brandenburg about 50 per cent, while Silesia and Bohemia lost *only* 20 per cent. Not included in these losses are those sustained as a result of starvation and pestilence which raged at the end of the war. Overall, Germany lost between 22 and 35 per cent of its total population. This corresponds roughly with the loss currently calculated which would be inflicted upon Germany in case of war in Central Europe conducted with battlefield nuclear weapons.[30]

This war left an indelible mark on Friedrich Wilhelm, born in 1620, who succeeded his father in 1640 when the war had not as yet ended. The first fourteen years of his life were dominated by it, seven of them spent in virtual incarceration in the Fortress of Küstrin, to protect him from a ravaging *soldateska* from all the nations of Europe.

At the outset it had been a war of religion, a civil war; but it became a struggle to decide who would determine the future of Central Europe, the Habsburgs on the one hand, or France and Sweden on the other. In the light of the politics of the last two decades, a new and perverse interpretation has been put forward: it was a war for the preservation of the *Teutsche Libertät*,[31] the German liberty. By this nothing other is meant but the fragmentation of Central Europe, the liberty of well over 300 princes and lesser dignitaries to do as they pleased within their territories.

Even the Peace of Westphalia is now put forward as a model for rational peace-making.[32] Of course it was welcomed in order to put an end to a seemingly endless slaughter. But if it was an example, then certainly it had no durability within the context of seventeenth- and eighteenth-century European politics. The central power of the Empire had been destroyed and although the danger posed by the Ottoman Empire temporarily united most of the German princes, the threat posed by France in the west and by Sweden in the north resulted in a new arms race and more wars. Apart from other wars in Europe, Germany was involved in the struggle against the Swedes and Poles between 1655 and 1679, in the wars against Louis XIV between 1667 and 1697, in those against the Turks between 1663 and 1699, in the Nordic Wars from 1700 to 1721 and in the Wars of the Spanish Succession from 1701 to 1714. If Münster and Osnabrück were to be signposts for the future, then all that can be said about them is that those who made them forgot to set them up for others to read.

III

Against that background the problem of *absolutism* in Brandenburg-Prussia will now have to be examined. It is not without interest to note that one of the most esteemed historical dictionaries contains no entry under this word.[33] The deficiency is made good by a less well-known volume which defines *absolutism* as a monarchic form of government, based on the assumption that the monarch enjoys an unlimited exercise of power, but also mentioning its institutional limits, the countervailing forces and other restraints.[34] Jean Bodin's dictum; *Maiestas est summa in cives ac subditos legibusque soluta potestas*[35] thus points to a potential rather than an actual reality. Still, the popular notion of *absolutism* appears to endow it with characteristics hardly distinguishable from those of totalitarian states of the recent past or of the present day (although even these had their inner restraints).

At the outset two points must be stated quite clearly. Firstly, that the 20-year-old youth who assumed office as Elector of Brandenburg did *not* see himself as an *absolute* ruler; secondly, that he became an absolutist after 20 years in office and as a consequence of circumstances *not of his own making*. His entire upbringing had been determined by influences hardly conducive to absolute rule.

As an electoral prince Friedrich Wilhelm had spent his time from 1633 to 1638, between the ages of 14 and 18, at the University of Leyden in the Netherlands and with the family of the *stadhouder* Frederick Henry of Orange.[36] Dutch statesmanship, commerce and prosperity were to become for him the models he wished to emulate once he had assumed responsibility for his electorate.

Leyden University was a centre of intellectual and spiritual reform in Protestant Europe. It provided the intellectual armoury of the Dutch movement for independence, breaking with the

Spanish branch of the House of Habsburg. Among its leading lights was Justus Lipsius, a philologist who rediscovered some of the works of Roman antiquity and was a protagonist of the Netherland Renaissance, together with Cornelius Kilianus, who in 1574 had published his renowned Dutch dictionary.[37] They entered into the ferment of Dutch intellectual debate, insisting that the precepts upon which the civilisation of antiquity had become great should be the foundations upon which to build the independent Dutch Netherlands. Of course Lipsius was not the only humanist to draw from the sources of antiquity, but the German humanists concentrated in the region of the upper Rhine had, as Pieter Geyl rightly observes 'rarely made so immediate a connection with practical life' and thus avoided the pitfall 'into mere subjection to pure Latinity'.[38] The Stoic philosophy as expounded by Seneca, with its emphasis upon the simplicity of manners and ethics, modesty and frugality, the rejection of luxury and waste, ready obedience towards the law and the temporal powers, the fulfilment of duties towards God, one's neighbour and the commonweal, 'a voluntary ethic of duty with an ascetic inclination'[39] left an especially deep impression on Lipsius' thought.

Added to this was the profound influence of Calvinism. The Genevan reformer used the classics of antiquity to substantiate his own religious postulates before having recourse to the Bible. Although Calvin was only too aware that an emphasis upon the precedents of antiquity carried with it the danger of seeming to slight Christianity, he nevertheless followed in the footsteps of Stoic philosophy by insisting that the purpose of natural law is to make us responsible for our deeds. This line of argument made it easy for the propagators of predestination, knowingly or unknowingly, to make use of Stoic philosophy,[40] as was shown in these islands by Oliver Cromwell's private secretary, John Milton.

The fusion of elements of Calvinist theology with Stoic philosophy produced a brand of Puritanism which, while not neglecting the hereafter, placed the here and now in the centre of man's endeavour. The 'reformed Protestants', as the Calvinists called themselves in Germany, confronted Lutheran acceptance of the world as it is, and the submission of the individual to it, with demands for thorough reform in all walks of life. They did not oppose Luther's emphasis on the Day of Judgement, but they penetratingly criticised man's social environment. To Luther's call for a reform of the church, they added a call for a reform of the world and its social institutions.[41] In both the Dutch Netherlands and England this brand of reformed Calvinist Puritanism coincided with the emergence of a modern capitalist economy.[42] In Germany, and there almost exclusively within Brandenburg-Prussia, its specific derivative, the Pietist movement, produced the foundation of an early species of state socialism.

It is significant for our purposes that Friedrich Wilhelm's grandfather, Johann Sigismund, had become a Calvinist in 1613; the entire Hohenzollern dynasty followed in his footsteps, while the majority in Brandenburg and Prussia continued in a firm adherence to Lutheranism. The impulses which Friedrich Wilhelm received during his stay in Holland proved decisive. Here he was confronted with a model state which had liberated itself from Spanish overlordship and whose merchants and soldiers had come to dominate Europe commercially and built up an overseas empire. This model was worth emulating in north-eastern Europe.

IV

However, the conditions accounting for the rise of the Dutch Republic were completely lacking in Brandenburg and its possessions. Geographically there was a marked lack of territorial unity and consolidation; economically the contrasts between the urban centres of its western provinces and barren Brandenburg or agrarian-orientated Prussia were too great to allow an easy fusion. The so-called 'Germanic liberties' acted as a centrifugal force as well as affording some impetus towards local political consolidation. The overall territorial unity which had provided the Dutch with a foundation for political unity was thus absent. To form a common identity between Rhinelanders, Brandenburgers and Prussians was a task which no genius, even under the most favourable circumstances, could have achieved in one lifetime. And circumstances were anything but favourable for the Hohenzollerns as the Thirty Years War drew to its end.

One step of far-reaching political wisdom had already been taken by Johann Sigismund: when converting his house to Calvinism he had not applied the principle of *cuius regio eius religio*. In this way a policy was inaugurated which was to lead in practice to religious toleration. Nevertheless initial tensions were endemic between a ruling house belonging to the reformed faith and an essentially Lutheran population. The highest governmental institution, the Privy Council, consisted almost exclusively of Calvinists. The exception was the head of the Council, Count Adam zu Schwarzenberg, a devout Roman Catholic from Jülich, a man of considerable administrative ability, though not always matched with political acumen.[43] Since Brandenburg's neutrality had been untenable anyway, it had been upon Schwarzenberg's advice that Elector Georg Wilhelm finally chose the side of the Emperor in the war, which only made things worse since Wallenstein's demands were as exacting as would have been his exploitation of an enemy. Moreover, Brandenburg's population in the main supported Gustav Adolf against Emperor Ferdinand; in addition Georg Wilhelm was the Swedish king's brother-in-law. In these circumstances he changed sides, only to return to the imperial camp in 1635, after the Swedish defeat at Nördlingen.[44] Schwarzenberg virtually dispensed with the Privy Council and governed solely with the War Council, which brought the Hohenzollerns into their first major conflicts with the estates of Brandenburg, a clash in which Schwarzenberg prevailed.[45] But generally it can be said of the Brandenburg estates and especially of the nobility, that they at no time showed any determination to gain political power. Neither did they have any political programme, and between 1600 and 1640 they expressed themselves forcibly only on matters such as taxation and the administration of the state debts.[46] No doubt the war seriously affected the economic power of the nobility, and Catholic and Protestant military forces alike ignored any institutions when it was a matter of collecting contributions and supplies. Ancient, old-established privileges counted for little or nothing, though to raise taxes by open force was naturally felt to be obnoxious. But Schwarzenberg's policy in supporting the Empire was dictated not only by his religion but also by his endeavour to maintain the unity of the Empire. Added to this must be the inheritance in 1637 of Pomerania by Brandenburg, a territory which could not be taken over, as it was occupied by the Swedes. In order to escape the Swedish menace the Elector departed for Königsberg, leaving Schwarzenberg to rule Brandenburg until his death in 1640.

Upon taking over the reins of government in 1640 Friedrich

Wilhelm confronted a situation in which he had either to succeed or face total ruin.[47] He had spent the two years before his father's death in Königsberg, but was prevented from actively participating in government.[48] Virtually unprepared, he had to deal with realities. The stark alternatives confronting him in 1640 continued throughout his rule. Although in terms of territory the Hohenzollerns had moved into second position behind the Habsburgs, there was no assurance that they could hold on to their gains, for their actual power over the new territories was minimal. Brandenburg was dependent for its survival upon the goodwill of its neighbours, which initially put the estates of the various territories in a strong position, as they could act as mediators, arbitrators or even blackmailers, as did the estates of Prussia when they tried to play off Brandenburg against Poland and vice versa.

Yet it was Prussia which was of particular importance to the Elector. Here the state had greatly benefited from the settlement policy of the Teutonic Order, which had kept most of the land in its own hands. Secularisation did not change that and so the personal domain of the Elector in Prussia was considerably larger than in Brandenburg. As we have already noted, the originally free peasantry had long since been reduced to a condition of servitude, though this state of affairs cannot be compared with that prevailing in Poland or Russia where servitude was actual slavery. Since Prussia had never been part of the Empire, imperial laws did not apply. The peasants could be ordered to perform services and pay taxes without the estates having to be consulted first.[49] But the mere fact that the peasants could be made to pay taxes demonstrates that they cannot have been serfs in the literal meaning of the term. A further major advantage, producing additional revenues, was the commercial significance of Königsberg, the outlet to the Baltic not only for the Duchy of Prussia but also for Lithuania, the main commodities being timber, grain, furs and hemp. Initially the Swedes had benefited from the tolls charged there, but by 1629 they had had to cede these to the Poles. Since King Vladislav IV was the Elector's liege lord, the latter had to share the revenue with him. That was the situation inherited by Friedrich Wilhelm; Prussia constituted an economic asset, but at the same time a political problem, since the question of who was to be sole ruler of Prussia demanded a decision sooner or later.[50]

Not dissimilar in principle was the position in Cleves, Mark and

Ravensberg, though the Elector's position there was even more tenuous than in Prussia. At the outset the inheritance of these territories was disputed, and since they were within the Empire, the imperial courts were invoked and deliberately delayed their final decision. The cities of Cleves on the right bank of the Rhine were of particular importance, not only because of their participation in the Rhine trade and the revenues derived from tolls, but also, having been garrisoned by Dutch forces which were regularly paid, they suffered little from the war, unlike those of the left bank where Xanten had been garrisoned by Hessian forces, ill-paid and a plague on the land.[51] On the other hand the economic importance of Mark still lay in the future, its mining industry as yet of purely regional importance. But it, too, had not fared badly in the war, having lost only about 10 per cent of its population.[52] In the easternmost part, in the county of Ravensberg, cloth manufacture prospered unimpeded throughout the war. But throughout the first half of the seventeenth century, Cleves and Mark displayed greater affinities with their lower German Dutch neighbours than with their new masters in Brandenburg. The estates there played a similar role in relation to Brandenburg and Holland, as did those of Prussia in relation to Brandenburg and Prussia.

Naturally, these problems did not exist to the same extent in Brandenburg, where the Hohenzollerns were acknowledged (after more than two centuries) as the rightful sovereigns. Economically barren, Brandenburg's strength as well as its weakness lay in its geographic position, as the major route of transit from south to north, profiting particularly from river tolls levied along the Elbe. But the mouths of the Elbe and Oder were under the control of Hamburg and Pomeranian Stettin respectively. To turn Brandenburg's position from a weakness into a strength it was imperative to acquire military power. Given the emphasis of politicians and jurists on the *ius belli*[53] an army was vital for mere survival, not to mention consolidation and expansion. The lack of an effective army had condemned Brandenburg to virtual impotence between 1618 and 1648.[54] The Elector's father, Georg Wilhelm, had in 1637 raised a force of some 12,000 men, nominally still on a feudal basis, but in practice consisting of mercenaries because of the increasing unwillingness of the towns and the nobility to fulfil their obligations. The need to pay these mercenaries caused difficulties with the estates, especially in the new territories along the Rhine, as well as in Prussia and Brandenburg itself.[55] What army there was in 1640 differed in no respect from the roving gangs of marauders which were the scourge of Central Europe in the final phase of the Thirty Years War.

Friedrich Wilhelm, who in the early years of his reign relied heavily on the advice of his mother, Charlotte of the Palatinate, the grand-daughter of William the Silent, received through her a memorandum penned by Major-General von Wedel, who the year before had left Brandenburg to take up service with Brunswick. In it von Wedel outlined the existing political alternatives, emphasising, however, that none of these could be pursued without a strong and loyal army, though this should be raised in cooperation with the estates.[56]

But for the moment the young Elector had other worries, above all that of extricating Brandenburg and its possessions from the war. His position was still too weak to risk a direct confrontation with the pro-imperial policy pursued by Schwarzenberg in Berlin. In order to neutralise his role, Friedrich Wilhelm, probably on the advice of his mother, reappointed Sigismund von Goetzen as chancellor.[57] The Elector continued to reside in Königsberg, from where he could act without the pressure to which he would have been subjected in Brandenburg. Schwarzenberg also circumvented the Elector's instructions to ensure at all costs that the fortress of Küstrin would remain closed to imperial troops. An outright dismissal of Schwarzenberg was out of the question, since this would have alarmed Vienna. The war was to be conducted on a purely defensive basis against the Swedes. Schwarzenberg himself remained at Spandau, where he believed himself to be unassailable, and ignored invitations to come to Königsberg. On the one hand his mere presence obstructed any understanding with the Swedes, on the other he was still needed as a mediator with the Emperor. The problem was resolved when he died of a stroke in March 1641. The cause of this stroke was thought to be a stormy confrontation with the officers of the army demanding their pay as well as with the military commander of Spandau, who declared that unless funds were forthcoming to complete the building of fortifications he would blow the place up.[58]

The demise of Schwarzenberg did not make Friedrich Wilhelm his own *absolute* master, but it simplified his political course, in which a rapprochement with Sweden had the first priority. Here the military played a key role. The Elector, realising that Brandenburg's army as it stood was more of a liability than an asset, and that a new one would have to rest on entirely different foundations, followed Goetzen's detailed instructions and reduced the infantry to 16 companies, each with 150 men, and the cavalry to 300 men. The surplus, of little value anyway, was transferred to the Emperor.[59] This measure was meant to pave the way towards an understanding with Sweden, while at the same time leaving his relations with Vienna unimpaired. Friedrich Wilhelm let the Emperor know that contingents of the Brandenburg army were being transferred to him, but Brandenburg itself was no longer in a position to contribute anything to the war effort.[60]

The immediate outcome of these measures was a two-year armistice concluded in Stockholm on 24 July 1641.[61] It was a beginning; the Swedes were still in possession of Brandenburg's strategic key points, while imperial troops were formally prohibited from Brandenburg as a transit area. The Electorate's unarmed neutrality produced respect for it neither in Stockholm nor in Vienna. But it provided a necessary breathing space, though one in which both Swedish and imperial troops continued to ravage the country, causing several peasant uprisings.[62] When peace negotiations began at Münster and Osnabrück in 1644 Brandenburg could not throw any armed force into the scales. The Swedish presence made the raising of a new army there an impossibility. Modest beginnings of rearmament could be carried out only in Brandenburg's Rhenish and Westphalian possessions, which from 1644 were evacuated by the Dutch, Hessians, Swedish and Imperial troops. The recruitment of a new force, however, was opposed by the estates, who would have preferred to see no army at all on their territory and were particularly anxious that troops should not be raised from their own population. Moreover, not without justification, they feared that these steps were only the thin end of the wedge, at the end of which there would be a standing military force. Friedrich Wilhelm's pleas that what was done was for the security of all his possessions were ignored.[63] The question of finance did not yet arise, since the costs were in the main carried by Prussia. Here the estates responded to the appeal by a member of the Privy Council, Konrad von Burgsdorff, to provide his master with 'respect and authority by means of the sword'[64] no doubt aware that a financial contribution was preferable to raising forces within Prussia herself.

Although a modest army, still consisting of mercenaries – the change towards a permanent standing army was not made until 1660 – it showed distinctly new features. Otto Hintze quite rightly describes it as the product of 'the nationalisation of the *soldateska* of the Thirty Years War'.[65] From a weapon of the military entrepreneur it was transformed into an instrument of state. Severe discipline was introduced. The field chaplains, including Catholics, had to announce to the soldiers that any act of plundering would be punished by hanging. Any officer who physically attacked a civilian would be stripped of his rank for a year and have to carry the musket as a common soldier. Every unit, down to platoon level, was issued with a Bible and a religious service was to be held every morning and evening. The army was not yet officered by the Prussian nobility. The officers' social origins were as heterogeneous as were their local ones. The specifically Prussian officer corps still lay in the future. What was new was the rigid command structure and the principle of unquestioning obedience to orders.[66]

Some of these measures did not survive Friedrich Wilhelm's reign. For instance, he proscribed corporal punishment for soldiers by their officers and prohibited running the gauntlet. Even deserters no longer went automatically to the gallows – manpower had become too scarce to waste in Central Europe. Every court-martial sentence had to be confirmed by the Elector personally. All recruitment was to be carried out in the Elector's name, not in that of a *condottiere*. Artisans and peasants were exempt from recruitment: they were needed elsewhere. In other words, the Elector tried to professionalise the army and infuse it with the degree of respectability which other trades and professions enjoyed. A common soldier's pay in the Brandenburg army varied from 2¼ talers to 4 talers per month in 1655, by the end of the century it averaged 7 talers, with variations between the branches – infantry, cavalry or dragoons.[67] At the other end of the spectrum, a colonel in 1638 was paid 205 talers per month in both infantry and cavalry, but by 1685, only 80 and 81 talers respectively.[68] The decline of pay at this level may well reflect the market fluctuations and the changing importance of rank,[69] but this explanation misses one additional point: the high inflationary rate prevailing in Brandenburg towards the end of the 1630s, with much debased coin in circulation.[70] A Prussian taler in 1700 had more than three times the purchasing power it had had in 1640.[71] For the administration of the army war commissaries were established in each province, the first institutions making for unity of the Elector's possessions, leading to centralisation and forming the nucleus of what was to become a unified and centralised bureaucracy.

The model which guided the Elector's organisation of his army was that of the Dutch, a small, well-disciplined and regularly paid force, as introduced by Prince Maurice of Nassau. It was hardly a 'military revolution',[72] but part of an evolutionary process imposed by dire necessity, first in the Netherlands, then in Sweden and in Wallenstein's army.[73] But the fragility of this evolutionary process is shown by the collapse of discipline among the imperial and Protestant forces as soon as regular pay was no longer forthcoming. The Thirty Years War was an unforgettable lesson to all powers of what was likely to happen if, firstly, a ruling house did not exercise direct control over its forces, and secondly if it became insolvent.

V

Given the diverse character of the territories involved, their different social structures, traditions and historical development, the establishment of a unified administration was slow and difficult. Initially relying heavily on the sound commonsense of his mother, Friedrich Wilhelm governed through his Privy Council, assuming personal responsibility for every decision,[74] and consulting the estates of his territories when necessary. Officially it was the Privy Council of the *Kurmark*, that is Brandenburg, but gradually its powers began to reach further. In Brandenburg as in Prussia it was the nobility who dominated despite their relative poverty in the former which by the late eighteenth century had earned them the nickname of *Krautjunker*, noblemen able to grow only cabbages. In Prussia they were the *Grafenfamilien*, the families of counts mostly deriving their status from the Polish crown which had become proverbial for granting an abundance of noble titles. Below them were the knights, formally still bound to them by feudal obligations, the lower nobility from which in the course of the seventeenth and eighteenth centuries the chief administrators of an area, the *Landräte*, were recruited. But the sheer number of the lower nobility in this period ensured their dominance in the Prussian Diet, in which they entered into a lasting alliance with the higher nobility.[75] Prussia's nobility enjoyed a dominant economic position largely due to demesne farming. But besides the nobility, expertise was increasingly in demand, especially in the legal sphere with trained jurists, but also in the technical and commercial sphere. Here are the beginnings of the Brandenburg-Prussian bureaucracy, the avenue of advance for its small but growing bourgeoisie as well as for talent coming from outside. But throughout the seventeenth century 'demand' outstripped 'supply'. Hence recourse was taken to whatever talent was available, between 1640 and 1680 preferably Dutch.[76]

The privileges usurped by the nobility, usually at the expense of the peasantry, were confirmed by the Elector in 1653, the first bond of the alliance between crown and nobility, forged finally on the battlefields of the Seven Years War. These privileges mostly remained unchanged until the Prussian Reform movement in the early nineteenth century, some of them surviving well into the last part of that century, for example certain policing and jurisdictional powers. The population of the countryside east of the Elbe was mainly composed of four categories. There were the peasants, each possessing between 30 and 60 hectares of land, their service obligations to the local landlord consisting of supplying between two and four horses and one or two agricultural labourers. Secondly there were the cottagers, most of whom held no more than 30 hectares of land and were compelled to render manual service. Thirdly there were small cottagers, who had little more than a small garden and supplied casual as well as full-time labour at harvest time. Fourthly there were the servants, and those peasants who served their lord directly and lived on or near his demesne. Apart from those services mentioned, the peasants had also to pay dues in cash or in agricultural produce to the lord of the demesne. Such peasants were subject to the lord, or to the administrator of the electoral domain. They were not allowed to leave the demesne without permission from their lord and could marry only with his consent; neither could they practise a trade without his permission. They were all subject to patrimonial justice, all police and judiciary power over them being concentrated in the lord's hands. Actual serfdom existed in Pomerania and the *Ukermark*, where the lord could do with his serfs as he pleased, buying and selling them like livestock; such serfs had no right of appeal to any court. Towns and cities which had lost their independence to the lord of the demesne were in a similar position, the burghers being bound to render services required. In general, conditions for the peasantry were harsher the nearer they lived to Poland and Russia, until Friedrich Wilhelm, Friedrich Wilhelm I and Frederick the Great put an end to the worst excesses.[77] Hence if we refer to the attribute *absolutism*, we find it in existence in Brandenburg and Prussia's social structure and practice long *before* the actual system of government became an absolutist one. It must be added that it was on the domains of the Hohenzollerns that an enlightened policy towards its tenants provided an example long before the nobility followed suit. But the prevailing system in the seventeenth century was a consequence of a perverted *feudalism* whose original justification had already disintegrated, in addition to being influenced by the social arrangements prevalent in Russia and Poland.

Such quasi-feudalism in the East served for decades as a warning of what might be in store for Brandenburg's western provinces. There Friedrich Wilhelm endeavoured to govern in conformity with the more liberal constitution, a trend that seemed to be strengthened when the Elector married Louise Henrietta of Orange in 1646, though the close alliance with the Dutch which Friedrich Wilhelm had hoped for did not at first materialise. Indeed in his alliance policies the Elector's experiences led him to write in his testament of 1667: 'Alliances may be good, but one's own strength is better because it is more reliable.'[78] Collaboration between him and the estates of his western provinces functioned only as long as he made no demands on them. But while the army had been raised primarily with Prussian funds, it had also to be sustained financially. Friedrich Wilhelm had originally agreed that in Cleves and Mark only well-endowed natives should be entrusted with public office, but their backing was found wanting when he required funds for the army, and his insistence on the necessity of an army for the security of these provinces as well as those in the East was dismissed as a mere pretext,[79] the first step towards introducing Prussian conditions there.[80]

No reliable figures can be given for the population of the Elector's possessions. For Brandenburg alone, figures vary between 300,000 and 400,000,[81] though this may still be too high. Estimates for all the territories hover around the 2.2 million mark; even before the Thirty Years War Brandenburg and Prussia were marked by a low density of population, with 10.6 per square kilometre, whereas for the rest of Germany the average was 17.9 to 22.4 per square kilometre.[82] Much the same problem exists regarding the population of the cities. To cite one example, Berlin-Cölln, which in 1600 numbered 12,000 souls, in 1640, 6000, in 1680, 9000, had risen in 1700 to 29,000.[83] Of course this drastic reduction in the mid seventeenth century here and in other cities cannot be solely attributed to the war. Equally strong inroads were made by epidemics. But as a matter of comparison France, Brandenburg-Prussia's most powerful neighbour, had a population of 23 million.

The everyday life of the population, its food, clothing, housing, religion, work, community life, the family and so forth are topics beset with comparable obscurity. No doubt conditions varied greatly throughout Germany, even where the basic means of nutrition were concerned. Probably eating habits differed to a greater extent among the working population than they did for men of substance and the nobility, who could use imported spices, and the means of production differed vastly between the countryside and the towns.[84]

Even in the sixteenth century Germany, like England, had more than its fair share of beggars, not necessarily because of lack of work, but because begging was apparently an existence preferable to that of a dependent peasant. Most recent research has concluded that widespread begging was the result of equally widespread apathy, cutting across all sections of the population.[85] In Brandenburg-Prussia a whole host of statutes were enacted to curb and eliminate begging, but without result.[86]

In an age still dominated by theology, and even more by religious controversy and by continuous uncertainties of one kind or another, *fear* played a dominant role. Religion and superstition were inextricably intertwined; the fear of God and witchcraft went together and with them a belief in powers not explicable by the natural sciences,[87] a complex phenomenon to which recently only Jean Delumeau has addressed himself.[88] In that context the *age of absolutism* as a whole can be seen as a successful process of social discipline affecting all orders of society and this process became the precondition without which the Industrial Revolution would have been unthinkable. This discipline relied on religious orthodoxy, whether Roman Catholic, Lutheran or Calvinist, and was embodied in as well as projected by a rationally operating bureaucracy and a standing army.

VI

Friedrich Wilhelm of Brandenburg-Prussia was not the first to have set this process in motion; he always had the Dutch example before him. His near-contemporary Wallenstein had much the same in mind and might have gone further if he had had firm roots in the Germanic body politic. But, upstart that he was, he lacked the power to overcome the resistance of those whose influence was deeply anchored in centuries of the Empire's political life, though in the main with centrifugal effects. Hence the Elector of Brandenburg-Prussia was the first on German soil who provided this necessary and influential example, though there is little evidence to suggest that he did so in full awareness of the scope and consequences of his actions. He reacted to the prevailing forces in society with the ways and means which, in his view, the situation required – ways and means never out of proportion to the challenge he had to meet.

Unable to convince his estates of the essential identity of interests between *his aims* and *their own welfare*, confronted by interest groups which had only their own short-term advantage in mind, he felt himself compelled to do without them. But here too there was give and take, or an accommodation with the existing social structure. The Diet of Brandenburg met for the last time in 1653, in return for a confirmation of its privileges, the beginning of alliance between crown and nobility already mentioned, which was to last for 250 years. The diets in the western provinces continued to meet and to debate, but increasingly without any power of decision. What was left of them was finally swept away by Napoleon.

The Electorate made only modest gains at the Peace of Westphalia. After the first Nordic War (1655–60) when Brandenburg's new army received its baptism of fire it showed the first signs of its excellence. Friedrich Wilhelm now established his full supremacy over Prussia. No longer was he Poland's vassal, but full master in his own house. Imperial as well as French diplomatic support, as occasion required, had assisted, and his triumph was sealed by the Peace of Oliva on 3 May 1660. What he still needed was the assent of the estates of Prussia, the councillors, *Landräte*, knights and burghers, notably those of Königsberg. At the Great Diet from 1661 to 1663 Friedrich Wilhelm was quite prepared to confirm the privileges of the estates, but their objection to his exercise of direct sovereignty was summarised thus:

> There can be no *tyrannis* or *dominat* [sic!] worse than that in France. There the burghers have been forced to accept that the King of France alone is sovereign, with such power that if he requires money and asks someone how much money he has, that person loses his head if he does not immediately reply with the truth.[89]

Count Schwerin, one of the Elector's closest advisors, pointed out to him that the estates feared the same would happen to them if they acknowledged the Elector as their full sovereign, and he suggested avoiding the term *Souverän*, adopting instead *Supremus et directus dominus*. But if this did not suffice the Elector would have to use force, because Prussia was declining into the same condition as Poland, and it would require very able people to restore her economic prosperity.[90] The burghers, led by the Chairman of the Königsberg City Court, Hieronymus Roth, argued that the Elector had usurped the role of *Dominum directum* and concluded pacts and agreements without having first consulted the estates.[91] Roth rejected any claim that the Elector possessed the *ius supremi at absoluti domini*[92] and did not shrink from conspiring with the Poles; the Elector had to assert his claims by force.

In October 1662 he sailed from Danzig with an army of 2000 and entered Königsberg whose citizens opted for passive resistance rather than open hostility. Roth was captured and charged with treason. He was found guilty, but in view of the complex circumstances mercy was recommended. This Friedrich Wilhelm was ready to grant, provided that Roth formally pleaded for it. Roth refused and was confined (in relative comfort) in the fortress of Peitz until he died in 1678.[93]

But this was not the end of the Elector's troubles with Prussia. In 1669 he asked the estates for a new grant for military purposes. This was refused and tension grew. One of the main opponents, Christian Ludwig von Kalckstein, was actually a colonel who had previously served in the Elector's army and had just been dismissed the service because of embezzlement; he was convicted of *lèse-majesté* but escaped to Poland, where he acted as a self-appointed spokesman for the Prussian estates. As the Polish crown turned down the Elector's request for extradition he was abducted by the Elector's men, taken to Prussia, tried for treason and beheaded at Memel in 1672.[94] With that the resistance was broken, and in 1673 and 1674 the first taxes were levied without the consent of the estates. These included excise duties, an indirect consumer tax upon urban dwellers which was one of the mainstays of Brandenburg-Prussia's fiscal system until the early nineteenth century. Thus *absolutism* had come about by circumstances rather than as the result of a deliberate long-term design.

1660 in many respects represents the watershed in the Elector's policy. Up to then he had endeavoured to reign with the consent of the estates, but had failed to convince them that there was an identity of interests between them all. Cleves and Mark endeavoured to obtain backing from the Dutch Republic, Prussia from Poland; only in Brandenburg was he undisputed master. To avoid a return to impotence a strong army was essential, though even with this new system of taxation the Elector never had enough funds to sustain one and was dependent on subsidies promised by the Dutch, the Empire and even the French but rarely fully paid. It became clear that strength could be provided only out of his own resources, by an army backed with a centralised and efficient administration. To levy and collect taxes such as the excise, land tax and land contributions, the General War Commissary was created in 1660, with authority over the provincial war commissaries. This was accompanied by the establishment of a central administrative agency for the Elector's domains. The Privy Council thus declined into insignificance. Instead, Friedrich Wilhelm ruled through a cabinet, below which centralised institutions operated on the basis of collegiate responsibility. As noted before, it was out of the war commissaries and the General War Commissary that the agencies of a central administration emerged.

This was the Elector of Brandenburg-Prussia's form of *absolutism*, an absolutism which only partly penetrated to the provincial level, and to the local administration not at all.[95] At that level the independence of the judiciary, of church and school, administration and police, maintained themselves, the term *police* having a different connotation from that which it has today, embracing such matters as local welfare, sanitation and similar concerns. Neither was *centralisation* quite what it connoted in the nineteenth and twentieth centuries. The bureaucratic hierarchy of the seventeenth and eighteenth centuries was far from all-embracing. Brandenburg-Prussia's *absolutism* was by no means a thoroughly organised system, or an order based on rule without extensive delegation of powers and privileges. In the seventeenth century the absolute ruler governed in accordance with the privileges he had confirmed in his lands and those granted to the nobility through a complex arrangement of central power, the power of the nobility, urban magistrates and local administrations. At each level these exercised their judicial powers over the land and its inhabitants, powers of patronage and police with which the central administration rarely interfered. Venality existed in office-holding, but had virtually disappeared by 1730, since the office-holder in the final analysis was judged by his performance. Incompetents could very quickly lose their offices irrespective of what had been paid for them, because the primary concern was for attainment and efficiency. The qualifications made with regard to centralisation applied in general to absolutist rule in Europe, but also to the Dutch Republic, the Scandinavian countries, and England, countries which either had only brief experience of absolutist government or none at all.[96]

Theology had divided the states of Europe against each other. Consequently religious co-existence within each state was a major problem. Such co-existence required agreements and mutual guarantees between the different parties, but these could not always be relied on. To remove theology from the centre of public debate and controversy could only take place with the support of *absolutism*. Hence Hobbes's call for a strong state, capable of suppressing divisive religious debate. Within that context a strong disciplined army was considered as one means of solving the problem. Both the military and the bureaucracy were closely connected with the deconfessionalisation of popular thought, and the consequent introduction of religious pluralism.

In Brandenburg-Prussia, in accordance with the *absolutum decretum* as preached by the Calvinists, the corporative three-estates doctrine of the Middle Ages was rejected, and the judiciary and policing power of the churches reduced. The Elector acted as *Summus episcopus*, as the religious sovereign, claiming in the theological sphere the same rights as he held in the secular one. The reformed church was his domain, but his ecclesiastical authority did not extend over the Lutherans who were the majority of his subjects, and still less to the Catholics, whose rights and existence were safeguarded by the terms of Westphalia. In other words, the limits of princely interference in confessional matters were clearly and narrowly drawn.[97] Practical considerations served to narrow them still further. A state like Brandenburg-Prussia, extensively depopulated, had to attract new settlers if it was to grow and prosper. Religious exclusiveness would only constitute a barrier; religious toleration of all Christian denominations, and non-Christian minorities such as the Jews, who especially in Prussia were instrumental in 'fostering the growth of industry'[98] was part and parcel of *raison d'état*. Brandenburg-Prussia profited considerably from the influx of Huguenots after the revocation of the Edict of Nantes by Louis XIV. Throughout the second half of the seventeenth century, and the whole of the eighteenth, Brandenburg-Prussia was one of the largest havens for those persecuted on account of their faith. That these minorities also possessed special skills in all walks of life was a bonus.[99] Only the rigorous methods used in recruiting the army worked against this policy of attracting settlers and this constituted a serious problem, not solved until 1740.[100]

The future of any state depends to a large extent on its standards of education. But education in Brandenburg-Prussia is a topic which glaringly shows up the divergence between *absolutism* in theory – especially when defined 200 years later – and in reality. Brandenburg-Prussia, in the field of education, was anything but an interventionist state. Its 'lower schools' were not deliberately structured so as to produce submissive subjects and the state did virtually nothing in this sphere of elementary schooling in the seventeenth and eighteenth centuries. This left the initiative to local and private bodies as well as to individuals, be they noble patrons, officials of the Hohenzollern domains, urban and rural communities, or the clergy. It was generally recognised that extensive public education would have a significant influence 'upon the general welfare and that of the state', but nevertheless education was left in the hands of highly motivated individuals and corporate bodies, leaving a wide area in which private tuition and instruction flourished.[101] This applies equally to university education – where the University of Halle, a Pietist institution, rose to pre-eminence, and from it during the last decade of the seventeenth and the first half of the eighteenth centuries important reform impulses emanated, affecting all spheres of Brandenburg-Prussia's life.[102]

1660 and the Peace of Oliva marked another divide in the Elector's policy. Construction and completion of the Müllroser Canal, which connected the rivers Oder and Spree and thus opened a direct waterway to the Elbe for the trade of southern Poland and Silesia, had symbolic as well as practical value.[103] The fact that Friedrich Wilhelm could construct it at all was in no small measure due to the increased reputation he had attained in matters of foreign policy since 1660. Sweden, still in possession of Germany's Baltic coast, tried to object, since it expected only disadvantages for its port of Stettin, but the Elector could afford to ignore this. The canal also raised Berlin's importance, since that town was the point of transit where goods coming from the Oder were transferred into the Havel ferries.

Within his possessions the Elector was anxious to abolish or reduce tolls which might have impeded inland commerce, but he encountered opposition. Frankfurt-on-Oder tried in vain to maintain its right of deposit and the revenues deriving therefrom. Problems were still caused by the territories along the Elbe where the number of tolls was considerable. The argument that their reduction or abolition would be more than matched by increased commerce convinced only some of those concerned and all that could be achieved was their marginal reduction.[104]

But at the back of the Elector's mind was still emulation of the Dutch: Brandenburg-Prussia's expansion into an overseas and colonial power. Plans for this, inspired by Gijsel van Liers, a Dutchman in the Elector's service, date back to the early years of his reign.[105] In 1664 the Dutch built two 'men o'war' for the Elector: the *Herzogtum Kleve* and the *Grafschaft Mark*. They could also be used as merchant vessels. Of necessity their crews were Dutch, but they sailed under the Brandenburg flag, officered by men in the Elector's service. Here Brandenburg-Prussian *Weltpolitik* for the first time in history stumbled across English objections. Both vessels were temporarily interned in Falmouth on suspicion that Dutch vessels under the Brandenburg flag were trying to enter the Channel, since Britain and Holland were then at war. Only reprisals against English merchant vessels in Königsberg caused the English to give in. But on the return journey the same thing happened, the whole venture ending with a net loss of 240,000 guilders.[106]

This incident, combined with the continuing threat from Sweden, convinced Friedrich Wilhelm of the need for naval strength; he set about building a fleet in 1665, in the first instance by hiring the vessels from another Dutchman, Benjamin Raule, and buying eight by 1684. At that time Brandenburg's navy consisted of sixteen frigates and eighteen other, smaller vessels.[107] Raule became its director and Admiralty offices were installed at Emden, Pillau and Kolberg. This navy first saw action against the Dutch: the Elector hoped to coerce them into paying subsidies that were still outstanding.[108] But his and Raule's ambition was to open the avenue of international overseas commerce to Brandenburg-Prussia, and especially to find a foothold on the Gold Coast. A Brandenburg-African company had been founded in 1682 and in October of the same year the vessels *Kurprinz* and *Morian*, accompanied by the Elector's confidant, Major Otto von der Gröben, a widely travelled man, sailed to West Africa. This and subsequent journeys to Africa led to the founding of *Neu-Friedrichsburg* which seemed a promising venture but which was impeded by an endemic lack of capital and English and Dutch obstruction. Only with a tenfold increase in capital could this venture have become profitable, and that would have been at the cost of continuous conflict with Holland.[109] *Neu-Friedrichsburg* lasted no more than half a century: it was sold by Friedrich Wilhelm I.

In the County of Mark the Elector gained an increase in production of iron, laying a base for industrial expansion. On the other hand Cleves declined, the major factor here being the economic stagnation of the Dutch Republic.[110] The case was much the same in Prussia, which was seriously affected by the war between Poland and Sweden, leading to a sharp decline of commerce in Königsberg. Genuine prosperity was reached only in the west, in Ravensberg with its production of cloth, a major export commodity.[111]

Within Brandenburg itself, Berlin prospered, not least because of Electress Louise Henrietta, who introduced the first sanitary measures, had houses built and improved, and laid out tree-lined avenues, among them 'Unter den Linden'. She also strongly backed the foundation of the University of Duisburg, as a countervailing influence to the Jesuit school at Emmerich.[112] Already ailing, she bore her husband a son in 1666, but died in June 1667. Though deeply affected by her death, in little more than a year the Elector married Dorothea von Holstein-Glücksburg, the widow of Christian Ludwig von Lüneburg, in order, as he put it, to have company around him.[113]

Friedrich Wilhelm's foreign policy cannot be treated here at any length. For eleven years of his reign he was compelled to wage war, mainly in the interest of his own survival. Such meagre territorial gains as he made came from the Peace of Westphalia. His policy was one of security from war and external pressure; this was the essential precondition of all-round progress. His frequently changing alliances and alignments only reflected the politics of his age. From Vienna he received no support, nor was any gratitude to be expected from the Habsburgs, who were determined to prevent the emergence of another 'Vandal kingdom' in the north. Within the context of the Empire, the Habsburgs pursued a policy which put dynastic interests before those of the Empire; Brandenburg-Prussia was no exception. The treatment it received from its allies, whether France, the Dutch Republic or England, left much to be desired. The only great but decisive victories Friedrich Wilhelm won were over the Swedes at Fehrbellin in 1675, at Stettin in 1677 and in the campaigns of 1678/9 across the Frische and Kurische Haff. Thanks to these the reputation of the army of Brandenburg-Prussia was established and Friedrich Wilhelm became 'the Great Elector'.

In his economic policies he operated like any power at the time, with openings and restraints which neither he nor his contemporaries recognised or analysed. The economic bases of his possessions dictated a largely agrarian policy of self-sufficiency, though the international market stimulated the export of grain and cloth. The Thirty Years War had thoroughly disturbed, even destroyed the finely balanced consumer-producer relationships, concentrated as they were within small territorial areas. For the second half of the seventeenth century the economic decline of Holland had an equally disastrous effect on the Rhenish provinces, as the war between Sweden and Poland had on Prussia. The consequences could be mitigated by a wise economic policy within the prevailing mercantilist system; the cure was a matter of long-term development. Economically Friedrich Wilhelm brought commerce back to life, and Brandenburg in particular profited, especially from the further development and expansion of the inland waterways. Projects which went beyond these territorial confines had in the final analysis to be abandoned. The country was not only short of natural resources, above all it was lacking in capital. In this respect as in many others, Friedrich Wilhelm could not act as an *absolute* monarch, as this cliché is generally interpreted. Apart from his immense personal efforts, he was dependent on initiatives taken by a multitude of others, from his close advisers down to the village level. In so far as towards the end of his reign members of the War Commissary and later the Court Chamber became active, one notes a general consistency of economic endeavour. But besides the shortage of capital there was also a shortage of the economic expertise that might have provided long-term planning. Men rich in projects and visions existed in abundance, and some of them were very realistic, but hard cash for the long-term investment was lacking.

Much foresight has been attributed to the Great Elector for making timber available to rebuild devastated villages, though this was a practice common throughout Germany. More remarkable was his success in attracting new settlers to depopulated areas, especially in the agrarian sector but also to work in infant industries. But here too, results were forthcoming only over the long term.

Only with hindsight might it be said that Friedrich Wilhelm fought for the preservation of the traditional social structures. What else could a prince of his time seek to do, if not to ensure the stability of that which for 30 bloody years had been severely shaken? His outlook, like that of his contemporaries, was guided by what was believed to be a divinely ordained framework. Dependence of the peasant on his landlord could mean *servitude*, but at the same time it also provided *security*. Against the background of the peasantry's recent experience, the restoration of order and security was preferable to anything else. In the last analysis, to the common man as well, what happened was divinely ordained. Moreover, wherever the Great Elector could personally intervene, and this was usually only within his own domains, conditions were less harsh than elsewhere. One may well praise the Prussian reformers of 1807–15 for the peasant emancipation but the initial results were a loss of personal and economic security, and a landless peasantry, deprived of their livelihood and the roof over their heads.[114] However, and this needs stressing again, the social structure of *absolutism* was no longer *feudal*, the contractual bonds which had characterised *feudalism* had forever disappeared, giving way to dependence of the weak on the socially and economically strong.

It was precisely this social structure that operated as a restraint on the exercise of *absolute* power. But these were not topics on which rulers and ruled spent much time pondering, especially when, as in Brandenburg-Prussia in contrast to France, there was relatively little abuse of power and none of the tyranny that had driven peasants to despair and open rebellion more than a century earlier.

The Great Elector realised only too clearly that all was not as he would have wished it to be. In 1688 he died, a deeply disappointed and frustrated man, feeling betrayed by all from whom he had sought support. He was aware of leaving only a fragmented achievement, and could not foresee that these fragments, the administrative structure, the army, the bureaucracy and the judiciary were strong enough to serve as cornerstones for the future Prussian state.

His heir, Elector Friedrich III, had no such visions. It says much for the achievement of his predecessor, that 25 years of financial misrule left those cornerstones essentially undisturbed. He was a true child of the age of the baroque, surrounding himself with the outward trappings of *absolutism*, but without the *substance*. He was inclined to an excess of luxury quite out of proportion with the resources of his land. It would even be less true to describe him as an *absolute* monarch, he enjoyed life and left the task of government in the hands of others. But he did take one wise step, namely the establishment of primogeniture in Prussia. What political weight he possessed rested with his army, drilled and trained to near perfection by Prince Leopold von Anhalt-Dessau. The army was unaffected by his extravagances and made Brandenburg-Prussia a valuable ally, sought after by the Emperor.

Under the influence of his Hanoverian wife Sophia Charlotte, Friedrich became a patron of the arts, drawing such famous names as Leibniz and Samuel Pufendorf to his court as well as architects like Andreas Schlüter, who rebuilt Charlottenburg and Berlin's *Zeughaus* (the Royal Ordnance) as well as creating impressive sculptures which still adorn Berlin. That town took on the character of a capital city, even if only a modest one. He not only founded the Prussian Academy of Sciences, but with his assistance the Pietists built their University of Halle where Spener and Francke taught, although their importance was only to emerge under his successor.[115] His one supreme aim was a royal crown, which could be attained only with the Emperor's consent. His advisers were against it since Brandenburg-Prussia's economic foundations would be unable to carry the burden of kingship. It might lead to a neglect of the army, and Friedrich might demote himself from a strong electoral position to a mediocre royal one. But he would not abandon his aim. Here the performance of the Prussian army in the War of the Spanish Succession on the side of the Emperor proved decisive. It brought him the crown, though not *of* but *in* Prussia. But this made no difference to him; he had his royal dignity, albeit anything but an *absolute* one, in 1701.[116] That dignity as yet required substance, a process beginning 12 years later, when a new phase of *absolutism* began in Prussia which was to last until 1786.

VII

To conclude, if the reign of the Great Elector had made one thing clear it was the predicament as well as the paradox which at first affected only Brandenburg-Prussia and two centuries later Germany as a whole: its geographic position called for a policy which would not threaten any of its neighbours, while on the other hand it was exposed to lethal danger as long as it could still be subjected to external pressure. For its rulers there were only two choices. The first was submitting to the political pressures of its neighbours who were seeking to control its policies and destinies, at least partially. Brandenburg-Prussia's neighbour Poland chose that avenue. The consequences were the erosion of its sovereignty, domestic anarchy and ultimately its partition between its stronger neighbours. The second choice was strict rational organisation and a military policy which would allow the state, if necessary, to wage war along its distant borders against any coalition. Any war in which Brandenburg-Prussia was involved would be a war for its survival. Room for political manoeuvre was thus reduced to the barest minimum.

6. The Austrian Lands: Habsburg Absolutism under Leopold I

JEAN BÉRENGER

I

WHILE it is certain that to strengthen the authority of the monarchy remained the Habsburgs' ideal, an absolute monarchy can be seen only as a distant goal, given the peculiar structure of the Austrian monarchy, composed of a number of kingdoms forming a free alliance in which the various estates (*Stände*) remained powerful.[1] Eager to play their part as heads of state, the Habsburgs had always been concerned to strengthen the monarchy's power, but they had been obliged to content themselves with the Bohemian model. The power of the estates in turn reflected that of the aristocracy (*Herrenstand*), which held absolute supremacy, for the person who owned the landed property controlled not only the production of primary foodstuffs, but also a major part of the economic activities and authority over his subjects which the state had more or less devolved upon him. One's experience of the world was undoubtedly gained within the boundary of the great landed estates; in Bohemia, the peasant's outlook coincided exactly with the limits of the estate he lived on. In Hungary or in Austria, even if the peasant was not legally bound to the landlord, he never considered leaving the village over which the vicar and the landlord held control. By means of the right of patronage, the landlord had succeeded in making the minister of the Church into a subordinate, and in the peasant's mind it was not the distant king, often remote in terms both of language and of culture, who was his absolute sovereign, but the landlord who collected the tithes, the state tax and dues in the local village; he dispensed justice and often used his position of economic monopoly for his own benefit. Above all he was an entrepreneur who used his peasants' service to exploit directly a part of his own lands; the benefit was considerable since he paid nothing for labour and no taxes (the lord's estate was actually free of tax). The aristocrat was not merely a landed gentleman of means but the owner of a farming concern and a businessman, who enriched himself by supplying the imperial army. In many cases the landlord was also an industrialist and the more enterprising lords even set up factories. They reinvested a part of their profits in government funds and helped to support the building industry. The lords' sole competitors were Jewish or Italian merchants to whom the Emperor had granted privileges as court bankers (*Hofhandelsmann*).

This crushing supremacy of the landlords in the economic sphere was exemplified by the fact that they owned two-thirds of the property of Bohemia. With the exception of Hungary, where the gentry remained powerful, the aristocrats easily dominated all the other Estates, as the clergy was composed of prelates drawn from the aristocracy; royal boroughs counted for very little and the lower nobility had been reduced in Bohemia and Austria to a virtually insignificant role. The Diets were controlled by the aristocrats who, in the final analysis, paid or refused to pay their taxes to the Emperor. They held local administration tightly in their grasp, together with a large number of the governorships of the respective countries and the financial decisions of the local Diets. It must thus be admitted that they held the real political power in most of the countries of the Austrian monarchy.

Faced with the problems posed by the power of the aristocracy and of the estates, one possible solution was offered by the theories of Justus Lipsius,[2] involving on one hand granting a large measure of autonomy to the Estates and the Diets (*Landtage*) and on the other hand bringing about religious unity by the conversion of all subjects to the Catholic faith. The 'renewed' Constitution' (*verneuerte Landesordnung*), which Ferdinand II granted Bohemia in 1627 presented a model which Leopold I was to try to impose upon Hungary. When, at the age of 17, Leopold succeeded his father, Ferdinand III, the young sovereign benefited from the positive results of his grandfather's policies in Bohemia and Inner Austria and also from the policy of Counter-Reformation which his father had implemented in Lower Austria. Would he succeed in applying this model to Hungary? What were the results by 1700, or still better 1705, the year of Leopold's death?

II THE AUSTRO-BOHEMIAN PATTERN[3]

The Emperor's religious policy was aimed at bringing all his subjects back to Catholicism on grounds of conscience and for political motives. Profoundly influenced by family tradition and by the 'Princeps in compendio', Leopold declared to the Nuncio, from the outset of his reign, that he would do his utmost to eradicate the public exercise of the Lutheran cult in his hereditary lands (*Erblande*), for fear that the people might otherwise rapidly fall back into Lutheran practices.[4] He felt himself to be personally responsible for his subjects' salvation and 'could not risk damnation by allowing himself to become a party to such non-Catholic gatherings and forms of worship in his hereditary lands',[5] adding on the same issue that he drew his inspiration from the example of his ancestors, 'who had taught him to beg rather than allow the spread of heretical practices among his States'.[6] For him, the defence of the Roman Catholic faith was an integral part of his duties.

This religious policy was not merely intended to promote the spiritual well-being of his subjects, but was also a response to an imperative political necessity. In a monarchy in which so many diverse states, nations and cultures existed side by side, a shared religion could serve as a cohesive force. Similarly, religion was not merely a private matter, but a means of demonstrating opposition or of conveying an aspiration to autonomy. In the seventeenth century, the discontent of a particular social group found itself expressed in a change to heterodoxy, be it in Christendom or in the Islamic world. A case in point is the Croatian nobility of Slavonia which remained Roman Catholic because the magnates were being won over to Protestantism.[7] Allegiance to Roman Catholicism was at once a means of showing one's allegiance to the Habsburg dynasty and a way of expressing hostility towards the Hungarian magnates and the Hungarian state. Following the principles expressed by Justus Lipsius,[8] the Viennese court allowed for the Roman Catholic religion to be a basic principle of unity within a political entity which embraced so many different states and peoples, for without it, the prince could not fulfil his duties and there could be neither allegiance nor justice, but merely disorder: *religion became the binding force and support of the State*. The religious policies of the time should therefore not be seen merely in terms of freedom of conscience, as religion was still far from being a private matter.

Leopold I was thus presented with the task of completing the work of his father and grandfather. In 1670, Lower Austria can be considered as having become Roman Catholic once again, at least as far as the masses were concerned, although some families among the nobility remained faithful to the Augsburg denomination. According to the report of 85 priests, there were no more than 354 Lutheran subjects in 1675, the last of whom left the country in 1697.[10] This rigorous policy was extended to the Jews: in 1670, 1400 of them were expelled from Vienna, the synagogue being converted into a church in honour of St Leopold.[11]

Without unduly exaggerating the depth of the Catholic restoration in the hereditary lands, it can be asserted that by 1700 the House of Austria had achieved the almost total elimination of Protestants from Bohemia, Moravia and Austria; at the beginning of the eighteenth century, government circles considered that the hereditary lands were now Roman Catholic, the repressive policy having borne fruit.

But this point of view was far too optimistic, because the supervision of the recently converted populace remained insufficient. If the Jesuits played an educational role among the ruling classes, they lacked the means to take control of the parishes. That is the main reason why the Emperor was obliged to call on the assistance of the Estates to put the crowning touch to his attempt at Counter-Reformation, and the result was failure.

In Bohemia the political situation was relatively simple after the achievements of the repression in the 1620s; the Catholic Estates were invited to join in the process of restoring the old religion. The Emperor was first to engage hostilities in his 'proposal' (*kayserliche Proposition*) for the session of 1651 of the Bohemian Diet. The first article stipulated that 'all must be of Catholic religion, no non-Catholic shall be suffered and the cure must be occupied in every locality'.[12]

The first two points of this programme were achieved within a relatively short space of time, to the detriment of economic rebuilding;[13] the vast majority of Protestant subjects fled the country (about 100,000 people), which thus became populated exclusively by Roman Catholics, in theory at any rate, for the emigration, though complete, lasted longer than is generally realised. In 1676, the political speech delivered at the opening of the session came as solace to those Estates which approved of His Majesty's intention to expel the last remaining non-Catholic subjects still living along the border. The conclusions of this session reminded the Bohemian lords of their obligations to enforce the general decrees relating to the 'Reformation' (i.e. to the Counter-Reformation).[14] There were differences between the great principles expounded in the Meeting Hall of the Estates[15] and concern about the economic interests involved. It is a revealing trait: royal authority was treated with indifferent respect even in an area towards which the Emperor felt attached, and then only if the Estates assured him of their cooperation in the enforcement of the law. Can one rightly speak in this instance of an *absolute* monarchy in the French sense of the term?

The third point of the 1651 programme proved even more difficult to achieve, namely the vital necessity of reinstalling a priest in every parish, so as to strengthen the convictions of the recently converted, as well as to develop those of the more established Catholics. It thus proved necessary to instal priests who would apply the directives of the Council of Trent. If these demands appear legitimate to us, they nonetheless met with the greatest difficulties, with members of the Catholic clergy (also of the first Estate of the realm) often displaying the mentality of beneficiaries little concerned about the spiritual development of their flock. In fact a parish could maintain a priest only if it had sufficient means to ensure a decent living, far above that of the peasantry and comparable to that of a country gentleman (member of the third Estate or *Ritterstand*). It was not merely a question of the priests' comfort, but essentially a matter of prestige in the eyes of the population. Poorly endowed parishes did not keep educated priests and if the curate wished to avail himself of casual offerings (*Stolageld*), he automatically lost the trust of the recent converts. The real solution lay in endowing the parish in rents and in recuperating the tithes – both of which had been usurped by lay lords in the fifteenth century (in Bohemia) or in the sixteenth and were rarely restored, even when the lords had become fervent

Roman Catholics once again. The House of Austria itself was powerless to resolve rapidly and efficiently this economic problem, which appears to be of vital significance: thus Ferdinand II reinstalled a curate in Hollabrunn (Lower Austria) in 1625, but it was not until 1660 that his successor completely recovered the parish property.[16]

The unwillingness with which the Catholic Estates restored the clergy's property was a widespread phenomenon in Austro-Bohemian lands. The members of the committee appointed by the Bohemian Diet to investigate the rebuilding of abandoned parishes gave the following report in 1668: out of a total of 77 lords questioned, 50 gave no answer, 21 answered that the matter was being pursued by the relevant authorities (the archbishopric committee) and a mere 3 lords had re-established a total of six parishes.[17] Prince Lobkowitz, who was not renowned for his clerical leanings, personally rebuilt four of these, including the parishes of Lobkovic and Roudnice. The two remaining lords to display such a keen awareness of their duties were Count Czernin and the Grand Prior of the Order of Malta. These, it ought to be said, were the exceptions. Among those who displayed their superb indifference to this essential aspect of the rebuilding of the Church, one meets not only such mighty and devout lords as Prince John-Adolphus Schwarzenberg or Count Ignatius Sternberg, or enormously rich ones such as the Liechtensteins or the Eggenbergs, but also the Chamber of Bohemia (*böhmische königliche Kammer*), which ought to have made a point of implementing the sovereign's own policy, and especially religious Orders. That the Chapter of Prague Cathedral or the canonesses of St George's Convent in Prague – affluent bodies with little concern for the spiritual needs of rural folk – should not have deigned to answer the investigating committee's questions can be understood, but the Dominicans and the rector of the Gladstan Jesuits also refused to answer.[18]

After the failure of the measures jointly taken by the Emperor acting as king of Bohemia and the Diet, Leopold set up a committee of inquiry 'in order to ascertain which *inhabitants* (i.e. members of the Estates) illegally possessed tithes and other property belonging to pious foundations and to bring them to restore them – all this being in direct contravention to the warnings issued by the previous Diet'.[19] Created in 1651, this committee was composed of members of the clergy appointed for a two-year period and the first article of the conclusions of the Bohemian Diet dealt with benefices and parishes (*Von denen Collaturen und Pfarren*).[20] From 1660 to 1700, the same article appears, year after year, without exception, proving that the question had not been resolved and was becoming a matter of pure routine. Ought the declaration, which Count Breuner, the Archbishop of Prague, made in 1697 to be taken as an admission of failure? He had declared himself disposed to make a certain sum available to the clergy, but felt that the essential task was the recovery of the landed property,[21] 45 years after the first measures were taken by the Diet and 77 years after the victory at White Mountain. The usurpers were in effect being requested to restore the belongings they had granted themselves, while the aristocrats did not feel such a renewed pastoral initiative to be at all necessary.

The Bohemian clergy had almost found a solution in the 1680s. In 1667, the committee issued a reminder of the necessity of furnishing pastors for the abandoned parishes; in cases where the income should prove insufficient, the solution proposed by the Roman Congregation for Propaganda would have to be adopted: namely the use of salt tax revenues, as after the report of 11 March 1669 nothing further could be expected from the lords. Certain usurpers of Church property had answered that it was impossible to re-establish the parishes because of lack of means.[22] Such blatant cynicism left no room for hope and the Estates, serving the roles of both judge and judged in the matter, eagerly accepted this solution which was intended to protect their interests and the landed property formerly confiscated from the Roman Catholic clergy. Rarely had such a conflict been witnessed between material interests and religious feelings. They were able to ease their consciences at the royal treasury's expense, the salt tax revenues (*Salzgeldern*) being an integral part of the king's ordinary revenues (*regalia*). For this reason, the Diet appointed a study commission 'in order to gather vital additional information and to give their verdict on the matter as soon as possible'.[23]

Presided over by John-Frederick, Count Wallenstein, the Archbishop of Prague, the commission presented its conclusions in 1681: the special fund, which had been established to create new bishoprics and which was funded by a part of the salt-tax revenue, could be utilised. A clumsy solution, which involved fighting one problem of undermanning at the expense of another. The Diet adopted this report and asked for the Emperor's approval.[24] The session of 1682 registered the Emperor's agreement with satisfaction, and especially that of Pope Innocent XI. The Diet also appointed a commission which it charged with a detailed visitation, which would study particular circumstances 'on a case-by-case basis'.[25]

The Roman Catholic Church was dogged with bad luck, because the return to a situation of open war against the Ottoman Empire mobilised both the funds of the Austrian monarchy in general and of the Church in particular towards other ends. Pope Innocent XI authorised exceptional levies on the clergy's property in the hereditary lands, thus favouring the war effort against the Turks and contributing to the relief of Vienna and to the liberation of Hungary. Opting for the more urgent priority, the Holy See provisionally renounced its idea of concerted pastoral action and the parishes were never re-established.

It nevertheless remains that the action of the Bohemian Estates in the entire affair had been ineffectual, to say the least. They had shown themselves to be in no hurry to act, once it became a case of restoring Church property. On this point, the Diet successfully defended its members' interests and the sovereign's authority was severely damaged.

In purely political terms, the 'renewed Constitution' of 1627 had brought some satisfaction to the Habsburgs in Bohemia, the importance of which liberal historiography has greatly exaggerated since, in practice, it was a case of genuine collaboration between the Estates and the crown.

The crown of Bohemia, from 1627 onwards, was hereditary within the House of Austria, which meant that there were no longer any negotiations between the king and the Diet at the time of his election, as had been the case the last time in 1617; most importantly, there was no longer a contract (*Wahlcapitulation*) restricting the power of the monarch. Henceforth the crown held real executive command, since it was the king who appointed the Grand Officers of the crown – Grand Burgrave, Grand Chamberlain, Grand Judge, Marshal, etc. (*Oberstburggraf, Oberstkämmerer, Oberstlandrichter, Landmarschall*) – who constituted the government and the Lieutenancy Council (*Statthaltereirat*) in the event of the king of Bohemia's absence. But as a practical restriction, these dignitaries were all chosen from the country's nobility, as were the judges of the supreme court of Prague (*Appellationsgericht zu Prag*) and the kingdom's chancellor. The Diet, however, was not permitted to present its grievances at the beginning of each session, as these were consistently critical of the government's policy.

The crown shared legislative power with the Estates. The king alone held the right to propose bills, which he put forward at the beginning of the session (*Landtagproposition*), which was generally held once a year. In Lower Austria, the collaboration reached such an extent that the Estates themselves were left on their own to codify laws in the 1670s, the crown contenting itself with sanctioning the Diet's proposals.[26]

Above all the crown needed the permanent collaboration of the Estates for the vote of the land tax. The revenues of the so-called *regalia* accounted for scarcely 20 per cent of the crown's resources, the remainder coming from a land tax voted and collected by the Estates themselves. This explains why it was necessary to convene a session of the Diet every year, as the Emperor could not subsist without his subjects' money.

Lastly, the crown did not have control over local administration, since the power of the nobility over the peasants had been strengthened after 1620. It was the Diet which divided the tax among the various branches of the nobility and it was the lord's steward who collected the tax from the peasant. The peasant practically never fell within the jurisdiction of the royal tribunals, except on appeal and even then, only in Lower Austria.

The application of the theory of forfeit (*Verwirkungstheorie*), according to which the Estates had, in 1618, unilaterally broken the contract binding them to the crown, thereby authorising it to make Bohemia a patrimonial state, yielded only limited results in practice, if one compares the Czech or Austrian lands with France under Louis XIV. Even the apparent success of the Counter-Reformation leaves many questions unanswered and the persistence of a hard core of crypto-Protestants[27] can largely be explained by the inadequacy of pastoral guidance, linked in turn to the selfishness of both prelates and aristocracy, a problem which would only be resolved by Joseph II.

We turn now to the question of how Leopold I attempted to apply the same policy of Counter-Reformation and constitutional reordering in Hungary and look at the results of such a policy.

III AN ATTEMPT TO TRANSFORM THE KINGDOM OF HUNGARY

Even after the successes of Cardinal Pázmány, the kingdom of Hungary, supported by the principality of Transylvania, remained a bastion of Calvinism in Europe and within the Austrian monarchy. Calvinism drew its support from the gentry (*közepnemesség*) who wielded considerable economic and political power and took particular advantage of the Diet's sessions in order to voice their grievances, alarming the Viennese government by the violent tone of the debates.[28] The Emperor, as king of Hungary, ceased summoning the Diet from 1662 to 1681, thinking thereby to eliminate the gentry as a political force; the gentry however were intent on defending their religious and political freedom, and in so doing, making themselves the champions of independence for the Hungarian state.

The general tendencies of the government of Vienna were expressed by one of Leopold's counsellors during the 1662 session of the Hungarian Diet: 'We need to do to the Kingdom of Hungary what we did to the Kingdom of Bohemia.'[29] However, the Hungarian constitution did not allow the Emperor to intervene directly and he had to content himself with supporting the Roman Catholic elements, that is the prelates, the converted magnates and the Jesuits.

These elements had strengthened considerably in the course of the seventeenth century. Towards the end of the sixteenth, they were composed primarily of prelates who had mostly been deprived of their livings and had sought refuge in the western counties of Upper Hungary; the Primate of Hungary, the Archbishop of Strigonia (Estergom) had withdrawn to Trnava, close to Pressburg (Bratislava). Confirmed supporters of the Counter-Reformation, they were nevertheless firmly rooted in the society and government of Pressburg; the chancellor of Hungary had always been a bishop and in the event of the viceroy's post being vacant, the Lieutenancy Council was presided over by the Archbishop of Strigonia.

The clergy represented the first Estate of the realm and the bishops, like the magnates, sat in the Upper Chamber of the Diet. The higher clergy were linked to the aristocratic families who held seats in the government, such as the Forgáchs and the Pálffys. Furthermore the social group of the magnates had made peace with the Habsburgs after 1608 and had not been unappreciative of the talents of Cardinal Pázmány, who had brought many a Hungarian aristocrat to the Catholic faith. In 1660, the Upper House and government of Hungary consisted of zealous Catholics engaged in converting their Protestant subjects. The two most famous examples are those of Francis Nádásdy, Lord Chief Justice (*Judex Curiae*) and of Sophia Bathory, widow of George II Rákóczy, prince of Transylvania. Francis Nádásdy is reputed to have caused the ruin of about 200 Protestant parishes in western Hungary through a mixture of threats and persuasion. In eastern Hungary Sophia Bathory expelled all reformed vicars from her deceased husband's demesnes.[30] The Roman Catholic lords found the backing of the Jesuits everywhere, the latter having founded houses across the entire territory of the kingdom.[31]

The success of the Counter-Reformation would thus have been assured, had the crisis of 1664 not cast doubt over the whole situation. It is well known that the Hungarians unanimously condemned the peace which the Emperor signed with the Ottoman at Vasvár. They accused the Habsburgs of leaving their land a prey to Ottoman incursions despite the Christian armies having been victorious, and of sacrificing their country to dynastic interests.[32] The Catholic magnates, the members of the Pressburg government and the Archbishop of Strigonia himself gathered in a vast conspiracy against the Austrian rule, to which the Viceroy Count Francis Wesselényi lent his name.[33] The Habsburgs thus managed, for the first time since 1526, to unite the whole of Hungary against them, Catholics and Protestants alike, regardless of which Estate they belonged to.

The movement led to open revolt only in 1670, however, because the main leaders, who wished to give themselves either a national or a French king, were vainly searching for external support. Louis XIV allowed his envoy Grémonville to string the conspirators along until 1668, at which juncture he considered it better for his interests to enter into direct negotiations with the Emperor.[34] The governor of Croatia, Count Peter Zrinyi, had the unfortunate idea of turning towards the Turks for support and offering them a treaty which would make Croatia a Turkish protectorate. Betrayed and exposed, Peter Zrinyi thus provoked a serious political crisis; the kingdom of Hungary was occupied by imperial troops; all Hungarians suspected of being rebels together with the main leaders (counts Peter Zrinyi, Frangepani and Francis Nádásdy) were arrested, tried, sentenced to death and executed at Wiener-Neustadt in April 1671. Through Peter Zrinyi's blunder, the very people who had hoped to spare Hungary Bohemia's fate now plunged their country into a situation similar to that which Bohemia had experienced in 1620. By rebelling, the Hungarians had broken the agreement which bound them to their Habsburg king, who was now entitled to apply the theory of forfeit (*Verwirkungstheorie*), since the Emperor's reaction had for once been forceful and the military occupation of the country left the sovereign in an exceptionally strong position.[35]

Once the initial days of anguish of the spring of 1670 had passed, the event must have seemed an unexpected blessing to the Viennese court. Firstly the main body of the imperial army was stationed in Hungary, where it was behaving like an army of occupation, and secondly the sovereign was no longer bound by any law, since he had become *absolute* monarch through the Hungarian default. Until then, he had had to respect the Constitution and in particular the 'Royal Diploma', which he had accepted before acceding to the throne in 1655.[36] Respectful of the letter of the law, the king let the Catholic elements pursue their activities and refused to hear grievances of a denominational nature.

Henceforth Leopold I would reveal his true colours and implement the programme of the Hungarian clergy which Bishop George Barsony had exposed in his book *Veritas toti Mundo declarata*,[37] in which he denied non-Catholics any rights on the grounds that the Peace of Vienna of 1606, which remained the basis of Protestant privileges, was null and void since, according to him, it had been signed under duress by the Emperor Rudolph. Moreover the kingdom of Hungary had been Roman Catholic since St Stephen's conversion and the king could make no concessions to heresy, if he wished to respect the spirit of the fundamental laws of the state. This work was a subject of much discussion among the Hungarian prelates and the Jesuits and was abundantly debated by the Protestants.

The Emperor's entourage had already been won over to these ideas. Leopold's Jesuit confessor, Father Müller, took care to read Stephen Werböczi's *Opus tripartitum*,[38] which remained the basis of Hungarian common law and concluded that the Hungarians were rebels and deserved that the Viennese government should enforce the theory of forfeit. In 1673 he declared to the Swedish minister Esaias Pufendorf that the Hungarians had forfeited their privileges and were now ordinary subjects.[39] During the privy council's meetings, the Austrian Chancellor John Hocher expressed extreme hostility towards the Hungarians in general, for political motives. As chairman of the special tribunal (*Judiciume delegatum*), which had sentenced the rebel leaders, he felt that conversion to Catholicism alone was capable of making them into subjects as obedient as the rest.

In a *Memorandum* destined for the privy council (*Geheime Konferenz*), Chancellor Hocher argued that full advantage ought to be taken of the opportunity to crush the rebellion, deprive the Hungarians of their freedom and occupy the country militarily. He justified sweeping changes which would force the Hungarians to accept German garrisons, and then the German language, customs and clothing. Field-Marshal Montecuccoli, acting as President of the Council of War (*Hofkriegsratspraesident*) insisted on the religious aspect and vaunted the merits of Catholicism. He considered above all, basing his view on Justus Lipsius, that unity of religion made for unity of minds, and that confusion would thereby disappear, removing with it the causes of rebellion and unhappiness. The Catholic party was supported by the Papal Nuncio, Pignatelli, who urged a resolute policy of Counter-Reformation against the Hungarian Estates, in order to obtain the highest possible number of conversions.[40]

The Viennese court's action was initially of a repressive nature, so as to deprive the Protestant communities of their churches and above all of their pastors. The latter were held responsible for the unrest of 1670. They were accused of having turned people against the Habsburgs, of having spread prophecies and of having publicly hoped for a Turkish victory over the Christian forces at Candia. The king appointed a special tribunal headed by the Archbishop of Strigonia; in 1673, 26 pastors were sent to the galleys, not as Protestant clergymen, but as political agitators.[41] In all, 733 Protestant academics (vicars and schoolteachers) were rendered unable to practise through either exile or imprisonment. It was a clear victory for the Catholic Church, since both Lutherans and Calvinists lost a considerable number of their clergy in the process. The Catholic Church was simultaneously doing its utmost to recover both churches and landed property. Quarrelling over this issue had been continuous for many years and the number of churches recovered by Roman Catholics between 1670 and 1680 is estimated at 800. Bishop Leopold Kollonich, chairman of the Royal Hungarian Chamber, expelled the Lutherans from the church in royal free boroughs and often led expeditions to take possession of country churches.

The Viennese court entrusted to the Jesuits the vital task of converting the masses to Catholicism but, for security reasons, their action was concentrated in the cities, where the results, at least in appearance, were satisfactory.[42] But of what benefit was this success in statistical terms in a country with an urban population as small as Hungary's was in the seventeenth century? The towns did not amount to very much, either in terms of population, economically or politically. In point of fact, the gentry gave no support to the action of the Jesuits, whose results, in pastoral terms, remained modest.

But those results were brought about at exorbitant expense, for the means used to secure them aroused the unanimous displeasure of all the Hungarian Estates, regardless of religious differences. The military occupation demanded by Leopold's counsellors angered even those most favourably disposed towards the king. The imperial forces pillaged, raped and even committed acts of sacrilege against Catholic churches. These methods had been advocated by Montecuccoli and Hocher, who considered that terror would make the Hungarians give way.[43] In fact all those behind this policy had little or no knowledge of Hungary and imagined that the Hungarian Estates would react in similar fashion to those of Bohemia after the battle of the White Mountain. They had completely misjudged the Hungarian mentality: the inhabitants began to resist and avenge the abuses which they were suffering. From 1672 onwards, armed soldiers took to clandestine warfare, gaining control of the most important routes, taking reprisals against priests and especially against any Jesuits they might capture.[44]

Originally recruited among nobles whose property had been confiscated by the Royal Chamber, these partisans (*bujdosok*) were joined by large numbers from the border garrisons who had been dismissed for religious reasons. The Viennese court's blunders were thus responsible for fuelling rebellion. The Catholic clergy was more and more reticent in the face of Bishop Kollonich's abuses of power,[45] and national unity tended to forge itself against the House of Austria. The partisans became more organised and found outside support, that of Transylvania from the outset, from 1675 onwards that of France, and finally from 1679 onwards that of the Ottoman Empire.[46] Under Count Thököly the *Kuruc* movement became a military and political force in the field of Eastern European affairs. The great policy launched in 1670 was now a failure – instead of ending the Hungarian problem, the military repression had succeeded only in creating a second front during a European war, the one thing the Viennese government had feared all along.

From 1678 onwards, the more clear-sighted of the imperial counsellors had begun to realise that the policy they had been following for eight years had failed and that a compromise solution with the Hungarian Estates was urgently needed. The Nuncio Buonvisi approved of the idea of negotiations as did Father Sinelli, a Capuchin, personal counsellor of Emperor Leopold, who had always preached moderation. Chancellor Hocher himself was too intelligent to oppose a change in policy; only stubborn Hungarian prelates and the Jesuits remained intransigent, as they felt that if the kingdom of Hungary could only be forced into obedience, the position of Roman Catholicism would also be strengthened in the hereditary lands.[47]

In negotiating a compromise, Leopold I was admitting the failure of one of his government's central aims: to unify the Habsburg monarchy by means of religion. The situation, however, was a serious one, since a failure to reach an accommodation on his behalf might have resulted in the entire kingdom falling under the authority of Thököly and being transformed into an Ottoman protectorate. For this reason the Emperor, in spite of his personal feelings, convened a Diet at Sopron, in May 1681, to negotiate a compromise.[48] Thanks to the determination of Father Sinelli, who had become Bishop of Vienna, the moderates prevailed and the imperial court gave substantial guarantees to Hungarian Protestants.

The conclusions of this session maintained article I of the Peace of Vienna of 1606, and granted religious freedom to the Estates and to Hungarian soldiers from the military border. Even if he did not restore the Protestant churches confiscated since 1671, Leopold allowed for a church to be built in each county; magnates and gentlemen were entitled to maintain oratories and chapels in their residences.[49]

This compromise did not entirely end Catholic encroachments,[50] but when one considers the aims which the Emperor had set himself in 1672–3, it must be recognised that he had made enormous concessions, even if the Roman Catholic Church did draw considerable advantages from the operation. The Emperor, by accepting the principle of multidenominational practice, was abandoning all hope of one day unifying the monarchy by religious means. Hungary would now have a special status of its own. It was a severe setback for the Viennese court, and fraught with dire consequences for the future of the Habsburg monarchy.

During the session of the Diet at Sopron, the Emperor made important political concessions. He suppressed the *Gubernium* and reinstated the position of Viceroy in favour of Count (later Prince) Paul Esterhazy, a Catholic magnate, whose family was devoted to the Habsburgs. He agreed to dismiss the president of the Hungarian Royal Chamber, as Kollonich's excessive zeal had aroused Catholic enmity. He even went so far as to accept the principle of withdrawal of German troops, a promise he failed to keep because of the rise of the Turkish threat. He furthermore gave an undertaking to examine in detail the grievances which the Estates had presented, also promising to restore the property confiscated by the Chamber.[51] In the king's relations with the Estates over the years, he often made promises designed to calm the discontented, but which the Viennese government rarely kept. On this occasion, however, he was obliged to back down and give the Hungarians full autonomy as before. Germans found themselves removed from positions of high authority and the Emperor lost all chance of introducing the system of collegial government closely dependent on the Chancellor and the king: a system which existed in Lower Austria with the 'Government' (*Regiment*) in Bohemia, in Moravia with the so-called 'Tribunal' and in Silesia with the 'Lieutenancy' (*Statthalterey*).[52] Yet again the Hungarian Estates had succeeded in maintaining the separate character of that state by preserving the institution of the Viceroy elected by the Diet.[53]

On this point again, the concessions made by Leopold I at Sopron, in 1681, proved decisive, for even if he was in a strong position in 1687, he was more eager to dismiss the members than to impose reforms upon them. It is known, furthermore, that the commission of *Neo-acquistica* published a report on the 'reorganisation' (*Einrichtungswerk*), which was never implemented.[54]

In 1696, Cardinal Kollonich attempted to impose moderate taxation on the Hungarian Estates (4 million florins per year, about 20 per cent of the total revenue of the Emperor) and gathered together an assembly of magnates and prelates in order to avoid convening the Diet. This proved a complete failure, as the Viceroy Paul Esterhazy led the aristocratic opposition and pursued a policy of painting things as black as possible for his own ends: better to make the peasants pay a military tax and subject them to requisitioning on the part of the imperial forces than to renounce the country's fiscal privileges. The 1698 session of the same 'assembly of notables' (*Concursus palatinalis*) also resulted in an obstinate refusal on the part of the Hungarians. This calling into question of the nobility's fiscal immunity contributed to the success of the insurrection of Francis II Rákóczy. In 1711, at the end of the war of independence, the Viennese court was forced to recognise the fiscal privileges of the Hungarian Estates and it was an important facet of the first 'Austro-Hungarian' compromise. Despite Leopold's attempts to impose the Austro-Bohemian model on Hungary, the latter country still enjoyed a full measure of autonomy in 1700.

The king's authority could only in fact be imposed by means of force and only the presence of the imperial troops on Hungarian soil could initially defeat the resistance of the Estates; even then, the latter did not shrink from an armed struggle to see that measures affecting their political, religious or fiscal privileges were repealed. They did not hesitate to call on their king's enemies, the Turks or the French, for assistance.

IV CONCLUSION

The notion of absolute monarchy is inappropriate when speaking of the government of Leopold I. The only achievement of his reign concerned Hungary, upon which, following the liberation of Buda in 1686, he managed to establish, during the session of the Diet of 1687 that the crown should be hereditary in the House of Austria. Otherwise his attempt to extend the Austro-Bohemian pattern to the whole of the Austrian monarchy was a failure. He did not succeed in fulfilling the original programme of the Styrian branch of the House of Austria, namely the integration of different peoples and cultures through Roman Catholicism. We shall conclude with Robert Evans: there was a limited integration for the Austro-Bohemian lands and a refusal of integration for Hungary.[55] The truth was that the crown remained weak in the face of the Estates, who possessed overwhelming political and economic power. Indeed, in 1700 the Estates were more powerful than ever and shared power with the crown, which had not even been capable of universally imposing the strength of the Roman Catholic Church.

7. The Emergence of Absolutism in Russia

PHILIP LONGWORTH

WHETHER Russia was a truly absolutist state[1] and if so when it became one[2] have been matters of dispute among historians. One must begin, therefore, by considering what the essential components of absolutism are and in which period of Russian history they are first to be observed. There is general agreement that absolutism is a form of monarchical power untrammelled by any other institution, whether noble privilege, representative assembly or the Church; that it is supported by a justificatory ideology and exercised by a professional bureaucracy (as well as by armed force). Furthermore absolutism is commonly associated with the codification of laws applicable to the entire realm, with the organisation of a professional standing army, and with the pursuit of 'mercantilist' policies designed to enrich the ruler and the state.[3]

In the case of Russia absolutism is commonly associated with the country's westernisation and particularly with the period 1700–25, in the reign of Peter the Great. However, while Peter placed the coping stone on the absolutist system, the chief elements of absolutism (as defined above) were already established by 1700. The period 1650–1725, favoured by some historians,[4] is therefore a more accurate designation, and the reign of Peter's father, Tsar Alexis (1645–76), can be taken as decisive, since it was in those years, particularly after 1652, that the various elements of absolutism were introduced or entrenched.

However, all this grew out of features present earlier in Russian history. These must be examined if one is to understand why absolutism took on a more complete form, and lasted longer, in Russia than in any other European state. At the same time they suggest why neighbouring Poland, which shared many of Russia's characteristics (economic backwardness, demographic weakness, a poorly developed legal system and an unbalanced society dominated by the land-owning nobility), took a different direction. Poland became decentralised to the point of being unable to maintain its integrity as a state at precisely the same time as absolute royal power was consolidated in Russia.

The roots of Russian absolutism are to be found in the confluence of several developments in the later fifteenth and sixteenth centuries. Of great importance was the fact that (unlike Poland) the state won its competition with the Muscovite seigneurs for the lion's share of the peasantry's surplus product, and was able to increase the value it extracted from the overwhelmingly agrarian economy.[5] At the same time territorial expansion increased the resources available to the state,[6] allowing the ruler to grant land tenures in return for personal service to him without the right, as formerly, for the grantee to take employment with another prince. In the 1480s and 1490s Novgorod, a city-state which enjoyed profitable trade with the West, was captured and Mongol suzerainty over the Russian lands came to an end.[7] Together, these developments were crucial to the growth of Moscow's power.[8]

Territorial expansion continued through the sixteenth century with the conquest of the Tatar khanates of Kazan, Astrakhan' and eastern Siberia. However, the costs of war, not least Ivan IV's ultimately unsuccessful attempt to gain an outlet to the Baltic, increased the financial pressure on the state. It responded by increasing the squeeze on both the peasantry and the seigneurs; and by leeching resources from the extensive monastic estates. Other important developments were associated with these trends: the state intruded into the area of rent-fixing, the distinction between land held in heredity and in return for service began to disappear, and the traditional customary law began to decline.[9] Meanwhile the bureaucracy expanded and the military establishment was increased. Ivan IV (1530–84) founded a corps of musketeers (*strel'tsy*) and tripled the number of service gentry to some 1600, allocating them lands for their support within a day's ride (*c.* 42 miles) of Moscow. He nevertheless experienced difficulties in maintaining the growth of the state apparatus and at the same time keeping the loyalty of some of his servitors, particularly sections of the higher nobility (some with princely titles and considerable hereditary estates).[10] It is in this context that the reign of terror which he carried out, against both refractory aristocrats and cities, notably Novgorod and Pskov which sought to preserve vestiges of their traditional rights, must be considered. Ivan also disposed of the head of the Russian Church, Metropolitan Philip, who protested against his raw exercise of power and, not least, his battening on the resources of the Church.

It should also be noted that the growing power of the monarch was supported by a justificatory ideology which drew increasingly on the Byzantine tradition. The fall of Constantinople to the Turks in 1453 had raised Muscovy to the status of the leading power in the Orthodox Christian world; and the marriage of Ivan III to Zoë Palaeologus, niece of the last Emperor of Byzantium, in 1472 enhanced Muscovy's prestige.[11] It also brought many more Greeks to Moscow where they were to play a significant role in developing the nascent bureaucracy and in introducing the idea of Byzantine autocracy to the Muscovite court.[12] At the same time ideas imported from the Romanian lands bolstered the idea of the monarch's supremacy over the Church as well as the laity.[13]

The successes and failures of Ivan IV contributed to a series of disasters which overtook Russia in the second half of the sixteenth century. The pressure on the peasantry, who were obliged to pay dues according to their capacity rather than any fixed norm,[14] continued to grow, as many lords increased their burdens in order to support their own obligations to the state. In reaction peasant flight increased, both to larger landlords who were able to offer better conditions and to unpoliced Siberia or the Cossack communities in the south.[15] In turn, this led to increasingly vociferous demands, especially from the smaller service gentry, for the peasants' right of movement to be withdrawn. At the same time there was a marked fall in the productivity of the central agricultural region, partly because of the depredations of Ivan's *oprichnina*, partly because of a change in climate (the advent of the 'Little Ice Age') which caused serious famines and consequent rebellions at the beginning of the seventeenth century. These disorders were compounded by the death of Ivan's successor, the childless Fedor (1598), which ended the dynastic line, called the legitimacy of his successor Boris Godunov (1598–1605) into question, encouraged Polish intervention in support of the impostor Dmitrii, Fedor's step-brother who had died in 1591, and led to a Polish occupation of Moscow itself.

After much tumult a rising patriotic movement succeeded in expelling the Poles and Michael Romanov was installed as tsar in 1613. But the intervening 'Time of Troubles' had eroded the chances of establishing the absolutism which Ivan IV had fostered. The legitimacy of tsars continued to be questioned:[16] and it had become the practice to call an Assembly of the Land (*zemskii sobor*), an institution established by Ivan IV to provide a counterweight to the aristocracy, in order to elect tsars or confirm them in office. As in Poland, where elective kingship had been established since 1570, this allowed the Assembly to place limitations on the monarch's powers. There is evidence that Tsar Michael was barred from dispensing personal justice in cases involving noblemen and that he had to seek the Assembly's consent before declaring war or concluding a peace.[17] Furthermore, the regency of the Patriarch Filaret (Michael's father) during the tsar's minority and the considerable political authority he exercised thereafter served, as we shall see, as a precedent for the Church to assert its authority *vis à vis* the tsar.

Nevertheless, some foundations on which absolutism might be constructed had survived the Time of Troubles. The bureaucratic system had not only survived but been extended.[18] The power of the old aristocrats had not been revived (although they continued to jockey for high office), and the memory of Ivan IV continued to serve as an inspirational model for centralising tsars.[19] Furthermore it can be argued that the Time of Troubles created a popular, though by no means universal, yearning for order – fertile soil for absolutism. However, in 1645 when the 16-year-old Alexis mounted the throne, absolutism was no more than a potentiality and there were a number of obstacles that blocked its realisation.

Although Alexis was the first tsar since Dmitrii to succeed by hereditary right and without election, the essential vulnerability of his position constrained him to call Assemblies of the Land before enacting important legislation or declaring war. Respect for his person was anything but universal, as was respect for authority in general. The immense size of the state (by 1649 Russian explorers had penetrated as far as the Pacific[20]) and slow, difficult communications made for ineffective administration. Localism was still rife, pagan practices commonplace in the rural outback, and religious piety on the wane in the towns. The law itself was a farrago of canon law and edicts, unevenly enforced, while, despite its decline, customary law remained strong in the countryside. The tsar's youth encouraged factional fights at court, and the conflicts became open during the Moscow uprising of 1648.[21] Nevertheless, within three decades all these obstacles had been swept aside and the tsar's power was absolute.

In examining how the situation was turned round we shall first examine how the monarchy promoted deference and order, and then how the institutional constraints were overcome. Finally, the questions of military and economic policies will be considered.

One of the tsar's first steps to promote authority was to support a movement for religious revival which in several respects resembled the Counter-Reformation backed by the Habsburgs in Austria, Bohemia and, less successfully, in Hungary.[22] Alexis sponsored a missionary movement, known as the 'Zealots of Piety', among the clergy, let it be known that his own religious observance was extremely strict, and used public occasions, such as his marriage in 1646, to set an example of decorous abstemiousness. Edicts were issued that enjoined the public at large to sobriety, sabbatarianism and avoidance of 'godless amusements'.[23] That of December 1648 condemned witchcraft, a variety of popular customs of pagan origin, and the activities of itinerant minstrels (*skomorokhy*) whose entertainments included subversive satires against the powerful.[24] Popular preachers were encouraged in the cities, while missionising zealots, often supported by troops, were sent into the countryside.[25] At the same time the miraculous discovery of icons and the miraculous cures effected by holy relics were publicised by lavish ceremonies and by pilgrimages to the shrines of saints who were reckoned to have a desirably exemplary effect upon the public. The tsar himself often participated in these.[26]

This reflected a symbiosis between State and Church, which, to judge from both his writings and his actions, formed an essential part of the tsar's political philosophy, and was largely Byzantine in its origins. The stress on ceremonial probably derives from the *Book of Ceremonies* of the tenth-century Emperor Constantine VII Porphyrogenitus. According to this, ceremony reflected 'the harmonious movement of . . . the Creator around the universe' and helped to preserve 'Imperial power . . . in proportion and order'.[27] Certainly Tsar Alexis' writings frequently refer to good order and proportion.[28] Furthermore, he not only acquired replicas of the Byzantine imperial regalia,[29] but subscribed to the Byzantine view of divine right. This held that the monarch was God's sole agent on earth and answerable only to Him. However, the tsar's view of his role also drew on other sources – on the purported advice of Aristotle to Alexander the Great,[30] on stories about the fifteenth-century prince of Wallachia, Vlad Tepes (Dracula);[31] and on the Russian religious tradition. Though the latter taught that to wield power inevitably involved sinning, it was also understood that disobedient subjects forced the monarch to punish them by way of fulfilling his divine charge; and that although the stern punishments he meted out put his mortal soul in jeopardy this in itself gave him something of a Christ-like aura since he suffered for the sins of his subjects. The ideology also gave him the right to reward and punish without reference to other authorities, including the Church. The fact that he acted on these assumptions is shown by the long lists of promotions and demotions which Alexis dealt with personally; by an extraordinary admonition he composed, threatening perdition to as well as ordering the imprisonment of, a senior monk who had acted against a section of musketeers stationed at his monastery;[32] and by his Latin motto 'By forbidding and commanding he alone rules and protects'.[33]

However, an absolutist ideology does not necessarily imply absolutist rule, and in fact as a young man Alexis had had difficulty in asserting his personal authority, especially once his childhood governor and Chief Minister, Boris Morozov, was forced to step down as a result of the uprising of 1648. The turning points came in February 1652 when Alexis dismissed the head of the Palace Office, Prince A. M. L'vov, and in 1654 when he set up a Private Office. This office was staffed initially by only three bureaucrats, the chief of whom was given the title 'Secretary in the Sovereign's Name',[34] but the staff tripled within five years and it continued to grow thereafter. Steps were also taken to give the Private Office staff special training, and from 1664 a school was set up for new entrants who, among other subjects, were taught Latin and grammar.[35] Meanwhile the influence of the office grew as able men who had served in it were posted to senior bureaucratic positions in various key departments of state.

The tsar's Private Office was the motor of absolutism in Russia.[36] It gave the tsar direct and immediate communication with all parts of the bureaucratic system, by-passing normal hierarchical channels, and allowed him to intervene directly in any kind of matter, whether sensitive Church affairs or foreign intelligence operations. It was the tsar's instrument for exercising personal authority, not least in gingering up the entire government machine. Through the few remaining records of its activities it is possible to reconstruct the monarch's personal involvement in government, at least in the latter part of his reign.[37] Yet there were important developments even in his first years as tsar, not least the first thorough codification of the laws of Russia in 1649.

This was an essential prerequisite for orderly government and again it was inspired by the Byzantine example. Earlier attempts had been made to establish the law and bring order to the legal system. The most recent was Ivan IV's *Sudebnik* of 1550. Since then, however, the accumulation of decrees and judicial decisions, many of them conflicting, had promoted a good deal of confusion and a lack of uniform application across the realm. The new Law Code (*Ulozhenie*)[38] included some important new legislation, but its major purpose was to establish what the law actually was and the principles by which it should be administered. Drawing both on canon law and on the corpus of Roman Law, notably the legislation of Leo the Wise, it prescribed standard procedures, ordained that justice be applied without regard to rank, and laid down punishments for aberrant judges. It also served the cause of absolutism by setting down strict rules to protect the monarch's security and honour. The implementation of the sovereign's will was not to be influenced by any powerful person who might stand in its way, but the Code gave no indication that the tsar himself was legally bound.

The reforms concerning townsmen, monasteries and serfdom that were incorporated into the Code are also significant in the context of this essay. Protests by townsmen who were aggrieved by having to carry a high taxation burden while their competitors who happened to be subject to the Church or to individual magnates were exempt, loomed large in the riots of 1648. The Code rectified the position by confiscating hitherto untaxed urban Church and seigneurial property to the crown. In addition a new department of state was established to administer, and tax, estates belonging to the Church. However, the tsar, by special dispensation, was to exempt the property of the Patriarch from taxation and allow him to carry out some of the new Monastery Office's function. There was to be no outright dissolution of the monasteries as in England, and indeed monastery property continued to increase through legacy, gift and purchase during the reign.[39] Nonetheless the resources of the Church were made available to the monarch and were exploited in times of exigency, particularly for war.

A more significant measure, and one frequently associated with the establishment of absolutism in Russia, was the Code's final imposition of serfdom on the peasants. It has been claimed that absolutism in Russia was nothing less than 'a device for the consolidation of serfdom'.[40] In fact the opposite is true. The culmination of the enserfment process was prompted by representations from the service gentry who needed a captive labour force to maintain the incomes from their land allotments (*pomest'e*) at a level adequate for them to sustain their service obligations to the state.[41] Furthermore, placing peasants under the jurisdiction of the seigneurs eased the state's task of keeping effective control of the rural population. In any case the enserfment of the Russian peasantry was a means of strengthening the state.

While the Private Office provided a means of direct monarchical interference in every aspect of the country's life, the Law Code of 1649, and the supplemental criminal code of 1669, countered the notorious instability of laws,[42] providing a framework of common law applicable throughout the realm that was not to be superseded until the nineteenth century. It was a fundamental support both to the monarch's attempts to knit his vast and heterogeneous possessions together and to the establishment of absolutism itself.

However, laws can be superseded and government machinery dismantled or destroyed. Historians of Russia have customarily pointed to institutions which had a capacity to challenge or impede the rise of absolutism: (i) the aristocracy and the system of precedence governing appointments (*mestnichestvo*); (ii) the Council of State (*Duma*); (iii) the Assembly of the Land (*zemskii sobor*) and (iv) the Church. The potential which each of these institutions had to limit monarchical authority is worth examination.

The aristocracy in Russia is difficult to define. The only hereditary title before the eighteenth century was that of prince. This denoted descent from the legendary Varangian ruler, Riurik, but since primogeniture did not exist in Russia (or anywhere else in the Slavonic world) the title was no indication that the bearer possessed sufficient wealth to sustain his status, or that he wielded political power. The descendants of the old appanage princes' retainers constituted another 'noble' element (sometimes termed 'untitled aristocrats'); there were also a number of families, such as the Morozovs, who had risen to prominence comparatively recently, thanks to gaining high political offices. The power of the aristocracy to impede the monarch rested on the extent of their landed property and the offices they held, especially in so far as this was governed by the rules of precedence (*mestnichestvo*), but above all by their capacity to act together as a coherent interest group.

However, though substantial landed magnates were to be found in Russia in the mid-seventeenth century, there was none to compare with those of Poland-Lithuania who (like the Radziwills for example) were not only immensely wealthy, but also hereditary office-holders and possessors of private armies. Furthermore Russia's great landlords seem to have had no sense of common interest or identity as did the service gentry. Since the aristocracy presented him with no coherent challenge, the monarch was able to deal with them on an individual basis. Thus, Prince Iakov Cherkaskii, who opposed certain clauses in the draft Law Code, was simply dismissed from office in 1648, as Prince L'vov was to be subsequently. On the other hand Prince Nikita Odoevskii, also a member of the old, titled elite and a personage of considerable landed wealth, who was a devoted subject of the tsar, was given a variety of high offices during his long career and enjoyed the monarch's confidence and friendship. In short, social status and wealth constituted no obstacle to absolutism. The institution of *mestnichestvo*, however, did.

This was a complicated system of allotting court and military duties in accordance with precedents decided by the positions one's ancestors or relatives had held; it may have served to satisfy aristocrats' senses of honour and contain feuding between them;[43] it certainly interfered with the monarch's freedom to make appointments. However, although the Books of Precedence on which the system was based were not to be ceremoniously burned until 1682, *mestnichestvo* had been inoperative in determining appointments and promotions of any consequence for several decades before that. Military campaigns and important ceremonial occasions at court were regularly proclaimed to be exempt from the rules, and though many appeals were made on grounds of precedence, there seems to be no record of any of them being upheld, while there is evidence that many of the appellants were punished. The tsar's own attitude was clearly expressed in 1667 when an old aristocrat protested at being placed below the recently appointed foreign minister who came of much humbler, gentry stock. In delivering judgement the head of the office governing appointments declared that ancestral precedents in such cases 'had not counted, do not count now, and will not count in future'.[44]

It had also been customary to expect promotion to the rank of *boiar* (the highest of the Council, or *Duma* ranks)[45] if one's father had held it. However, in a letter to V. B. Sheremet'ev in 1658 the tsar explained that the son of a *boiar* should neither expect to reach that rank nor boast about it if he did.[46] In fact the composition of the Council changed considerably between the 1640s and the 1670s, from a membership which was 70 per cent aristocratic to one that was barely 25 per cent aristocratic. At the same time members of gentry origins increased from barely a quarter to over half the total number, while the number of commoner bureaucrats rose from one to five.[45]

The role of the Council of State (*Duma*) has often been misunderstood. From the beginning of the seventeenth century, if not earlier, it had the character of a Council of Ministers. Although the first four ranks in the service hierarchy are termed 'Council ranks', generals, administrators with postings outside Moscow, and others who held one of these ranks but did not head important government departments (*prikazy*) did not normally attend Council meetings. It is worth noting that in the earlier part of his reign Alexis made almost a hundred appointments to the first two Council ranks (*boiar* and *okol'nichii*), which had the effect of diminishing the honour, while between 1660 and his death in 1676 he made only thirty-six such promotions (besides at least one demotion). More significantly, the tsar preferred to consult his Councillors individually or in committee, and discouraged them from discussing state affairs with each other when he was not present.[48] Full Council meetings were held progressively more rarely, and chiefly for ceremonial purposes. While there are good grounds, then, for believing that in the first half of the century the tsar did not act without the Council, from the early 1650s, in the words of a contemporary observer, he governed the state 'as he wished'.[49]

Similar tendencies are to be observed in respect of the Assembly of the Land. This 'parliament' usually included representatives of the gentry and townsmen, from both Moscow and the provinces, as well as Councillors and, when occasion called for them, clergy; but never peasants. The Assembly has often been regarded as a socially representative institution which had the potential to develop into a genuine parliament. However, this view seems to have stemmed from the wishful thinking of pre-Revolutionary liberal historians who were searching for precedents to justify Russia's conversion into a constitutional democratic state. It must be doubted if the Assembly of the Land ever had such a potential. From its very foundation in 1549 it had been an instrument of the monarchy. It was summoned on an irregular basis; its membership was defined according to the particular purpose for which it was called; and it never had any defined powers of its own. It served variously from time to time as a sounding board, as a means of gauging the acceptability of a proposed measure, of assuaging discontent, establishing what the customary law was, and of drumming up support. Convened quite frequently until 1653, when it was used to endorse the decision to go to war with Poland-Lithuania over Ukraine, it was not resorted to again until the early 1680s, on the last occasion, in connection with the conclusion of a peace with Poland.[50]

In Poland, by contrast, the *Sejm* had developed into a powerful force, dominated by the landed nobility and gentry (*szlachta*), that was able to block all attempts to develop an effective centralised government. Polish influence may well have led the Russian Assembly of 1613 to impose limitations on Tsar Michael's powers as a condition of his election, but there is no evidence of its exercising any power thereafter. Indeed, it seems to have become an unspoken assumption that Russia must not follow the Polish example. The Assembly was fundamentally a support for absolutism and by the end of the century it had been abandoned, there being no further need for it.

Of all the institutions that might have prevented the establishment of absolutism, the most important was the Church. In Russia, as in Byzantium, Church and Emperor were supposed to work in symphony together, though in practice the Emperor usually prevailed in any dispute between them. However, the Church's role as a focus for patriotic feeling during the Polish intervention at the beginning of the century, and the fact that Tsar Michael's father, the Patriarch Filaret, ruled the country during the early years of the Romanov dynasty gave the Church greater political potential. This was heightened by the prominent role given to the Church in promoting the religious revival of the 1650s. At the installation of the Patriarch Nikon in 1652 courtiers as well as clerics who were present were called upon to kneel and swear to obey him as their archpastor and spiritual father. The fact that the tsar himself had knelt at the tomb of the newly canonised St Philip, the Metropolitan whom Ivan IV had had murdered, has given credence to the view that the Church was gaining an ascendancy over the state, even though the tsar intended to use the canonisation of St Philip as a symbol of reconciliation between the victim and his murderer.[51]

However, although in 1654 Nikon was accorded the same high title that Filaret had borne (*velikii gosudar'*) and which tsars themselves used, it reflected no more than the fact that he was designated regent while the tsar himself was away on campaign (1654–6). Shortly after his return to Moscow Alexis broke with Nikon. When the latter abandoned his see in protest at the tsar's disfavour and laid down conditions for his return, the tsar refused to accede to them;[52] despite canonical difficulties, he had the Patriarch deposed by a special synod held in Moscow in 1666.[53] The fact that Nikon attracted scant support from either clergy or laity may be explained in part by his association with the liturgical reforms which he had forced through at the tsar's behest in the 1650s and which were highly unpopular with Russian traditionalists. However, these were confirmed by synod (with the tsar's approval) at the beginning of 1667, soon after Nikon's condemnation.

The long *apologia* which Nikon composed after he lost the tsar's favour betray distinct theocratic tendencies.[54] However, there is no evidence that he held such views, which were not usual in the Russian Church, while he was serving as Patriarch. The tsar himself had little difficulty in imposing his own choice of Nikon's successor upon the synod; and at the next patriarchal election of 1672 the synod openly declared its readiness to elect whomsoever the tsar chose.[55] The Church had been confirmed as an instrument of the state, even though the patriarchate itself was not to be abolished, and its role transferred to a largely secularised Office of the Holy Synod, until the reign of Peter.

One notes with interest that the spate of canonisations of the early 1650s, chiefly of patriotic Church hierarchs who would serve as exemplary models in the war against Poland, was to be the last. This is one index of a secularising trend to be observed from the 1650s and which is also seen in a degree of free-thinking and a rejection of icon-veneration on the part of sections of the urban population. This has been attributed to economic growth and the concomitant development of city life.[56] Secularisation may not always be associated with absolutism, but in the case of Russia the tendency (which was to reach its apogee under Peter) was associated not only with urbanisation and the promotion of secular ideas at court, but with one of the chief characteristics of absolutist states, the creation of a 'modern' (and in the Russian case, a 'westernised') army.

Although this phenomenon is commonly associated with Peter, it had its origins in the sixteenth century when Ivan IV established a corps of musketeers (*strel'tsy*) and when a government department was set up to regulate the employment of Polish mercenaries (*Panskii Prikaz*). The Office was subsequently renamed the 'Foreigners' Office' (*Inozemskii Prikaz*), to reflect the fact that professional soldiers were being engaged from many countries apart from Poland, not least Irish and Scots 'wild Geese'.[57] This influx of foreign officers and NCOs saw a very considerable increase in the 1650s and 1660s,[58] and was to have great importance for the development of the state.

Modernisation was not confined to improving weaponry and tactics; the army was to a large extent regularised too. The service gentry levies and peasant recruits were gradually formed into up-to-date cuirassier, dragoon and infantry regiments, subjected to strict discipline and proper training, in order to make them capable of fighting modern armies like that of Sweden as well as the traditional cavalry armies of Poland.[59] Due to the exigencies of war, with Poland (1654–67) and with Sweden (1655–7) and the financial difficulties which flowed from it, the modernisation proceeded by fits and starts rather than at an even rate, but it was to have profound political as well as social, economic and cultural consequences.

In the short term it provoked disaffection and then rebellion on the part of some traditional military elements who perceived themselves to be obsolescent, especially the *strel'tsy* who bore some resemblance, not least in their trading privileges, to the janissaries of Ottoman Turkey. They proved unreliable in the Moscow risings of 1648 and 1662, and downright rebellious in the 1680s and later 1690s.[60] Resentment of 'regularisation' also gave rise to more diffuse protest, including mass desertions, on the part of other categories. The service gentry, however, remained loyal to the crown out of economic self-interest, because of their dependence on serf labour and for fear that the crown would punish disobedience by sequestering their lands. Also the troops of 'new formation', officered chiefly by foreign mercenaries who subjected their men to draconian discipline, constituted a powerful instrument for imposing civil order, as they proved in suppressing the Moscow rising of 1662.[61]

In the longer term the influx of foreign experts, not only of soldiers but also of physicians, entrepreneurs, horticulturalists and professionals of all kinds,[62] had the cumulative effect of breaching the walls of Russian isolationism and, in so far as they were introduced by the crown, gave Russian absolutism a distinctly western character. Incipient westernisation aroused popular xenophobia. In attempts to assuage these feelings, foreigners in Moscow were confined to a special suburb in 1649,[63] and decrees were subsequently issued restricting the wearing of clothes cut in the western fashion.[64] However, the tsar himself remained committed to the West, partly because it was a source of modern technology and expertise, partly for reasons of his international prestige. The embassies he sent to England, France, Venice, Florence and Spain, as well as to the Habsburg court, Denmark and elsewhere, were intended to assert Russia's interests, raise the profile of the tsar internationally, and to gather information, not least on how western monarchs bore themselves.[65]

The tsar's foreign agents (for example the Englishman John Nebdon) were asked, among their other commissions, to report on the panoply of western courts[66] so that the tsar might emulate his peers.

Emulation of the West is observable in policy as well as in outward show, and the programme of military reconstruction had its parallel in economic policy – notably the adoption of 'mercantilism'. In implementing its policies Russia had an advantage in that the crown itself was the largest merchant in the realm, controlled the silk trade with Persia, and held monopolies of rhubarb, furs and other products. It was also in a much better position to determine the terms of its international trade, notably with the English and Dutch at Archangel, than the Poles could theirs through Gdansk. Furthermore the most substantial Russian merchants (*gosti*) worked closely with the crown, which they served in the capacity of customs officers, agents and commercial advisers.[67] On the other hand Russia was at a disadvantage in lacking a port on the Baltic, in being comparatively backward industrially, and in having an internal market which despite its growth was still comparatively underdeveloped. The measures adopted by the state to overcome these disadvantages in the third quarter of the seventeenth century suggest the extent to which it embraced the philosophy of 'mercantilism'.

The war of 1655–7 with Sweden aimed (as Ivan IV's Narva campaigns had done) to gain an outlet to the Baltic and hence a much more direct, and cheaper, access to the West than through Archangel, which was iced up for most of the year and involved a dangerous voyage round the North Cape. The attempt to capture Riga failed; so did a diplomatic offensive to obtain docking rights there for Russian ships.[68] It was not until the beginning of the eighteenth century when St Petersburg was constructed on a tract of marshland wrested from the Swedes, and when the powerful naval base at Kronstadt was built, that Russia obtained a Baltic port and the opportunity to become a naval as well as a land power. Meanwhile, however, a flotilla of modern warships, including a frigate, had been built by Dutchmen specially engaged for the purpose. It was based at the Caspian port of Astrakhan' and the intention was to use it both against the pirates who were plaguing the trade route to Persia, and to find (as it was hoped) a route across the Caspian to the East Indies. However, the flotilla was destroyed by the Cossack rebel, Stepan Razin, in 1670.[69]

Although, for the moment, Russia was incapable of competing with Holland, France and England as an international trading power, attempts were made to generate more industrial activity. Mineral prospecting had long been encouraged for obvious military and financial reasons, and the state had also established an arms-manufacturing centre at Tula, to the south of Moscow. This centre saw a considerable expansion during the century, but the state's efforts to promote industry were not confined to those projects with a military purpose. It also established glass, brick and textile manufactories and another for making agricultural implements. Most of these enterprises were run by the crown, which already possessed the best crafts centre in the country, the Kremlin Armoury, as well as a state pharmacy (*Aptekar'skii Prikaz*) which was to some extent a centre for scientific research, not least of the hermetic kind.[70] At the same time, traditional industries (salt-gathering, potash-burning, tanning, distilling, etc.) also saw further development.[71] More remarkable, perhaps, were the state's attempts to develop what might be termed a 'mercantilist agriculture'.

This involved the introduction of new crops (sometimes, as in the case of mulberry trees for silk-worms, on an experimental basis) or better strains of crops (spring wheat, melons, peas, vines, flax, hemp, etc.), chiefly on lands owned by the crown. The court estates were also used for the improvement of dairy-farming, stock-rearing and horse-breeding. Irrigation systems, powered by windmills as well as by the already customary water-mills, were installed, fenlands drained, fishponds dug, and an experimental five-field system of crop rotation was also introduced.[72] Large estates had always spearheaded agricultural improvement, and it is hardly surprising that the crown estates should have been used in this way. Nevertheless a change can be detected in the seventeenth century, from the exploitation of crown lands and workshops merely for the purpose of maintaining the court's economic autarchy to their use in promoting economic improvements for the state as a whole.

Another means employed to promote economic development was legislation. In 1665 the city of Pskov was granted a measure of self-government and a series of commercial privileges including the right to hold two fairs a year.[73] The architect of this experiment was a man of gentry origins whom the tsar had promoted to high office, Afanasy Ordyn-Nashchokin. Nashchokin was also largely responsible for the Commercial Statute of 1667. This set out (after the manner of Colbert) to protect trade both from foreign competition and from Russian officialdom. Foreign merchants were confined to dealing at ports and frontier towns unless they paid substantial additional taxes; they were barred from dealing with each other without payment of duty, and excluded from the retail sector. Duties were to be collected in gold or hard currency at artificially fixed exchange rates and the export of precious metals was banned. Sumptuary laws were also introduced (which dictated what clothing particular social groups could wear), associations of townsmen were encouraged to form banks, and credit was eased to help the formation of merchant companies.[74] The results of these policies, many of which were pursued into the eighteenth century, may have disappointed expectations (though they certainly helped to quieten native merchant protest). Nonetheless during the seventeenth century the Russian economy acquired a dynamism which was signally lacking in Poland. The internal market became state-wide, river traffic increased, and the urban classes grew in size, obtained greater privileges, and became more prosperous.[75] This formed a basis from which Russia was to rise to the status of a great power.

Much of the inspiration for the state's mercantilist policies came from abroad, through the mediation of men like Andrei Vinnius. Born in Amsterdam, Vinnius became both a registered merchant in Moscow and a Dutch translator in the Foreign Office (*Posol'skii prikaz*), rising to the rank of full secretary. He proposed several schemes for the economic betterment of the state to the tsar, and was employed by him on several head-hunting expeditions for foreign experts who might help realise them.[76] Vinnius, indeed, may have been one of those responsible for introducing the concepts of the 'police state' into Russia – that is, the notion (originating with the Jesuits in Peru) that it was possible to improve society through the application of rules.[77] These ideas, developed in a number of German states, practised by Colbert in France and in the Prussia of Frederick William I, also had their influence on the seventeenth-century Kremlin[78] and were to be observed, too, in the Russia of Peter I.

Given the weakness of all Russian institutions apart from the monarchy itself, the assumption and exercise of absolute powers might seem a straightforward matter and the genesis of the Russian police state an unremarkable concomitant. However, Russia faced one difficulty in implementing the absolutist programme that other European powers did not share, at least to the same degree – the problem of distance. In the conquest of Siberia (as in the American West) the state followed rather than led the pioneers.[79] Furthermore, effective control of its immense territories, always problematical, was often virtually impossible especially towards the periphery because of the distances involved and the difficulty of the routes. Even the central zones were covered to a much greater extent than today, with dense forests that provided cover for deserters, religious dissenters, rebels, and highwaymen.[80] Newly conquered territories like Ukraine proved difficult to digest while the Cossack settlements to the south remained virtually autonomous, and often rebellious, down to the early eighteenth century, and in the cases of Zaporozh'e and the Ural River until the 1770s.

The steps taken to remedy these problems were not entirely unsuccessful, however. In the third quarter of the seventeenth century the post system (inherited from the Mongols) was much improved and regular courier routes were established to connect Moscow with Siberia, Archangel, Kiev, Riga and points farther west.[81] Embassies sent to China and India were ordered not only to report on the best routes but to engage masons and engineers capable of building stone bridges. At the same time trees were cleared on either side of the roads leading to Moscow to preclude ambushes of travellers by robbers.[82]

By 1675, then, absolutism had been firmly established in Russia and absolutist policies were being implemented in many spheres. The state was greatly expanded, and several attempts to challenge the tsar's authority had been beaten down. After Alexis' death in 1676, however, the system he had erected seemed somewhat vulnerable. His eldest surviving son, Fedor (*regnat* 1676–82) burned the Books of Precedence, but felt the need to invoke the support of the Patriarch and an Assembly of the Land before doing so. The tsar's Private Office was dismantled; so was the Monastery Department. Then, on Fedor's death, rivalry between the families of Alexis' two wives, the Miloslavskiis and Naryshkins, created openings both for religious dissenters (the 'Old Believers' who rejected the reformed liturgy) and the aggrieved *strel'tsy* who took control of Moscow for several weeks under the ambitious Prince Khovanskii. This gave the Patriarch a heightened role as a political mediator.

It is an index of the fundamental strength of the absolutist state which Alexis had bequeathed, that it survived these turmoils. Under the regency of Alexis' daughter Sophia (1682–9) Khovanskii was executed and the arch-dissenter the Archpriest Avvakum burned at the stake. Westernising policies were continued under her chief minister, and devotee of Machiavelli, Prince

Golitsyn,[83] until his fall following an unsuccessful campaign against the Turks. Upon assuming power, Alexis' youngest son, Peter, followed most of his father's policies, even to the extent of reviving the Private Office under another name, and pressed them further. By his death in 1725 Russia's absolutist system had been perfected.

Absolutism was established in Russia at roughly the same time as in Denmark, Sweden and Prussia-Brandenburg. All four states were influenced by the example of Poland which, lacking the stimulus of powerful neighbours for too long perhaps, had sunk into an anarchy of localism. Its irreversible decentralisation turned it into a power vacuum which invited regular foreign interference in its affairs from the mid seventeenth century, though it was not to disappear from the political map of Europe until the late eighteenth century. By contrast, Russia's absolutist system was to survive, with remarkably little reconstruction, into the twentieth century, outlasting all others in Europe.

8. Britain

JOHN MILLER

I

IN THE major monarchies of continental Europe absolutism developed mainly in response to the need to mobilise the resources of disparate, often scattered territories for war. Monarchs owed whatever success they enjoyed partly to the creation of cadres of officials committed to the extension of royal power, partly to the acceptance by other social groups that absolutism offered advantages, in terms of either profit or security. England at first sight seems very different. First, it had been governed as a unit for centuries. Private jurisdictions and exemptions from royal authority had been relatively insignificant even before Henry VIII asserted control over the Church and extended the English system of local government into Wales. Second, England's rulers had more freedom to choose whether to make war. The complex and often ambiguous land frontiers of the major continental powers created constant friction and a sense of vulnerability which encouraged pre-emptive strikes; the sea offered a much more formidable barrier. Third, England had developed a system of government by consent which made the ideas and methods of absolutism not only less acceptable but also less necessary. The local self-government that was so widespread in late medieval western Europe had here developed on a national level. Its ultimate expression was Parliament: England's kings, unlike those of France, had managed to create a national means of securing consent to taxation and legislation. Under the Tudors monarch and Parliament cooperated in extending the crown's functions and powers and the monarchy was eventually able to secure many of the aims of absolutism – above all the mobilisation of resources for war – without recourse to authoritarian methods and the sacrifice of traditional liberties or local self-government.[1]

This happy picture of homogeneity and consensus cannot, however, be accepted without qualification. The need to seek consent led to debate about the way in which government should be carried on, which in turn could lead to acrimony and even civil war. Moreover, if we broaden our perspective to embrace all the lands of the British crown, we see rather more similarities to the continental picture. English kings had long ruled Ireland by right of conquest; from 1603 they were also kings of Scotland and ruled the two kingdoms quite separately. Scotland's laws and institutions were very different from England's; if the king was less able to enforce obedience north of the border, he could behave more arbitrarily against dissident individuals and groups.[2] The crown's attitude towards the infant colonies in North America combined authoritarian intentions and practical ineffectuality. Thus Britain in its widest sense was a multinational state whose constituent parts differed widely in culture and language, religion and institutions, liberties and autonomy.[3] In the pages that follow, we shall first consider England, then extend the discussion to the rest of Britain.

II

One reason for the wide acceptance of absolutism on the continent was the appeal of the ideal of a just impartial king, who put the interests of the whole kingdom before those of particular interest groups – nobles, town corporations, the church. This ideal appealed to officials, who could view their pursuit of greater power in terms of the public good; but it also appealed to the victims of noble caprice and brigandage or the corruption of urban oligarchs. In England such 'intermediate powers' were much weaker. Justice was dispensed not by private individuals but by men commissioned by the king; legal and fiscal privileges were few; in Parliament the king dealt with all his subjects through their representatives. Thus the best way of achieving the general good seemed to lie not in concentrating more power in the monarch, but in cooperation between king and subject. The English sought political legitimacy not in abstract theory but in historical prescription, in the 'ancient constitution'.[4] It was believed that the origins of the monarchy, Parliament and the common law were all lost in the mists of antiquity. They had grown together in a mutually sustaining relationship so that the king's powers and the subject's rights were complementary. Kings should protect their people against invasion and insurrection; maintain order and dispense justice; uphold true religion; promote prosperity and protect the weak. To fulfil these obligations it was accepted that they needed extensive powers, including a discretion to act above or outside the law when the public good required it. On the continent the crown invoked such powers when overriding particular privileges in the name of the general good. In England, by contrast, Parliament constructively helped the king to tackle practical problems and the legal rights most prized by Englishmen, notably trial by jury, were common to all. It could therefore be argued that English 'liberties' were not incompatible with the general good and that the ostensible objectives of absolutism – justice, plenty, success in war – could best be achieved by cooperation.

It was all very well, however, to talk of cooperation or of a balance between the king's powers and the subject's rights. In practice it was often difficult to agree on the terms of cooperation or the precise point of balance. If at any time the king's use of his powers seemed to threaten the subject's rights which should take precedence? This was a question which many preferred not to ask, trusting that the king would act for his people's good; but what if he failed to do so? Between 1603 and 1640 some advisers and spokesmen of James I and Charles I moved from conventional claims that the king enjoyed certain emergency powers to a view of the prerogative which can only be described as absolutist, in that overriding normal laws would cease to be highly exceptional and become something close to a regular practice. Such assertions were most common in wartime when the justification of urgent 'necessity' could most plausibly be invoked. Thus in 1626 the Earl of Dorset declared that if the people would not contribute voluntarily to the war against Spain Charles had the right to compel them to do so. Charles received similar advice from Strafford in 1640, who argued that he was 'loose and absolved from all rules of government' and should take from his people whatever the state's necessities required. This basic line of argument was elaborated by theorists and divines, who showed extensive familiarity with the work of Bodin and other absolutist writers.[5]

If absolutist arguments were often used under the early Stuarts, they did not sweep away older modes of argument (and those who used them often argued that consensual methods were preferable).[6] The most widely used images of royal power were of the king as father of his people or as the head of the body politic. In each case, the power of the king was innate, conferred by God and nature, not by the consent of those he ruled. But the same laws of God and nature restricted his use of his power: it would be an unnatural father who wilfully harmed his children, neither would the head deliberately injure any part of the body.[7] Such reassuring images, however, seemed increasingly at variance with reality, as the crown imprisoned men without due process of law and exacted money without Parliament's consent. As their apologists invoked the necessities of state, their opponents dug in around the common law's protection of property rights. Faced with the king's abuse of a discretion once accepted as necessary, many denied that he possessed any such discretion: liberty and property should be totally – 'absolutely' – protected by the common law.[8]

Before 1640 the critics of royal policy were on the defensive, clinging to a narrow interpretation of the ancient constitution in the face of royal innovation. From 1640 they became the innovators, stripping the king of his powers and then making war against him. Such conduct could not easily be justified by an appeal to the past. Some claimed to be defending the spirit, the fundamentals of the old constitution, others that the king was so misled by evil counsellors that he did not know what he was doing and that the Parliament that he had brought into being represented his true intentions. Many found such arguments unconvincing. To make war on the king was treason: the only way in which Parliament could justify its action was by arguing that, if the interests of king and people proved utterly incompatible, Parliament could take up arms as the people's representative. Many invoked the law of nature, the right of self-preservation. For more conservative Parliamentarians this argument contained a serious snag: what if 'the people' demanded more control over those who acted in their name? By the late 1640s Leveller writers were indeed demanding electoral reform and frequent elections so that MPs could be held accountable for their conduct.[9]

Thus in the 1640s Parliamentarian writers developed a potentially – then genuinely – democratic view of the constitution. The old ideals of balance and cooperation were challenged first by the absolutist arguments of the crown's apologists, claiming that no earthly power could limit the king's discretion, then by radicals who claimed that all authority originated with the people, who should be able to ensure that their rulers did not abuse their trust. Hitherto most had accepted that the constitution derived its legitimacy from God and prescription and was both sound and sacrosanct: if it failed to work, men blamed human error or wickedness, not structural weaknesses. The Levellers, however, argued not only that people possessed inherent natural (as opposed to legal) rights, but that no form of government was inherently better than any other: the people could change the government as they chose, in order to achieve the ends they desired.[10] If the government failed to fulfil its trust, or invaded the people's rights, they could resist and overthrow it and establish a new government which could better achieve the desired ends. Such arguments were to become widely accepted on both sides of the Atlantic in the eighteenth century, thanks to the likes of Locke, Sidney and Paine.[11] In the mid seventeenth they were far too radical for most Parliamentarians, let alone Royalists. The former had taken up arms to defend the traditional order against arbitrary taxation and religious innovation, only to find that Parliament's radical supporters (in the streets of London, in the New Model Army, among the Levellers and separatist sects) posed a far more drastic threat to that order. If Charles's fiscal methods affected their pockets, the radicals raised the spectre of the total expropriation of the propertied by the propertyless.

It is easy with hindsight to argue that such fears were exaggerated, but they were widely held and were given credibility by the rise of the New Model and abolition of the monarchy. This helps explain why Leveller ideas, so congenial to modern liberals, won limited support in their own time and were increasingly denied expression. The Restoration saw a conscious attempt to re-establish the pre-war consensus: from all sides came calls for a return to the good old ways.[12] In the early 1660s sectaries were harassed and radicals imprisoned without trial, with not a murmur of protest in Parliament.[13] There was an even more vigorous reaction against the perceived threat of civil war after the Exclusion Crisis of 1678–81. Tory writers strongly attacked the very idea of the ancient constitution. Some argued that laws could not simply develop – some authority had to enact and enforce them – and that kings had existed before laws. Others argued that history showed that no Parliament was called before the thirteenth century and that William the Conqueror had introduced new and alien laws. But if kings had created Parliaments they could presumably dispense with them; if they had made and unmade laws in the past, it implied that they could do so again. The publication of Filmer's *Patriarcha*, written decades earlier, so alarmed Locke that he set out to answer his arguments in his *Two Treatises of Government*.[14]

In fact, Tory writers rarely moved beyond the realms of history and philosophy to advocate practical extensions of royal power. In both the 1660s and 1680s royal propagandists (and Parliamentary statutes) confined themselves to denying that subjects could lawfully resist royal authority or that Parliament could legislate without the king.[15] In so doing, they reaffirmed the pre-war order, which had been challenged only when Parliament claimed a right of resistance and legislated without the king in the 1640s: the basic thrust of their writing, in other words, was conservative and defensive. Despite the effusions of overenthusiastic clerics (and the allegations of their opponents) most distinguished between non-resistance and passive obedience: if the king's demands were unjust, subjects should refuse to obey but then, like the early Christians under the pagan emperors, they should meekly accept the consequences of their disobedience.

Thus throughout Charles II's reign, most political argument took place within the framework of the traditional mixed and balanced constitution. His critics did not challenge that constitution, but claimed that he had failed to respect it. As Sir Francis Winnington told the Commons in 1680:

> The two great pillars of the government are Parliament and juries. It is these that give us the title of freeborn Englishmen, for my notion of freedom is this: they are properly so called who are bound by laws of their own, being tried by men of the same condition with themselves. These two great privileges of the people have of late been invaded by the judges who now sit in Westminster Hall.[16]

The more anxious the king's critics became, the more they insisted that he was morally obliged to follow the Commons' advice, to a point where they seemed to deny him any right to an opinion of his own. But, inhibited by memories of the 1640s, MPs rarely underpinned such arguments with a claim that the reason why the king should follow the Commons' wishes was that the Commons represented the people.[17]

Winnington's speech captures the essence of most seventeenth-century constitutional debate. Some, it was true, put forward arguments strongly influenced by theorists of absolutism; others advanced views whose implications were liberal and democratic.[18] In other words, some tipped the traditional balance overwhelmingly in favour of the king, others in favour of the people. But most apparently believed that the old constitution should continue to operate and this remained true well after 1688: Locke's utilitarian view of government and broad endorsement of a right of resistance at first won little support.[19] The old constitution had served well in the past: if it was not working properly now, that was because powers which were in themselves legitimate were being used illegitimately. Winnington saw the threat to liberty as coming not from absolutist theory but from the judges.[20] Let us, then, turn from theory to practice. Men often expressed fears of 'arbitrary government', threatening liberty and property, especially through the misuse of law. Were such fears justified?

III

When constitutional theories stressed cooperation and consent, they merely mirrored reality. Unlike their continental counterparts, English kings could make laws and levy taxes only with the consent of Parliament. Such consent was not a formality. Acts of Parliament were shaped by a complex process of discussion. Whereas now the British government pushes through a pre-packaged programme of legislation, relying on the Whips to maintain party discipline in divisions and buying off backbench revolts with token concessions, for much of the seventeenth century there were no parties. As one MP put it 'gentlemen come not here with resolutions, but to take them upon clear debate of things'. Where possible, especially on major issues, MPs preferred not to put the issue to a vote and tried to talk their way through to a form of words upon which all could agree.[21] The bill then went to the Lords, who usually proposed amendments, which the Commons considered; when the two Houses had reached agreement, the bill would go for the royal assent. The length of this process made it unlikely that any bill would become law which was widely unpopular: when in doubt, the Houses would enact a measure for a limited period, to give an opportunity for reconsideration. Moreover, it should be noted that the king's role in legislation was limited: he could either accept (and so give legal force to) or reject bills whose content had been determined by the two Houses; in France, by contrast, laws (so it seemed) were drafted by the king's council which might (or might not) amend them in the face of representations from the sovereign courts.

The amount of consultation involved in law-making might seem indicative of royal weakness, but it made sound practical sense. Laws were enforced not by professional magistrates but by leading members of the local community, country gentlemen or urban bigwigs: much the same sort of people as sat in the Commons. Since the government lacked an elaborate apparatus of supervision, it had to depend on the public spirit of these unpaid officials, who were most likely to act diligently to enforce laws of which they approved and about which their representatives had been consulted. Similarly ordinary citizens were far more actively involved in enforcing the criminal law, especially as jurors, than was the norm on the continent. If the English showed great respect for the law, this reflected the fact that it was in a real sense *their* law, not something alien imposed on them from above.

One major reason why the crown had to involve its subjects in administration was that it had very few professional officials in the provinces – and not many at the centre. This was in some ways a serious weakness: professionals might be expensive and sometimes obstructive, but they were more likely than amateurs to be technically competent and to enforce measures that were unpopular locally. On the other hand, the amateurs' wealth and standing gave them a natural authority, their local knowledge could be invaluable and in general if the monarch's council respected their prejudices and heeded their advice, the system worked tolerably well. Even when called upon to implement policies they disliked, many magistrates braved the wrath of their neighbours and doggedly did their duty.[22] Whatever the deficiencies of such a system, the Stuarts had no option but to make the best of it: they could not afford a standing army or a large paid bureaucracy.[23]

Their dependence on consent, in Parliament and the localities, meant that, paradoxically, the Stuarts were most powerful when they followed the wishes of their people.[24] The major expansion of the state after 1688 was to rest on a solid basis of consent.

English kings, unlike their continental counterparts, did not have to contend with vulnerable land frontiers, provincial particularism, unruly nobles or stubborn cliques of venal officials; but their powers of coercion were limited and they were unusually dependent on the active cooperation of their subjects. This meant that the constraints which they faced were less institutional (or physical) than political; they needed to keep their subjects' goodwill, which was a matter partly of public relations, but also of the content of their government. The need for political skills was all the greater in the absence of an objective set of rules governing the king's conduct. Ostensibly the common law provided one, but in practice it proved alarmingly malleable. A motley collection of customs, Parliamentary statutes and judges' decisions (which often contradicted one another) it lacked a clearly articulated set of principles against which particular cases could be measured. Judges habitually based their rulings more on technicalities, on what the precedents said,[25] than on wider considerations of justice; they were especially liable to do so when the king's powers were called into question. This was partly because they owed their jobs to the king, but they also regarded him as the fount of justice, who himself could do no wrong. Therefore if he said he was using a particular power for a particular purpose the judges usually felt that they had to believe him. They thus endorsed what many saw as abuses of power which threatened the liberty and property of the subject.[26]

If Stuart England were to move towards absolutism, then, this was likely to happen not through assertions of absolutist theory, or frontal assaults on established institutions, but through piecemeal extensions of power to which the judges gave a veneer of technical legality: 'What . . . all the . . . machinations of wicked men have not yet been able to effect may be more compendiously acted by twelve judges in scarlet.'[27] It was the Stuarts' misuse of law which focused so much political debate (especially before 1640) on seemingly narrow questions of legality. The growing divergence between the letter and spirit of the law, between what the judges were prepared to endorse and what seemed just, eventually led men, reluctantly, to consider the king's powers and his relationship with his people in wider political terms. Men talked of 'legality', but it became sadly clear that notions of 'legality' could be highly subjective. As the Stuarts' conduct came to be seen as 'illegal', so they eroded their subjects' support, to a point where in both 1640 and 1688 they offered minimal opposition to foreign invasions. This reinforces the point that the most important – if not the most obvious – constraints on the Stuarts were political. They could extend their powers, but their dependence on their subjects' cooperation could ultimately make it unwise to do so: 'when a king extendeth his uttermost authority, he loseth his power'. Moreover, without a measure of support – especially money from Parliament – it would be difficult to fight a major war, which imposed severe constraints on royal foreign policy in the 1630s and through most of the 1680s.[28]

None of the Stuarts fully came to terms with the constraints imposed by the need to maintain their subjects' goodwill. James I developed an authoritarian view of monarchy as king of Scotland. While accepting that he was obliged to rule according to law, he was impatient of legal subtleties and annoyed by his subjects' refusal to accept his interpretation of what seemed to him straightforward judicial rulings. Both Charles I and James II were temperamentally incapable of understanding any viewpoint which differed from their own and saw life in terms of polar opposites – right and wrong, legal and illegal. Both (apparently with a total conviction of their own sincerity) often acted in ways which others saw as duplicitous; and both blithely assumed that whatever the judges said was legal would be accepted as legal. Charles II was much more conscious of the dangers of opposition, but this did not prevent him from pursuing unpopular policies, either through miscalculation or from a vain hope of breaking free from what he saw as undignified constraints. None, therefore, accepted these constraints as a fact of life and set out to make the best of their position, as Elizabeth's ministers had done (at least until the mid 1580s).

One major reason for this was that all the Stuarts became disinclined to trust their subjects and their Parliaments. Having come south full of goodwill, by 1610 James I was heartily sick of what he saw as the Commons' neurotic suspicion of his intentions and venomous hostility towards the Scots. Thereafter he called

Parliament rarely and against his own better judgement. His son's honeymoon period was even shorter, ending when his first Parliament refused either to vote money for the war against Spain or to follow precedent and vote him the customs for life. By the end of the 1626 Parliament he was convinced (as he later declared) that the Commons sought 'to erect an universal overswaying power to themselves, which belongs only to us and not to them'. Given his dislike of what he (like James) called the 'popular' element in Parliament, the only surprise was that it was not until 1629 that he finally decided to do without it.[29]

James I and Charles I usually saw their subjects, and MPs, as basically well-intentioned, but led astray by a few incendiaries. Charles II and James II saw disaffection everywhere. Whereas in fact their father's trial and execution had been pushed through by a small minority of Parliamentarians, they saw it as the product of a broad hostility to monarchy and regarded all who had made war against Charles I as morally responsible for his death. Charles II was temperamentally distrustful and his fear of disaffection led him to seek conciliatory policies and to back down in the face of opposition. His brother, by contrast, believed that concessions encouraged opposition, which could be curbed only from a position of strength; he therefore sought to build up the army and the powers of the crown in order to crush its enemies.[30]

The first four Stuarts were thus ill-fitted to direct a system of government which depended, for its optimum operation, on trust and consent. This does not mean that they set out with a coherent plan to change that system or to establish absolutism. They might have toyed with the idea of doing so and chafed at the restrictions they suffered, but such a radical transformation was outside the scope of practical politics. Instead, they made the most of the powers they had (or thought they had) and usually professed respect for the common law and the ancient constitution. Their subjects, by contrast, often expressed fears that they intended to make themselves absolute and a beleaguered consciousness that 'We are the last monarchy in Christendom that retain our original rights and constitutions.'[31] As we shall see, there was considerable justification for such fears, but it does not follow that the extensions of power which cumulatively alarmed the political nation were all part of an articulated strategy; instead, kings reacted to events, and opportunities, as they arose. Neither was the question only political. From the late 1620s fears for Parliament and English liberties were usually entwined with anxieties about religion. In the popular mind absolutism was identified with the most authoritarian of churches, that of Rome, an identification later reinforced by the conduct of the self-styled champion of absolutism and Catholicism, Louis XIV. The linking of political and religious anxieties, as Charles I promoted Laud's Counter-Reformation within the Church of England and his sons flirted with or embraced Catholicism, compounded distrust of the Stuarts' intentions.[32]

To some extent this distrust was fuelled by their public utterances. James I's comparing kings to gods made more of an impression on his listeners than his subsequent stress on their duty to rule according to law; and there was nothing subtle about Charles I's threats of 'new counsels' should Parliament prove uncooperative.[33] But the impact of such rhetoric would have been limited had it not been matched by actions which also seemed to threaten liberty and property, Parliaments and juries.[34]

It had long been accepted that the Privy Council could commit to prison those seen as a serious threat to the monarch's person or to the state, such as the Gunpowder Plotters. The power of committal became contentious when it was extended to send to gaol those who refused to pay a forced loan. The Petition of Right of 1628, which Charles accepted, claimed that he had no such power, but this did not prevent Charles from imprisoning his more vehement critics on flimsy pretexts. He and his father also made more extensive use of Star Chamber. This consisted of the council sitting as a court, advised by two judges, and made no use of the cumbersome procedures of the common law (including the jury system). Its speed and informality were an asset when dealing with disputes between subjects, but proved far less acceptable when the king was a party, as in cases involving proclamations, or opposition to Laud's ecclesiastical policies or the crown's pet economic projects, like those for the draining of the fens.[35]

While Star Chamber seemed to threaten personal liberty, a variety of dubiously legal fiscal devices threatened the future of Parliament. The English crown had always been financially underendowed compared with those of France or Spain; the Tudors' plunder of the church had alleviated the problem only temporarily.[36] Moreover, the real value of the crown's revenue was eaten away by inflation, so by 1603 it urgently needed new sources of income. There were two possible options. The first was to persuade Parliament to grant more, but James was disinclined to show MPs details of his finances and his obvious generosity made it easy to blame his problems on extravagance. Besides, few MPs would relish justifying to their neighbours a massive increase in taxation: indeed, the Commons persistently failed to tackle the acknowledged problem of the underassessment of the taxes they voted. If the Commons could not or would not help the king, he would have to make what he could from his prerogatives. One fruitful device was the sale of peerages or baronetcies – not dignified, maybe, but nobody could say it was illegal. Others included the sale of monopolies and other economic concessions and fines for transgressing obscure – often long-forgotten – regulations. Those who had 'encroached' on what had long ago been royal forests were fined as much as £20,000. Such expedients brought the king much less than the courtiers and middlemen who promoted them and served to tarnish the king and his court with the stain of 'corruption'.[37] Often they penalised individuals without raising major constitutional issues, but there were some which did.

The first was impositions. Customs duties (tonnage and poundage) were normally voted by Parliament at the start of each reign, but there were occasions (for example in a tariff dispute with a foreign power) when it was accepted that the king needed to be able to levy additional duties without Parliament. His right to do so was confirmed by the judges in 1606, after a Mr Bate refused to pay such a levy; their judgement was quickly made the pretext for a growing range of non-parliamentary customs duties. MPs were quick to see the threat that this posed to Parliament: one explicitly compared impositions to the French *taille*, established as an emergency levy in 1451 and collected without consent ever since.[38] Anxiety about impositions underlay the refusal to grant Charles I tonnage and poundage for life in 1625; his response was to collect both impositions and tonnage and poundage without Parliament's consent for the next fifteen years.

These duties on trade were the only regular taxation that the crown received. Taxes on land (subsidies) were granted by Parliament on an *ad hoc* basis and suffered from two major weaknesses. First, assessment depended on taxpayers' giving in accounts of their net income – and not on oath; the more the Commons voted, and the more disgruntled taxpayers became, the lower their returns of income. Between Elizabeth's reign and 1628 the yield of one subsidy fell by about half. Second, the Commons expected the king to make costly concessions in return for subsidies; he must have wondered (in Conrad Russell's phrase) whether such paltry sums were worth bargaining for. (Between 1603 and 1620, subsidies brought in little more than the sale of baronetcies.[39]) Charles toyed with the idea of going over Parliament's head and demanding taxes from the freeholders of each county: the forced loan of 1626–8 was a watered-down version of this proposal.[40] But not until the 1630s did his advisers hit on a way of taxing land without Parliament, in the shape of ship money. This depended on the king's power – indeed duty – to defend the realm in an emergency. The practice of requiring coastal areas to contribute ships or money to defend against pirates or invaders was, with the judges' approval, extended to the whole country and became a regular annual event. As each county was given a quota which had to be met, underassessment was not a problem and the money came in much faster than subsidies had done. In theory it was not a tax, but an emergency rate, but many found it hard to accept the concept of a regular annual emergency. The judges' verdict for the king in Hampden's case highlighted the growing gulf between the letter and the spirit of the law.[41] Still more alarming were remarks like that of one of the judges: 'Many things which might not be done by the rule of law might be done by the rule of government.'[42]

By 1640 it seemed that Charles's reign had seen a systematic assault on England's liberties and religion.[43] Historians with access to the records of his government are more inclined to doubt whether he or his advisers had the vision or the application to formulate and implement imaginative policies: there was no restructuring of administration or finances, no extension of the armed forces. Their fiscal measures enabled them to keep going without Parliament, but little more.[44] When Charles's religious policies provoked a rebellion in Scotland, the disadvantages of alienating his English subjects became all too apparent and he was forced to throw himself on their mercy.

By contrast the years after 1642 saw major changes. Faced with the imperative need to win the war, MPs were forced (for the first time) to come to terms with the realities of war administration and war finance. The army and navy were greatly expanded and two major new taxes were introduced: the monthly (or weekly) assessment – a land tax, modelled on ship money, but much more onerous – and the excise, mainly on alcohol produced and consumed within England. (Charles had considered introducing an excise, but had not dared.) Both were unpopular, but Parliament (unlike Charles) had an army and no scruples about using it against recalcitrant taxpayers. Meanwhile Parliament fashioned a new executive based on a number of committees, headed by what became, in the 1650s, the council of state. So for all their talk of Charles I's changing the government, the first major surge of state-building in seventeenth-century England was undertaken by Parliament, which showed an intolerance of opposition which made Charles's rule seem mild in retrospect.[45] Meanwhile, fighting a war gave politicians and administrators a new sense of purpose, expressed in a growing professionalism and pride in serving the state.[46] For the first time England was able to offer a serious naval challenge to Europe's dominant maritime power, in the First Dutch War of 1652–4. Later in the decade the New Model acquitted itself well in Flanders and England gained Dunkirk. The experience of the 1640s and 1650s shows that in England war gave the greatest stimulus to the growth of the fiscal-military state and that this could happen independently of absolutism – or even of monarchy.[47]

Charles II inherited the fleet, the excise, the new professionalism and a (much reduced) army; when Parliament could be persuaded to vote taxes on land, they were usually based on the assessment. The Convention of 1660 and the Cavalier Parliament elected in 1661 were determined to re-establish a monarchy strong enough to guard against the danger of revolution from below but had no wish to relive the experience of the 1630s. The New Model was disbanded and the Commons pointedly ignored the king's hints that he needed a larger army: MPs preferred to put their trust in a militia officered by gentlemen like themselves. (They proved much more generous to the navy, which posed no threat to liberty at home; England's rapid commercial and colonial expansion in the 1670s and 1680s would have been impossible without strong naval backing.) The most fundamental limitation on the crown was not lack of military force but lack of money. After the legislation against ship money and the like in 1641, the king could, in effect, raise money only in ways approved by Parliament. The Convention was the first Parliament seriously to calculate the cost of government; it agreed to vote taxes to meet that cost, but these initially brought in much less than expected; this, together with war, extravagance and a growing burden of interest payments meant that for most of his reign Charles had to ask Parliament for additional grants.[48] Financial dependence (and his fears of disaffection) severely constrained Charles's policy-making. On the rare occasions when he and the Commons agreed he was able to reap the benefits of both the expanded state apparatus and the Commons' new financial realism. In 1664 they voted £2,500,000 for a war against the Dutch – a far cry from the £280,000 which Charles I had struggled to extract in 1628. The mismanagement of this war (and Charles's entering on another in 1672 without consulting Parliament) ensured that such generosity would not be repeated. Nor was it only Parliament's opinion that mattered. The need to borrow from London bankers, and so from those who deposited money with them, meant that the crown needed to keep the confidence of the business community: 'public credit' was becoming an important consideration in policy-making. Mutual distrust retarded expansion of the fiscal-military state, although there was some consolidation and even expansion in the navy, the ordnance and above all the revenue administration: by 1685 there were nationwide networks of customs and excise officials. But these developments meant no more than that the crown was managing better what it already enjoyed. There could be no further surge in state growth without a substantial increase in resources, which was not possible while the Commons had doubts about both the king's competence and his willingness to respect English liberties.

Distrust of Charles's intentions, while not absent in the 1660s, crystallised around 1672 in the form of fears that the king and his brother wished to establish 'Popery and arbitrary government'. First, Charles joined with the Catholic absolutist Louis XIV to make war on the Protestant Dutch. Second, he issued a Declaration of Indulgence, in which he claimed that he possessed the power to suspend all laws against Protestant nonconformity and to permit Catholics to worship privately in their homes. Third, James's conversion to Catholicism became apparent. He had long been regarded as an authoritarian figure, with leanings towards military rule.[49] As Charles had no legitimate heir, James's conversion raised the eventual prospect of the first Catholic monarch since Mary; more immediately, it seemed that he and Louis might push the easy-going Charles towards a more absolute regime. Such contentions rested less on hard evidence than on an assessment of James's character and assumptions about the necessary connection between Catholicism and absolutism. (There was, however, cause for concern about the systematic way in which Lord Treasurer Danby used places and pensions to undermine the Commons' independence.[50]) When Charles raised large additional forces for war in 1673 and 1678 anxiety reached fever pitch, compounded in 1678 by the Popish Plot, which forced people to consider what would happen if Charles were snatched from them. A majority of both electors and MPs decided that the prospect of James's becoming king was utterly unacceptable and sought to have him excluded from the succession. The attempt failed, but not before Charles and a large section of the political nation (the Tories) had become seriously alarmed by what they saw as the Exclusionists' (or Whigs') attempts to destroy church and monarchy, start another civil war and turn the world upside down (again).[51]

Although the purpose of Exclusion was to guard against a perceived threat of absolutism, the Whigs' conduct provoked the most authoritarian measures and most systematic misuse of law in Charles's reign. A strongly Tory bench of judges bent the law to punish Whigs and Dissenters. The king appointed Tory sheriffs, who chose Tory juries. In chartered towns, where elected magistrates were often loath to enforce the laws against Dissent, corporations were persuaded or forced to surrender their charters; they were granted new ones under which the king could remove members of the corporation at will. After a protracted legal battle, the judges declared that London's charter was forfeit on the grounds that the corporation had contravened its provisions; thereafter the City was governed by royal nominees.[52]

Such misuse of the law raised unpleasant echoes of the 1630s. Whigs and Dissenters depicted it as part of a wicked design (continued by James II) to establish absolutism. On closer inspection such claims seem dubious. The Exclusion Crisis had opened up bitter divisions. Neither Whigs nor Tories showed much scruple in the methods they used against their opponents: the Whig sheriffs of London were as partisan as any Tory in selecting jurors.[53] Much of the initiative in the repression of 1681–5 came from enraged or frightened Tories, convinced that they had narrowly escaped civil war and that they had to crush the Whigs in order to ensure that no such thing could ever happen again. Charles, too, wanted revenge, especially on London and individuals like Shaftesbury. There was, however, no coherent assault on municipal autonomy. On the continent, town corporations – important authorites interposed between king and subject – were among the main casualties of the drive to absolutism. But whereas Colbert tried to curb municipal spending and indebtedness, Charles's new charters rarely reduced and often extended the towns' powers of self-government: his prime concern was to ensure that those who exercised those powers were politically reliable.[54] Age and weariness exacerbated his habitual indolence and he was less inclined than ever to embark on a coherent, ambitious strategy; his ministers, imbued with legalism and fearful of being called to account in a future Parliament, were unlikely to encourage him to do so. The 'Tory reaction' was just that: a reaction against the perceived threat from Whig radicalism, which won wide support and involved only the intermittent and marginal abuse of traditional procedures. Given the subjective nature of 'legality', one must conclude that (in Tory eyes) the measures of 1681–5 were 'legal'.[55]

James II's reign was very different. He was always more authoritarian and energetic than Charles. Whether his primary aim was to promote Catholicism or to extend his prerogatives[56] does not in this context greatly matter, as the former could not be achieved without the latter. His soon realised that he would be unable to abrogate the penal laws and Test Acts (against Catholics' worshipping freely and holding public office) unless he also removed the laws against Protestant Dissent; so he set out to secure a Parliament that would repeal the laws against all religious nonconformity. This required two major extensions (or abuses) of his prerogatives. First, in 1686 he secured a ruling from the judges that he could dispense with the penalties of particular laws as he judged necessary. (He had first asked their opinions individually and sacked those who refused to comply.[57]) Kings had often dispensed with the penalties of law in the interests of equity, but the presumption had been that this power should be used sparingly, after careful investigation and not in cases of serious crime or where the penalty was due to someone other than the king. If suspicions of James's intentions underlay the judges' reticence, they were amply justified. He proceeded to dispense hundreds of Catholics and Dissenters from the penalties of the penal laws and Test Acts and appointed them to office, in flat contradiction to the intentions of the Parliaments which had passed those laws.[58] Early in 1687 he issued a Declaration of Indulgence, suspending all penal laws, pending their repeal by a Parliament, and announcing his intention to dispense all and sundry from the need to comply with the Test Acts. He did not consult the judges about this, apparently in the belief that he was merely exercising his dispensing power.[59]

James wished to admit Catholics and Dissenters to office partly in order to encourage closet Catholics to come into the open, but more so that they could help secure the election of a tolerationist House of Commons. Candidates committed to the repeal of religious legislation stood little chance in the counties, where the electorate was large and the Tory gentry powerful. But some 80 per cent of MPs served for boroughs, where the electorate was often small (sometimes only the corporation) and Dissent was often strong. James used the powers granted by the charters of 1681–5 to displace Tories and Anglicans and then (though the charters gave him no right to do so) put Dissenters and Catholics in their places. He subjected corporations and electors to a barrage of propaganda, harassing those who seemed hostile to his aims and bringing in soldiers to vote or to put pressure on other electors.[60]

Neither the king's use of the dispensing power nor his campaign to pack Parliament was wholly unprecedented, yet the differences of degree between James's conduct and previous practice were so great as to constitute differences in kind. To dispense individuals from the regulations governing Oxbridge fellowships was a far cry from suspending dozens of Acts of Parliament: had the principle been admitted, the king would have decided which laws should be enforced.[61] James's interference in the boroughs involved far more extensive changes of personnel than Charles's and deprived them of the right to elect replacements for those put out by the king. It would be naïve to suggest that seventeenth-century elections were free and fair, but (except in the 1650s, when severe political restrictions were placed on the electorate) they produced a House of Commons broadly representative of English opinion.[62] Had James secured a House ready to repeal the penal laws and Test Acts (which the bulk of the nation clearly opposed) the Commons would have ceased to be representative and would have become a rubber-stamp for the royal will, like the weaker French provincial estates (whose membership was equally carefully controlled).

James's conduct created fears of a sweeping extension of royal power and of the emasculation of the Commons: whether or not his intentions were absolutist, the consequences of his actions were likely to prove so and were perceived as such. Anti-Catholic prejudice led people to place the worst possible construction on whatever he did, but, even allowing for this, there was still good cause for alarm. In the Tory reaction the law had sometimes been misused, but the underlying aim had been to preserve the existing constitution: James threatened to overturn it.[63] Small wonder that the extensive support enjoyed by Charles and James during and after the Exclusion Crisis melted away, as James abandoned the Tories and showed open hostility to the Church of England. He was thrown back on his authority and the resources of the state, above all the army: but authority alone was not enough. In the face of William's invasion, James's subjects proved apathetic at best: his nerve broke and he fled to France.

1688 was seen in retrospect as England's definitive escape from absolutism, but had William not come or had James defeated him the situation could have been different. It seems probable that James's electoral plans would have ended in failure:[64] but what then? Would he have been forced to scale down his plans and seek a rapprochement with the Tories (as he did in the face of William's invasion)? Or would he have increased his reliance on his prerogative and on military coercion? Such speculations are bound to prove inconclusive, but it is worth remarking, first, that James mounted a far more sweeping and radical assault on the old constitution than his father or brother had done; second, that the threat posed by the subjugation of Parliament was more insidious than Charles I's attempts to rule without it, preserving the appearance of consent without the reality (rather like the Rump Parliament of 1649–53 and 1659–60); and third, James possessed a much stronger state apparatus than his father: extensive revenues collected by a large body of professional officials, backed by a standing army of 20,000 men which James sought to distance from civilian society.[65] James may have been none too bright and may have acted on assumptions that were wildly naïve: but the fears which he provoked were not unfounded.

After 1688, as in the 1640s, the defeat of what was seen as the threat of absolutism was followed by a large expansion of the fiscal-military state. James's flight forced England to join the war against France that had begun on the continent: although there was to be much disagreement about its conduct, few denied the need to fight, to prevent James's being restored as a French puppet. Similarly Louis XIV's recognition of 'James III' precipitated England's entry into the War of the Spanish Succession. The great wars of 1689–97 and 1702–13 were, in a sense, wars of the English succession, in which England dared not risk defeat. Unanimity on this point led to the sort of concerted effort seen in 1664–5, but which had thereafter been prevented by acrimony and distrust. Now the armed forces and taxation grew apace. The average revenue, in peace and war, between 1689 and 1702, was around £4,400,000 – roughly three times the average under Charles II. People grumbled but they paid: the alternative was to see James restored by a bloodthirsty Popish army. In addition a significant proportion of the cost of war was met by borrowing, with interest payments guaranteed by taxes voted by Parliament. Instead of raising loans from individual bankers, the government came to rely on big corporations – the East India Company, the South Sea Company and above all the Bank of England, founded in 1694. As the government's credit came to be accepted as rock-solid and the habit of investment in government stock grew, so the rate of interest fell to 3 per cent or less, enabling the government to mobilise far more money than would have been possible through taxation alone.[66]

The growth of the state after 1688 rested on Parliament's consent (which reduced the danger of resistance to taxation) and on the willingness of citizens to invest in the state's debts. That consent and that willingness reflected an awareness that the growth of the fiscal-military state was a regrettable necessity, a lesser evil than a Stuart restoration, but also a conviction that the threat which the enlarged state might pose to liberty could be contained. (In addition, it offered the ruling elite enhanced opportunities for employment and for profit, in the form of pensions and interest from government stock.) The key point here was that this enhanced state power was not under the unfettered control of the monarch, neither was he free to use his prerogatives as he wished. Legislation imposed some restrictions: the king had to be an Anglican; he could not keep an army in peacetime without Parliament's consent. But he retained in theory the power to direct the government, choose his ministers and command the armed forces; in practice he found it increasingly difficult to use those powers except in ways acceptable to Parliament. The Commons' refusal to grant William III an adequate revenue for life, plus the huge cost of war, made the monarch financially dependent on Parliament. This meant that Parliament's survival was assured and enabled the Commons to attach conditions to their grants of money and thus ensure that the king would not abuse his prerogatives. Executive interference with the judiciary and the rule of law ended after 1688 (although isolated and unpopular groups, like Catholics and Jacobites, might continue to be harassed). The gentry's local domination of administration and justice continued; many towns and other local authorities extended their powers through Acts of Parliament. Kings and ministers increasingly met trouble halfway by framing policies which they thought the Commons would approve. As Parliamentary acceptability came to be a (if not the) major criterion in policy-making, ministers used it as a trump card in their efforts to persuade the king to endorse their policies.[67] Moreover, the need to maintain 'public credit' also made ministers and MPs sensitive to opinion 'without doors'. The Duke of Newcastle, the most adept electoral manipulator of the eighteenth century, once remarked: 'If we go on despising what people think and say, we shall not have it long in our power to direct what measures shall be taken.'[68]

This is not to suggest that the growth of state power was accomplished without friction. William III was a tough authoritarian individual and concern at his possible misuse of the army led the Commons to insist that the bulk of it should be disbanded after the Peace of Ryswick in 1697. Even under his less abrasive successors, backbenchers often voiced fears of military rule and the military themselves proved reluctant to become involved in maintaining public order.[69] In general, however, politicians sought less to oppose the growth of the fiscal-military state than to contain it, so that it did not pose a threat to liberty. In England and the Dutch Republic, it proved possible to mobilise resources for war without the creation of absolutism; this suggests that war, rather than absolutist ideology or socio-economic change, was the major stimulus to the growth of state power in the seventeenth and eighteenth centuries.

IV

Scotland came under the same ruler as England in 1603 through the sort of dynastic accident that helped create multinational states on the continent, the death without heirs of all Henry VIII's children. Apart from the use of the English language, in the Lowlands, Scotland had little in common with England. The great nobility wielded power reminiscent of that of English magnates of the late middle ages, their economic hold over the peasantry reinforced by their own law courts. The lesser landowners, the lairds, were (in the Lowlands) emancipating themselves from the tutelage of the magnates, but in the Highlands and Borders clan chiefs feuded and plundered largely unhindered by the king's government. The crown was wretchedly poor – in the 1620s the king's revenue from Scotland was about one-fiftieth of his revenue from England – and its powers of coercion were correspondingly feeble: in effect, it had to employ the military power of one magnate against another. Government was thus a matter of balancing magnate interests: the bloody deaths of so many Scottish kings showed how vulnerable the king's person was. To compound the king's problems the Scottish Reformation took a direction very different from that of England. Whereas the English church had been subjected to much closer royal control, and was governed by bishops appointed by the crown, in Scotland episcopacy was abolished. In its place was established a Presbyterian system at whose apex was an elected General Assembly which claimed the right to direct the affairs of both church and state.

To offset its weaknesses, the crown had considerable assets. There was widespread respect for the institution of monarchy (although this did not necessarily imply compliance with the king's policies). The institutional (as opposed to practical) obstacles to royal power were weak. The Scots Parliament was less developed than the English and was dominated by the magnates. All the legislation which came before it was prepared by a committee, the Lords of the Articles; if the king controlled the Articles, he could push through measures of a kind which would never have passed in England, like an Act of 1669 allowing him to raise a militia of 20,000 men, to serve abroad if necessary. The weakness of Parliament reflected the weakness of all social groups other than the nobility: the peasantry were far more tightly under aristocratic control than was the case in England, the towns were small and impoverished and there was nothing like the English tradition of local self-government (or the consciousness of entrenched legal rights). Thus if the crown could control the magnates, and increase its powers of coercion, it might be able to extend its effective power much faster and further than would be possible south of the Border. In this it would not find too much of an obstacle in Scots law, which was relatively undeveloped: the first general survey appeared only in 1681. This lack of definition could prove a disadvantage when seeking to enforce the royal will in the localities, but gave the king considerable leeway, especially when dealing with dissidents: judicial torture became obsolete in England, but continued to be used in Scotland despite its uncertain legality. The extension of royal authority was facilitated also by the slow spread of English influence, economic and cultural, which undermined habits of violence and encouraged the transformation of the nobility (as in Tudor England) from a military to a civilian elite. Similarly, Lowland values slowly percolated into the Highlands: Gaelic chiefs sent their sons to be educated at Edinburgh or Glasgow.[70]

Thus the Stuarts possessed more sweeping powers in Scotland than in England, but faced more formidable obstacles in using them. Ruling Scotland required skills – of manipulation and persuasion and a shrewd knowledge of men – which James VI possessed in abundance. Although he visited Scotland only once after 1603, his record there was markedly more successful than in England.[71] Steady pressure and the occasional hanging helped bring a measure of order to the Borders. Making chieftains responsible for their followers' conduct encouraged them to maintain discipline among them. The introduction of JPs enhanced the influence of the lairds and accelerated their emancipation from the magnates. James even reintroduced bishops and transferred some of the functions of the General Assembly to the diocesan synods over which they presided.[72]

In all this James confined himself to the politically possible, avoiding confrontation with the magnates as a group, while picking off disruptive individuals. He understood Scotland: his son thought he did (as indeed he thought he understood England). Charles exploited grey areas of the law, as in England, shading off into what others saw as illegality. Insensitive as always, he united against him the two most powerful groups – the nobles and Presbyterian clergy – who were usually at odds with each other. By attempting to introduce an essentially English Prayer Book, he offended both national and religious sensibilities. But whereas the English response to his misrule was primarily one of sullen resentment, Scotland still possessed a military nobility which, with the clergy, led a major revolt which centred on the abolition of bishops and found its most formidable expression in the national Covenant.

If Charles I had positive aims in Scotland – religious reform, increasing the revenue – Charles II wished mainly to keep it quiet: fearful of disaffection in England, he had no wish to provoke trouble in Scotland. That was easier said than done. The civil wars had not only exacerbated the division between Presbyterian and episcopalian but had split the former into a dogmatic minority, who believed that the Kirk should direct the state, and a more moderate majority, ready to work within a system of limited episcopacy. At the Restoration Charles unwisely allowed himself to be persuaded by a group of nobles to establish a system of episcopacy much closer to the English model than to that of James VI. As there was little support for such a novel and alien system, Charles thus created a massive problem of nonconformity. Rough and arbitrary measures of repression provoked disorder and furious political resentment. Between 1663 and 1679 his chief minister, the Duke of Lauderdale, tried conciliation and repression in various combinations, in 1678 quartering a 'host' of wild Catholic Highlanders on the diehard Covenanters of the South West.[73]

The authoritarian measures used in Charles II's Scotland were not part of a coherent drive to strengthen the monarchy but unforeseen and unintended consequences of his decision to re-establish episcopacy, which he found highly embarrassing. Twice Lauderdale provoked open rebellion and his enemies continually encouraged complaints against his conduct in the English Parliament, amid insinuations that Charles might intend similar measures in England. His brother, first during a two-year stay in Edinburgh, then as king, pursued a more coherently authoritarian policy. The radical Presbyterians were brutally crushed. Office-holders – and all suspected of disaffection – were required to swear that they would not attempt any alteration in Church or State. In

1685 Parliament acknowledged the king's 'absolute prerogative' more explicitly than ever before, but watered down an attempt to reduce still further the flimsy protection accorded to those accused of treason. In all this the dominant theme was perhaps less an attempt to extend the royal prerogative or the resources of the crown than adding to its already considerable powers to deal with disaffection (about which James was always more than a little paranoid). After 1685 any advantage gained by the monarchy was quickly undermined by James's efforts to promote Catholicism, which alienated episcopalian and Presbyterian alike and ensured that his flight to France was initially generally welcomed.[74]

The first four Stuarts tried to rule Scotland separately from England, hoping that the government there would cover its costs and cause no trouble. English military force could be deployed against revolts – sometimes, as in 1639–40, with a resounding lack of success – but there was no question of using England's superior resources to impose English rule. James VI and Charles II both sought a peaceful union of the kingdoms, but their efforts foundered on English suspicion and contempt for the 'beggarly' Scots. It may be that the Stuarts realised that earlier attempts at conquest had failed; more likely they saw no point in wasting scarce resources in an attempt to conquer such an economically backward kingdom. Only Cromwell, determined to deny the Stuarts a springboard from which to return to England, embarked on a (successful) military conquest, in the process showing that the raw ferocity of clan warfare was no match for modern firepower. After 1688 one sees two seemingly contradictory developments. First, within Scotland the threat of absolutism ceased abruptly: the Claim of Right asserted subjects' rights more trenchantly than did the English Bill of Rights. Second, Scotland's affairs were influenced more directly and decisively by English military and economic power.

This was seen first in 1688, when William's invasion of England drove out James (who was, of course, also king of Scotland). For a while it seemed that the Revolution had emancipated Scotland. The Lords of the Articles were abolished and the Scots Parliament enjoyed a heady freedom – but soon found that freedom had its limits. After the English Parliament vested the succession in the House of Hanover the Scots claimed that they too could choose their own ruler. The London government, unwilling to tolerate the prospect of a Stuart king in Edinburgh, forced the Scots to enter into negotiations for a union. The terms, agreed in 1707, were not unreasonable: the Scots were to keep their Presbyterian Church (re-established in 1689) and their legal and educational systems; they were to enjoy the same rights as Englishmen throughout Britain and the empire.[75] The Union brought prosperity to Scotland's merchants and cities; the nobility scrambled for the places and pensions distributed in London to the politically amenable. English cultural and economic penetration accelerated; English (or rather German) troops finally brought order to the Highlands. But there was a price to pay. Scotland lost her Parliament, her privy council and (many believed) her identity. Ruled from London by a government concerned mainly to keep Scotland quiet – little had changed! – many Scots became resentful of being the junior partner. They might call Scotland 'North Britain' but they were not treated as equals by the people of 'South Britain'. While her religious and civil liberties had been preserved, in a fiscal and military sense Scotland had quietly been absorbed by England, to strengthen the British fiscal-military state.

V

If England's relationship with Scotland involved cultural penetration and partial absorption, that with Ireland rested firmly on conquest and expropriation. If the English regarded the Scots as uncouth, they saw the Irish as inferior beings, whose backwardness and Catholicism made them dangerous: the usual rules of civilised behaviour did not apply.[76] Although there had been a tenuous military presence for centuries, the subjugation of the island began in earnest after the end of the Nine Years War in 1603. By now religion as well as nationality divided conquerors from conquered – and the original conquerors (the Catholic 'Old English') from newer arrivals. In order to subordinate both Old English and native Irish to the crown, the Dublin government set out to destroy the Gaelic system of land tenure upon which the chiefs' influence rested. Knowing that no elected Parliament would sanction such changes, they were carried out through a series of legal rulings by the judges – all of them English and trained in the common law. Feudal tenures (including wardship) were substituted for the old forms, thus tying landlords more closely to the crown and weakening their hold over their tenantry. For good measure, further decisions declared certain valuable properties forfeit to the crown, including the best salmon fishery in Ireland.[77] Resentment at such treatment – and fear of worse at the hands of the English Parliament – led the Old English and Catholic Irish to rise in 1641, killing many English settlers. After almost a decade of confused warfare, the Irish were crushed by Cromwell and almost all of the Catholics lost their land. Some Protestants from the mainland had already settled on forfeited estates – mainly Scots Presbyterians in Ulster – and the republic urged more to go over, with partial success. With the return of the monarchy some Catholics adjudged 'innocent' of rebellion recovered their land, but 80 per cent was now in Protestant hands, together with all offices, civil and military. Under Charles II the Dublin government, caught between native Irish and Ulster Scots (it usually thought the latter the more dangerous) could do little more than hang on, fight off attempts further to weaken Ireland's economy for England's benefit and hope that it could deal with any trouble that might arise.

For both Old English and native Irish James II's reign offered a last chance to recover what they had lost. Egged on by the flamboyant Earl of Tyrconnell, James gave Catholics a virtual monopoly of offices, civil and military, and seemed prepared to contemplate Ireland's separation from England after his death.[78] After his expulsion from England, Ireland seemed the obvious base from which to recover his other kingdoms; the final phase of civil war in Ireland ended for James at the Boyne and for the Irish at the Treaty of Limerick (1691). Under its terms the lands of most Irish Catholics should have been safeguarded, but the Dublin Parliament (once again wholly Protestant) passed a series of penal laws designed to confiscate or break up the remaining Catholic estates. By the late eighteenth century less than 5 per cent of land remained in Catholic hands.

Unlike the rest of the British Isles seventeenth-century Ireland offers ample evidence of military coercion and expropriation, but it is a moot point whether it is helpful to view this in terms of 'absolutism'. To the English Ireland was a colony to be exploited for the benefit of the mother country: they viewed it as Spaniards viewed Peru, not as Castilians viewed Catalonia. As with the other colonies across the Atlantic, in the eighteenth century the Irish colonials became restive. When the London government summoned the Dublin Parliament to vote money to pay for Ireland's army and administration, MPs complained bitterly that their economy was subordinated to England's and denounced the Act of 1494 which required that Irish legislation had to be approved by the English privy council. The more vociferous the Dublin Parliament became, the more cautious and conciliatory the conduct of the British ministers, lavishing patronage on Irish peers and MPs, concerned only to keep Ireland quiet. As a result the bloodletting and expropriation of seventeenth-century Ireland were followed by a century of relative calm; and the growth of the British state was not matched on the other side of the Irish Sea. Only with the French Revolution and the rise of Catholic nationalism was the British government stirred to decisive action: the Act of Union of 1800 joined the Irish Parliament to that of Britain and so Ireland too was absorbed into the British fiscal-military state.

VI

In the seventeenth and early eighteenth centuries Britain developed certain characteristics of an absolutist state – notably those affecting its military and fiscal potential – but without any serious curtailment of property rights or individual liberty,[79] with the major exception of those of the majority in Ireland. Whereas the growth of the absolutist state on the continent usually implied the maintenance or extension of religious uniformity (Prussia was an exception), in England (though not in Scotland and still less in Ireland) the overwhelming majority came to enjoy religious liberty. Regional particularism was not eradicated in England because it had never really existed; although Scotland lost its separate political institutions, the Dublin Parliament (representing only a minority of a minority) maintained a vigorous existence: which (one might have asked) was the conquered kingdom? In England local self-government had never seriously been challenged, except perhaps in the 1640s and 1650s and briefly under James II. The rule of law had survived attempts by the Stuarts to manipulate it in pursuit of financial advantage, political vengeance or religious change. Viewed from the periphery – from Ireland or

North America – the government of Hanoverian England might seem 'tyrannous'; viewed from within England – and by the standards of most Europeans – its people managed to enjoy the self-confidence which came from being citizens of a great power combined with an unusual degree of freedom.

Bibliography

The place of publication of books is London, except where otherwise stated or for the publication of learned societies.

INTRODUCTION

Worthwhile studies of absolutism on a comparative basis (as opposed to single countries) are comparatively few. The pioneering essay by F. Hartung and R. Mousnier, 'Quelques problèmes concernant la monarchie absolue', *Relazioni del X Congresso di Scienze Storiche: IV Storia Moderna* (Florence, 1955) ought to have stimulated rather more debate than it has; the same is perhaps true of Perry Anderson's *Lineages of the Absolutist State* (1974; paperback edn, 1979) which is discussed at length in the introduction. One reason for this lack of interest may be the tendency of historians to concentrate on particular countries; there have been many excellent publications on France, Spain and so on since Anderson's work first appeared. (For an attempt at a bilateral comparison, see J. Miller, *Bourbon and Stuart: Kings and Kingship in France and England in the Seventeenth Century*, 1987.) Another reason is that in some countries the study of government is relatively unfashionable: historians are more interested in peasants (or witches) than in kings, more concerned with revolt than with authority: thus in France much of the best work on government has been done by American and British historians. Studies of revolt have indirectly addressed the problem of the nature of government, the debates on the subject being conveniently collected in T. Aston (ed.), *Crisis in Europe 1560–1660* (1965) and G. Parker and L. M. Smith (eds), *The General Crisis of the Seventeenth Century* (1978). Some general textbooks offer useful insights into the working of government: see J. H. Shennan, *Origins of the Modern European State 1475–1725* (1974); G. Parker, *Europe in Crisis 1598–1648* (1979); J. Stoye, *Europe Unfolding, 1648–88* (1969); E. N. Williams, *The Ancien Regime in Europe 1648–1789* (1972) and perhaps best of all G. N. Clark, *The Seventeenth Century* (2nd edn, Oxford, 1947). For one aspect of government that has been studied on a European basis see K. Swart, *Sales of Office in the Seventeenth Century* (The Hague, 1949). Finally, John Brewer's excellent *Sinews of Power: War, Money and the English State 1688–1763* (1989) continually compares the growth of the English state to similar developments on the continent.

1. THE IDEA OF ABSOLUTISM

Of the primary sources discussed in the essay, Bodin's *Six Books of the Commonwealth* is most readily available in the abridged translation by M. J. Tooley (Oxford, n.d.); a new translation (also abridged) is to be edited by J. H. Franklin for the series *Cambridge Texts in the History of Political Thought*. Hobbes's *Leviathan* is available in several paperback series, including Fontana and Penguin editions. Useful extracts from other English seventeenth-century sources are in D. Wootton, *Divine Right and Democracy* (1986) see esp. chap. 1, 'The Divine Right of Kings', also pp. 175–311 (Philip Hunton's 1641 *Treatise of Monarchy*). Filmer is well served by Peter Laslett's *Blackwell's Political Texts* edition (Oxford, 1949). European material, apart from Bodin, is less easily accessible for English readers. A facsimile edition of William Jones's 1594 translation of Lipsius's *Politics* has been published (Amsterdam and New York, 1970). Botero's *Ragion di Stato* is available in English in a volume edited for the series *Rare Masterpieces of Philosophy and Science* by P. J. and D. P. Waley (1956). A critical text of Bossuet's *Politique tiré de l'Écriture Sainte*, edited by J. Le Brun was published at Geneva in 1967; and for a selection of texts see J. Truchet (ed.), *Politique de Bossuet* (Paris, 1966).

In the secondary literature, pride of place may still be given to J. N. Figgis's classic study, *The Divine Right of Kings* (first published 1896: see now the edition with introduction by G. R. Elton, New York, 1965). For more recent scholarship, see W. H. Greenleaf, *Order, Empiricism and Politics* (Oxford, 1964) and F. Oakley, *Omnipotence, Covenant and Order* (Ithaca, 1984); also Oakley's 'Jacobean Political Theology: the Absolute and Ordinary Powers of the King', *Journal of the History of Ideas*, XXIX (1968) 323– 46. To these should be added J. Daly, *Sir Robert Filmer and English Political Thought* (Toronto, 1979); G. J. Schochet, *Patriarchalism in Political Thought* (Oxford, 1975); R. Eccleshall, *Order and Reason in Politics: Theories of Absolute and Limited Monarchy in Early Modern England* (Oxford, 1978); J. P. Sommerville, *Politics and Ideology in England 1603–1640* (1986).

Looking to continental Europe, see, on Bodin, J. H. Franklin, *Jean Bodin and the Rise of Absolutist Theory* (Cambridge, 1973). On French thought more generally, N. Keohane, *Philosophy and the State in France: The Renaissance to the Enlightenment* (Princeton, 1980). For 'Neostoicism' G. Oestreich, *Neostoicism and the Early Modern State* (Cambridge, 1982) is indispensable. On Boussuet, see J. P. Plamenatz, *Man and Society: A Critical Examination of Some Important Social and Political Theories from Machiavelli to Marx*, 2 vols (1963) vol. I, pp. 186–98; the whole of chap. 5, 'Divine right and absolute monarchy', pp. 155–208, is useful.

2. FRANCE

The best introductions to early modern French 'absolutism' are David Parker, *The Making of French Absolutism* (1983), and Richard Bonney, *L'absolutisme*, 'Que sais-je?' no. 2486 (Paris, 1989), both of which also examine the relevant medieval background. William Farr Church, *Constitutional Thought in Sixteenth-century France: a Study in the Evolution of Ideas* (Cambridge, Mass., 1941), summarises monarchical and resistance theories during the 'religious wars', and Charles Woolsey Cole, *Colbert and a Century of French Mercantilism*, 2 vols (New York, 1939; reprinted London 1964), examines the economic ideas and reforms associated with absolute monarchy. Relations between the crown and the *parlements* are discussed by A. Lloyd Moote, *The Revolt of the Judges: the Parlement of Paris and the Fronde, 1643–1652* (Princeton, 1971), who demonstrates the primarily legal priorities and methods of the judges, and by Albert N. Hamscher, who charts the re-establishment of cooperation in two books, *The Parlement of Paris after the Fronde, 1653–1673* (Pittsburgh, 1976), and *The Conseil Privé and the Parlements in the Age of Louis XIV: a Study in French Absolutism* (Philadelphia, 1987). The relations of the government with a provincial *parlement*, studied by Sharon Kettering in *Judicial Politics and Urban Revolt in Seventeenth-century France: the Parlement of Aix, 1629–1659* (Princeton, 1978), are shown to have been further complicated by the interference of other elites and institutions in the province, and she has developed this investigation, especially by examining the mechanisms of patronage, in *Patrons, Clients and Brokers in Seventeenth-century France* (Oxford, 1988). Other excellent studies of rivalries among provincial elites have been made by David Parker, *La Rochelle and the French Monarchy: Conflict and Order in Seventeenth-century France* (1980), and William Beik, *Absolutism and Society in Seventeenth-century France: State Power and Provincial Aristocracy in Languedoc*

(Cambridge, 1985), each based on a clearly defined geographical unit. Others have selected a group because of its function in the kingdom, the aristocratic governors in the case of Robert R. Harding, *Anatomy of a Power Elite: the Provincial Governors of Early Modern France* (New Haven, 1978), the varied people who acted as financiers in Daniel Dessert, *Argent, pouvoir et société au grand siècle* (Paris, 1984), and the judicial and mercantile families who administered the capital in Barbara B. Diefendorf, *Paris City Councillors in the Sixteenth Century: the Politics of Patrimony* (Princeton, 1983). A different approach has been taken by Eugène L. Asher, who has traced the provincial opposition to a single government policy in *The Resistance to the Maritime Classes: the Survival of Feudalism in the France of Colbert* (Berkeley/Los Angeles, 1960), while Joseph Bergin, in *Cardinal Richelieu: Power and the Pursuit of Wealth* (1985), examines the power base of a single minister and finds that he used traditional methods of clientage to establish his position. All these studies stress the importance of patronage, family influence and clienteles in the social and political mechanisms of early modern France, and Roger Mettam, in *Power and Faction in Louis XIV's France* (Oxford, 1988), incorporates their conclusions into a more wide-ranging discussion of power structures in seventeenth-century France. Local jurisdictional rivalries became even more complicated when the ecclesiastical authorities were involved, often forcing the crown to intervene and causing embarrassing dilemmas for the royal ministers. Two such confrontations are examined in all their complexity by Richard Golden, *The Godly Rebellion: Parisian Curés and the Religious Fronde, 1652–1662* (Chapel Hill, NC, 1981), and B. Robert Kreiser, *Miracles, Convulsions, and Ecclesiastical Politics in early Eighteenth-century Paris* (Princeton, 1978). Finally, the power of the crown cannot be understood without an understanding of the fiscal system and of the forces of order at the disposal of the king. Richard Bonney, *The King's Debts: Finance and Politics in France, 1589–1661* (Oxford, 1981), admirably describes the inadequacy and unpredictability of royal revenues, while André Corvisier, *Louvois* (Paris, 1983), shows that many reforms of the army were never implemented satisfactorily and that here too the effects of aristocratic patronage and of local interest groups remained strong.

3. CASTILE

Inevitably most of the pertinent writing on the subject is in Spanish and hardly any of it has been translated. Fortunately, the essential starting point, J. Vives's seminal paper at the Stockholm Congress in 1960, is available in English as 'The Administrative Structure of the State in the Sixteenth and Seventeenth Centuries', in H. J. Cohn (ed.), *Government in Reformation Europe 1520–1560* (1971), pp. 58–87. Of recent Spanish work, the most influential and most comprehensive are J. A. Maravall, *Estado moderno y mentalidad social, siglos XV a XVII*, 2 vols (Madrid, 1972) and F. Tomás y Valiente, 'El gobierno de la Monarquia y la administración de los reinos en la España del siglo XVII', in R. Menéndez Pidal, *Historia de España*, vol. xxv, *La España de Felipe IV. El gobierno de la Monarquí, la crisis de 1640, y el fracaso de la hegemonía europea* (Madrid, 1982) ch. 1, pp. 3–214.

On the formal political philosophy of the seventeenth century, J. A. Maravall, *La philosophie politique espagnole au XVII siècle dans ses rapports avec l'esprit de la Contre-Réforme*, (Paris, 1955) has not been superseded by J. A. Fernández Santamaría's more narrowly focused *Reason of State and Statecraft in Spanish Political Thought, 1595–1640* (New York, 1983). A clear account of the mainstream, academic ideas which were carried into our period is B. Hamilton, *Political Thought in Sixteenth-Century Spain* (Oxford, 1963). G. Lewy, *Constitutionalism and Statecraft during the Golden Age of Spain. A study of the political philosophy of*

Juan de Mariana, S.J. (Geneva, 1960), deals with the best-known, though by no means the only, or most radical, Spanish 'constitutionalist'.

An insight into the political function of the rituals of court and kingship can be gained from J. H. Elliott's two essays. 'The Court of the Spanish Habsburgs: a peculiar institution?', in P. Mack and M. C. Jacob (eds), *Politics and Culture in Early-Modern Europe* (Cambridge, 1987) pp. 5–24, and 'Philip IV of Spain, Prisoner of Ceremony', in A. G. Dickens (ed.), *The Courts of Europe, Politics, Patronage and Royalty 1400–1800* (1977) pp. 169–89. The propaganda uses of art are revealed in an original, interdisciplinary cooperation between J. Brown and J. H. Elliott, *A Palace for a King. The Buen Retiro and the Court of Philip IV* (New Haven, 1980). J. A. Maravall, *Culture of the Baroque* (Manchester, 1987), sees the entire culture of the age as serving the 'monarcho-seignorial regime' as an instrument of social and political repression.

B. Cárceles, 'The Constitutional Conflict in Castile between the Council and the Count-Duke of Olivares', *Parliaments, Estates and Representation*, vol. 7 (1987) pp. 51–9, is the only work in English on legalism, legislation, or the place of the councils in the Castilian constitution in this period. I. A. A. Thompson, 'The Rule of the Law in Early-Modern Castile', *European History Quarterly*, 14 (1984) pp. 221–34, introduces some recent work on lawyers and councillors and touches briefly on their political roles. The best general account of the conciliar system and of politics and government in the seventeenth century as a whole is J. Lynch, *Spain and America, 1598–1700*, vol. 2, *Spain under the Habsburgs*, 2nd edn (Oxford, 1981). C. H. Carter, 'The Nature of Spanish Government after Philip II', *The Historian*, 1 (1963) 1–18, is suggestive.

Against the conventional picture of parliamentary debility, a broadly similar revisionist view of the Cortes has recently been taken by C. Jago, 'Habsburg Absolutism and the Cortes of Castile', *American Historical Review*, 86 (1981) 307–26, and I. A. A. Thompson, 'Crown and Cortes in Castile, 1590–1665', *Parliaments, Estates and Representation*, 2, no. 1 (June 1982) 29–45, and 'The End of the Cortes of Castile', ibid., 4, no. 2 (Dec. 1984) 125–33.

The best beginning for an understanding of Church-State relations is J. Lynch's 'Philip II and the Papacy', *Transactions of the Royal Historical Society* (1961) 23-42. A. Domínguez Ortiz, *The Golden Age of Spain, 1516–1659* (1971) gives a superb account of the Church as an institution in society, while new approaches to the history of the Inquisition as a 'governmental' institution are included in B. Bennassar (ed.), *L'Inquisition espagnole (XVe à XIXe siècle)* (Paris, 1979), and summarised in H. Kamen, *Inquisition and Society in Spain in the Sixteenth and Seventeenth Centuries* (1985).

The politics of the Court and the councils after the death of Philip II, and the *valimiento* of the duke of Lerma are being re-examined by P. L. Williams, 'Philip III and the Restoration of Spanish Government, 1598–1603', *English Historical Review*, 88 (1973) 751–69, and 'Lerma, Old Castile and the Travels of Philip III of Spain', *History*, 73 (1988) 379–97. The 'absolutising' reform programme of Olivares has finally received magisterial treatment in J. H. Elliott's *The Count-Duke of Olivares. The Statesman in an Age of Decline* (Yale, 1986), or more briefly in his *Richelieu and Olivares* (Cambridge, 1984). R. A. Stradling, *Philip IV and the Government of Spain, 1621–1665* (Cambridge, 1988), deals also with the neglected second half of Philip IV's reign, while H. Kamen, *Spain in the Later-seventeenth Century* (1980) challenges most established views of the reign of Charles II. Lord Mahon, *Spain under Charles the Second* (1844), is a horrifying first-hand impression of the government of Spain in the last decade of the century.

Some sense of the collapse of Castilian finances, justice and government can be got from A. Domínguez Ortiz, 'La crise intérieure de la Monarchie des Habsbourgs espagnols sous Charles II', in J. A. H. Bots (ed.), *The Peace of Nijmegen 1676–1678/79. La Paix de Nimègue* (Amsterdam, 1980) pp. 157–67, for an overall perspective, and from C. Rahn Phillips, *Ciudad Real, 1500–1700* (Cambridge, Mass., 1979) (finances), M. R. Weisser, *The Peasants of the Montes* (Chicago, 1976) (crime), R. L. Kagan, *Lawsuits and Litigants in Castile 1500–1700* (Chapel Hill, NC, 1981) (justice), I. A. A. Thompson, *War and Government in Habsburg Spain, 1560–1620* (1976) (military administration), for their respective areas of interest. On the other hand, in *Six Galleons for the King of Spain* (Baltimore, 1987), C. Rahn Phillips takes a more optimistic view of the efficiency of the administration, and Charles Jago in 'The Influence of Debt on the relations between Crown and Aristocracy in Seventeenth-century Castile', *Economic History Review*, 2nd series, 26 (1973) 218–36, and 'The "Crisis of the Aristocracy" in Seventeenth-century Castile', *Past and Present*, no. 84 (1979) 60–90, sees fiscal pressure and aristocratic indebtedness rather as strengthening the hand of the crown.

4. SWEDEN

For those who cannot read Swedish, the possibilities of studying the history of seventeenth-century Sweden in any depth are limited, and even the coverage provided by Swedish historians is uneven. It is significant that the best comprehensive account of the period from 1654 to 1718 is still the classic multi-volume history by F. F. Carlson, *Sveriges historia under konungarna av Pfalziska huset*, published between 1855 and 1885. This has never been superseded and there is, sadly, nothing of comparable scale covering the earlier seventeenth century. For English-speaking readers there have been two major resources, both fortunately very good. Ragnhild Hatton has published the best modern study of the reign of Karl XII in *Charles XII of Sweden* (1968) and there are the many writings of Michael Roberts. The major works are the two volumes on *Gustavus Adolphus* (1953 and 1958), *Sweden as a Great Power 1611–1697*, which has an invaluable selection of documents in translation (1967) and *The Swedish Imperial Experience 1560–1718* (1979). There is also the collection of Roberts's *Essays in Swedish History* (1967) including two important pieces on the crisis of 1650 and the reign of Karl XI, and Roberts has edited the collection of essays, *Sweden's Age of Greatness 1632–1718* (1973). This includes a chapter of his own on the Swedish church and notable contributions from S. Dahlgren, 'Estates and classes', K. Ågren, 'The reduktion' and A. Åberg, 'The Swedish army from Lützen to Narva'. Beyond this K. Ågren has an article on the Swedish elite, 'The rise and decline of an aristocracy' in *Scandinavian Journal of History*, I (1976), there is a good chapter by J. Rosen in *Cambridge Modern History*, vol. V (1961) on the development of the absolutism, and some excellent material in the *History of the Swedish Riksdag* (Stockholm, 1988) a collective work with contributions by leading contemporary scholars. Finally there are the two articles by A. F. Upton, 'The riksdag of 1680 and the establishment of royal absolutism in Sweden', *English Historical Review*, CII (1987) and 'Absolutism and the rule of law: the case of Karl XI of Sweden', in *Parliaments, Estates and Representation*, VIII (1988). There is a major, though controversial study in German, by G. Barudio, *Absolutismus – Zerstörung der 'Libertären Verfassung'* (Frankfurt, 1976) on the creation of the absolutism in the years 1680–93: it is a strong and polemical critique of the prevailing school of interpretation among Swedish historians. It is also possible to get a taste of contemporary views on Swedish absolutism: there are Bulstrode Whitelocke's impressions of Sweden in the 1650s, *Journal of the Swedish Embassy* (1855), and the much more systematic, and usually well-informed account of another British ambassador, J. Robinson, *An Account of Sweden*, written in the 1690s and published in 1738. And there is a well-informed commentary on the reign of Karl XI, *Les Anecdotes de Suède* (1716). This polemical tract is anonymous, some authorities have ascribed it to the German scholar, S. Pufendorf, who was well informed about Sweden, but more probably the author is the highly-placed courtier and bureaucrat, J. P. Olivekrantz. After this, the student whose interest has been aroused by these works and would like to pursue the subject further will have to settle down to the task of learning to read Swedish.

5. BRANDENBURG-PRUSSIA

Unfortunately, readers not knowing any German are poorly served, compared with Prussia's history in the eighteenth century. The best introductions to the period in English are still contained in the *Cambridge Modern History*, vol. VI, J. F. Cooper (ed.), *The Decline of Spain and the Thirty Years War 1609–48/59* (Cambridge, 1970); vol. V, F. L. Carsten (ed.), *The Ascendancy of France 1648–88* (Cambridge, 1961); vol. VI, J. S. Bromley (ed.), *The Rise of Great Britain and Russia 1688–1715/25* (Cambridge, 1970); older but still relevant are C. J. Friedrich, *The Age of the Baroque 1610–1660* (New York, 1952); F. L. Nussbaum, *The Triumph of Science and Reason 1660–1685* (New York, 1953); J. B. Wolf, *The Emergence of the Great Powers 1685–1715* (New York, 1951) – all three titles available in the Harper Torchbook Series; the most recent standard of research is reflected in H. Schilling, *Aufbruch und Krise, Deutschland 1517–1648* (Berlin, 1988); Schilling, *Höfe und Allianzen. Deutschland 1648–1763* (Berlin, 1989). Unorthodox in approach, unreliable in its method of quoting sources is the introductory chapter of H.-U. Wehler, *Deutsche Gesellschaftsgeschichte 1700–1815* (Munich, 1987). For Prussia's history up to the reign of the Great Elector see F. L. Carsten, *The Origins of Prussia* (Oxford, 1954) though this study as well as Carsten's articles at the time still bear the psychological scars of the Nazi experience. For a general survey of Prussian history see H. W. Koch, *A History of Prussia* (1978).

Biographic studies in English of the Great Elector are few, though F. Schevill's *The Great Elector* (New York, 1947) seems to have withstood the test of time remarkably well. However, the great and definitive biography is by E. Opgenoorth, *Friedrich Wilhelm. Der Grosse Kurfürst von Brandenburg*, 2 vols (Göttingen, 1971–8); also G. Oestreich, *Friedrich Wilhelm. Der Gross Kurfürst* (Göttingen, 1971), a very brief but incisive study. See also G. Galland, *Der Grosse Kurfürst und Moritz von Nassau, der Brasialianer* (Frankfurt/M, 1893); O. Hoetsch, 'Fürst Johann Moritz von Nassau-Siegen als brandenburgischer Staatsmann 1647–1679', in *Forschungen zur Brandenburgischen und Preussischen Geschichte* (1906); M. Philipson, *Der Grosse Kurfürst Friedrich Wilhelm von Brandenburg*, 3 vols (Berlin, 1897–1907); W. F. Reddaway, 'The advent of the Great Elector', *Transactions of the Royal Historical Society*, n.s., 15 (1901); G. W. von Raumer, *Friedrich Wilhelms des Grossen Kurfürsten von Brandenburg Kinderjahre* (Berlin, 1850); von Raumer, *Friedrich Wilhelms des Grossen Kurfürsten von Brandenburg Jugendjahre*, 2 parts (Berlin, 1853–4); T. Saring, *Luise Henriette Kurfürstin von Brandenburg 1627–1667, die Gemahlin des grossen Kurfürsten* (Göttingen, 1941).

For administrative aspects see H. Rosenberg, *Bureaucracy, Aristocracy and Autocracy. The Prussian Experience, 1660–1815* (Cambridge, Mass. 1958), brief and somewhat superficial and by no means outdating O. Hintze's work, 'Der österreichische und der preussische Beamtenstaat im 17. und 18. Jahrhundert', *Gesammelte Abhandlungen*, 3 (1967); Hintze, 'Der preussische Militär- und Beamtenstaat im 18. Jahrundert', *Gesammelte Abhandlungen*, 3 (1967); some of Hintze's seminal essays have been translated and edited by F. Gilbert, *The Historical Essays of Otto Hintze* (Oxford, 1975); I. Mittenzwei, 'Theorie und Praxis im aufgeklärten Absolutismus in Brandenburg-Preussen', in *Jahrbuch für Geschichte*, vol. 6 (Berlin, 1972); E. Amburger, *Das Kammergericht und seine Präsidenten* (Berlin, 1955); H. Croon, 'Stände und Steuern in Jülich-Berg im 17 und vornehmlich im 18. Jahrhundert', *Rheinisches Archiv*, 10 (1929); E. Wyluda, *Lehnrecht und Beamtentum. Studien zur Entstehung des Preussischen Beamtentums* (Berlin, 1969); W. L. Dorn also throws light on the development of the Prussian bureaucracy during the outgoing seventeenth century in 'The Prussian Bureaucracy in the Eighteenth Century', *Political Science Quarterly*, 46 (1931); 47 (1932).

On military aspects see: M. Jähns, *Geschichte der Kriegswissenschaften, vornehmilich in Deutschland*, vol. 2 (Berlin, 1890); C. Jany, *Geschichte der königlich preussischen Armee bis zum Jahre 1807*, vol. 1 (Berlin, 1928). H. Delbrück's *Geschichte der kriegskunst*, vol. 4 (Berlin, 1920) is now available in an English translation, as are volumes 1–3.

On social and economic aspects see F. L. Carsten, 'The resistance of Cleves and Mark to the Despotic Policy of the Great Elector', *English Historical Review*, 66 (1951); Carsten, 'Die Ursachen des Niedergangs der deutschen Landstände', *Historische Zeitschrift*, 129 (1961); K. Breysig, *Geschichte der brandenburgischen Finanzen in der Zeit von 1640 bis 1697. Darstellung und Akten*, vol. 1. (Leipzig, 1895); H. Schnee, *Die Hoffinanz und der moderne Staat I. Die Institution des Hoffaktorentums in Brandenburg-Preussen* (Berlin, 1953); F. Wolters, *Geschichte der brandenburgischen Finanznen in der Zeit von 1640 bis 1697. Darstellung und Akten*, vol. 2: *Die Zentralverwaltung des Heeres und der Steuern. Urkunden und Actenstücke zur Geschichte der inneren Politik des Kurfürsten Friedrich Wilhelm von Brandenburg*, vol. 1, 2 (Munich/Leipzig, 1915); G. Vogler, 'Die Entwicklung der feudalen Arbeitsrente in Brandenburg vom 15. bis 18. Jahrhundert. Eine Analyse für das kurmärkische Domänenamt Badingen', in *Jahrbuch für Wirtschaftsgeschichte* (1966); J. B. Neveux, *Vie spirituelle et vie sociale entre Rhin et Baltique au XVIIe siècle* (Paris, 1967); H. Kellenbenz, *Der Merkantilismus in Europa und die soziale Mobilität* (Wiesbaden, 1965); F. Facius, *Wirtschaft und Staat. Die Entwicklung der staatlichen Wirtschaftsverwaltung in Deutschland vom 17. Jahrhundert bis 1945* (Boppard/Rhein, 1959); A. C. Carter, *Getting, Spending and Investing in Early Modern Times. Essays on Dutch, English and Huguenot Economic History* (Assen, 1975).

For cultural and religious aspects see F. Arnheim, 'Freiherr Benedikt Skytte, der Urheber des Plans einer brandenburgischen Universität', in *Beiträge zur Brandenburgischen und Preussischen Geschichte* Festschrift Gustav Schmoller zum 70. Geburtstag (Leipzig, 1908); P. Baumgart, 'Absoluter Staat und Judenemanzipation in Brandenburg-Preussen', in *Jahrbuch für die Geschichte Mittel- und Ostdeutschlands*, 13/14 (1965); J. V. Bredt, *Die Verfassung der reformierten Kirche in Cleve-Jülich-Berg-Mark* (Neukirchen, 1938); F. Dickmann, 'Das Problem der Gleichberedhtigung der Konfessionen im Reich im 16. und 17. Jahrhundert', *Historische Zeitschrift*, 201 (1965); R. Dietrich, *Berlin. Neun Kapitel seiner Geschichte* (Berlin, 1960); E. Kaeber, *Beiträge zur Berliner Geschichte* (Berlin, 1965); M. Lackner, *Die Kirchenpolitik des Grossen Kurfürsten* (Witten, 1973); G. Oestreich, 'Fundamente preussischer Geistesgeschichte. Religion und Weltanschauung in Brandenburg im 17. Jahrhundert', *Jahrbuch preussischer Kulturbesitz*, (1969); O. H. Richardson, 'Religious toleration under the Great Elector and its material results', *English Historical Review*, 25 (1910); H. Rothfels (ed), *Berlin in Geschichte und Gegenwart* (Tübingen, 1961); A. Woltmann, *Die Baugeschihte Berlins* (Berlin, 1872); S. Stern, *The Court Jew. A contribution to the history of the period of Absolutism in Central Europe* (Philadelphia, 1950); C. Sachs, *Musik und Oper am kurbrandenburgischen Hofe* (Berlin, 1910); H. Landwehr, *Die Kirchenpolitik Friedrich Wilhelm, der Grossen Kurfürsten* (Berlin, 1894); D. Joseph, 'Kunst und

Künstler unter der Regierung des grossen Kurfürsten', in *Mitteilungen des Vereins für die Geschichte Berlins*, XII (1895); O. Glasser, *Die Niederländer in der brandenburgisch-preussischen Kulturarbeit* (Berlin, 1939); G. Galland, *Hohenzollern und Oranien. Studien zur deutschen Kunstgeschichte* (Strassburg, 1911).

Foreign policy aspects: within this scope come Brandenburg-Prussia's relations with the Reich as well as with Germany's neighbours, which are adequately covered in the biographical and military aspects of this bibliography. Further guidance is supplied by the bibliographies of the three Harper torchbooks mentioned above.

6. THE AUSTRIAN LANDS

There is relatively little available in English (or French) on the history of the Austrian lands in this period. General studies of the Habsburg monarchy include H. G. Koenigsberger, *The Habsburgs and Europe 1516–1660* (1971); V. Mamatey, *The Rise of the Habsburg Empire, 1516–1815* (1971); V.-L. Tapie, *The Rise and Fall of the Habsburg Monarchy* (1971) and, most useful (and recent) of all, R. J. W. Evans, *The Making of the Habsburg Monarchy, 1550–1700* (Oxford, 1979). Relevant material on the reign of Leopold I includes J. P. Spielman, *Leopold I* (1977); J. Bérenger, *Finances et Absolutisme Autrichien dans la seconde moitié du XVIIe Siècle* (Paris, 1975); R. Wines, 'The Imperial Circles, Princely Diplomacy and Imperial Reform, 1681–1714', *Journal of Modern History*, XXXIX (1967); and J. Stoye, *The Siege of Vienna* (1964).

7. THE EMERGENCE OF ABSOLUTISM IN RUSSIA

The literature on Russian absolutism, like so much that deals with pre-modern Russian history generally, is on the whole unsatisfactory. Soviet historiography has long pretended that Peter the Great created Russia *ab initio*, while historians writing in English, when not following that interpretation, have often sought to show that Russia has never been 'European' and that its government was autocratic, not absolutist. These understandings are at long last beginning to change, but the legacy of misunderstanding (not least about ranks and institutions) continues to be repeated uncritically in the secondary literature, thereby acquiring a patina of spurious respectability. All this makes it difficult to recommend much for further reading on Russian absolutism that is not misconceived or riddled with errors. Fortunately, however, there are exceptions.

Philip Longworth's *Alexis: Tsar of All the Russians* (1984) is useful alike as a life and times of an important absolutist, for its treatment of Russian institutions and its bibliography. An adequate treatment of another key figure, Ivan IV, however, is still awaited, while the literature on Peter I and the 'Petrine Revolution' is too voluminous to deal with here.

Students who can read Russian may derive profit from N. U. Drushinin *et al.* (eds), *Absolutism v Rossii (xvii–xviii vv)* (Absolutism in Russia – 17th and 18th Centuries) (Moscow, 1964) and subsequent contributions by M. Ya Volkov and others to Soviet journals, especially *Istoria SSSR* and *Voprosy Istorii*. Those confined to English and French should not neglect the writings of three eminent Russian legal and constitutional histories of the pre-Revolutionary period: A Lappo-Danilevskij, 'L'Idée de l'état et son évolution en Russie depuis les troubles du xviie siècle jusque'aux réformes du xviiie', in Paul Vinogradoff (ed.), *Essays in Legal History* (1913); M. Kovalevsky, *Modern Customs and Ancient Laws of Russia* (1891); and F. Sigel, *Lectures on Slavonic Law* (1902). The works of R. E. F. Smith, *The Enserfment of the Russian Peasantry* (Cambridge, 1968),

Peasant Farming in Moscovy (Cambridge, 1977) and Smith and David Christian, *Bread and Salt: A Social and Economic History of Food and Drink in Russia* (Cambridge, 1984), are invaluable aids to understanding the development of the agrarian economy and institutions affecting the peasant majority. R. Hellie's new edition of the 1649 Law Code provides a good English translation, though Cherepiria's standard work on the Assemblies of the Land (Moscow, 1978) is available only in Russian. W. Palmer's *Patriarch and Tsar*, 6 vols (1871–6) provides a mass of original material on Church–State relations and the Schism, much of it unavailable in Russian, but it is unwieldy and marred by the compiler's lively religious prejudices.

Finally, mention must be made of a suggestive new work on the state's financial machinery in the fifteenth and sixteenth centuries, S. M. Kastanov's *Finansy Sredrevkoroi Rossii* (Moscow, 1988), which appeared too late to take account of in the preceding essay.

8. BRITAIN

If there have been few attempts to compare English monarchical government with that of the continent in this period, this probably owes less to English insularity than to a preoccupation with 1640–60, hardly a period when the monarchy was at its strongest. The best overall survey of government has long been J. P. Kenyon, *The Stuart Constitution* (2nd edn, Cambridge, 1986), while A. Fletcher, *Reform in the Provinces: The Government of Stuart England* (New Haven, 1986) offers a synthesis of recent work on local government and a good deal more besides. The first coherent attempt to argue that an English absolutism was a possibility was J. R. Western, *Monarchy and Revolution: The English State in the 1680s* (1972); others have elaborated on this theme, including J. Childs, most recently in '1688', *History*, LXXIII (1988); for a more sceptical view see J. Miller, 'The Potential for "Absolutism" in Later Stuart England', *History,* LXIX (1984). Historians of the early Stuart period have tended to fight shy of the term 'absolutism'. Those who saw the civil war as the product of long-term social and economic developments paid scant attention to government or kings, while the 'revisionists' of the last twenty years have been inclined to play down the divisions of the period and to see the civil war as the product of short-term misunderstandings. For forceful statements of 'revisionism' see C. Russell, 'Parliamentary History in Perspective 1604–29, *History,* LXI (1976) and K. Sharpe, 'The Personal Rule of Charles I' in H. C. Tomlinson (ed.), *Before the English Civil War* (1983); for a restrained but cogent criticism see D. Hirst, 'Revisionism Revised: The Place of Principle', *Past and Present*, 92 (1981). Studies of the Stuart kings tend to be mediocre. C. Carlton, *Charles I: The Personal Monarch* (1984) makes some wild errors, but also some shrewd points. The best overview of early Stuart monarchy is probably still S. R. Gardiner's magisterial *History of England 1603–42* 10 vols (1883–4); there is also a sophisticated analysis by M. Hawkins of 'The Government: its Role and Aims' in C. Russell (ed.), *Origins of the English Civil War* (1973). See also J. Miller, *Bourbon and Stuart* (1987) and *James II: a Study in Kingship* (new edn, 1989).

Historians of English political ideas have tended to fight shy of 'absolutism' or else to discuss it in hopelessly simplistic terms: two worthy exceptions are J. Daly, 'The Idea of Absolutism in Seventeenth-Century England', *Historical Journal*, XXI (1978) and J. P. Sommerville, *Politics and Ideology in England 1603–40* (1986).

Research on the growth of the state tends to be scattered in specialist monographs. There is useful material in Western and in J. Childs' books on *The Army of Charles II* (1976) and *The Army, James II and the Glorious Revolution* (Manchester, 1980). H. Tomlinson summarises 'Fiscal and Administrative Developments in

England' in J. R. Jones (ed.), *The Restored Monarchy 1660–88* (1979). There are massive studies of *The English Public Revenue 1660–88* by C. D. Chandaman (Oxford, 1975) and of *The Financial Revolution 1688–1756* by P. G. M. Dickson (1967); but there is unfortunately no work of synthesis on the period before 1688 comparable to J. Brewer, *Sinews of Power: War, Money and the English State 1688–1783* (1989).

Scotland and Ireland are generally less well served. R. Mitchison, *Lordship to Patronage: Scotland 1603–1745* (1983) offers a clear and perceptive introduction. On Ireland J. C. Beckett's *The Making of Modern Ireland, 1603–1923* (1966) is probably the most succinct introduction and should be supplemented by vols III and IV of the Oxford *New History of Ireland*.

Notes and References

INTRODUCTION *John Miller*

I am most grateful to Roger Mettam for reading and commenting on a draft of this introduction; any errors and misconceptions which remain are of course my own.

1. J. Daly, 'The Idea of Absolute Monarchy in Seventeenth-Century England', *Historical Journal*, XXI (1978) 250.
2. F. Hartung and R. Mousnier, 'Quelques problèmes concernant la monarchie absolue', *Relazioni del X Congresso di Scienze Storiche: IV Storia Moderna* (Florence, 1955) pp. 4–15; see Burns's chapter below.
3. Pepys, *Diary*, ed. R. C. Latham and W. Mathews, 11 vols (1971–83), VIII, 300; Daly, 'Idea of Absolute Monarchy', pp. 235–47.
4. G. Parker, *Europe in Crisis 1598–1648* (1979) p. 61.
5. Ibid., pp. 59–60.
6. See J. R. Major, *Representative Institutions in Renaissance France* (Madison, 1960), P. S. Lewis, *Late Medieval France: The Polity* (1968) pp. 328–74.
7. See M. Bloch, *The Royal Touch* (1973).
8 J. Brewer, *The Sinews of Power: War, Money and the English State 1688–1783* (1989) p. xvii.
9. P. Anderson, *Lineages of the Absolutist State*, Verso edition (1979).
10. Ibid, p. 429.
11. J. Ellul, *Histoire des institutions IV. XVIe–XVIII siècle* (Paris, 1956) p. 71. Ellul adds (pp. 72–3) that there were other important factors, including war and the king's acting as arbiter between different groups.
12. J. R. Jones, *The Revolution of 1688 in England* (1972) pp. 11–12; J. Childs, '1688', *History*, LXXIII (1988) 398–424.
13. Parker, *Europe in Crisis*, pp. 66–70.
14. J. Miller, 'Les États de Languedoc pendant la Fronde', *Annales du Midi*, XCV (1983) 45–6; R. Bonney, *Political Change in France under Richelieu and Mazarin* (Oxford, 1978) ch. 10.
15. Anderson, *Lineages*, pp. 198–202.
16. See T. C. W. Blanning, *Joseph II and Enlightened Despotism* (1970) pp. 10–20, for a useful summary.
17. Anderson, *Lineages*, pp. 240–5.
18. See Chapter 7, below.
19. See the large literature on revolt including Y.-M. Bercé, *Histoire des croquants* (Geneva, 1974); R. Pillorget, *Le Mouvements insurrectionnels de Provence entre 1596 et 1715* (Paris, 1975); P. J. Coveney (ed.), *France in Crisis 1620–75* (1977).
20. Anderson, *Lineages*, pp. 33–4, 97.
21. Ibid., pp. 52, 66, 26.
22. Ibid., p. 141. This comes from misreading G. E. Aylmer, *The King's Servants* (1961) p. 248: Aylmer is talking of fees charged by officials, not of sales of office; the fees were, in effect, a form of disguised taxation.
23. Anderson, *Lineages*, p. 66.
24. Ibid., pp. 137–8.
25. Ibid., pp. 31–3, 58.

26. Ibid., pp. 36–7, 58, 102–3.
27. P. Sonnino, 'Colbert and the origins of the Dutch War', *European Studies Review*, XIII (1983) 1–11.
28. Anderson, *Lineages*, pp. 104, 179, 198–202.
29. For an example of the importance of lust see J.-P. Babelon, *Henri IV* (Paris, 1982) pp. 953, 958.
30. Anderson, *Lineages*, p. 58.
31. For questions of precedence, see Public Record Office, SP 78/118, fo. 32; for giving priority to 'the flag' see SP 104/177, fo. 164.
32. Anderson, *Lineages*, p. 32; also pp. 18–20, 100–1.
33. Ibid., pp. 107–10, 231, 321.
34. See N. Steensgard, 'The Seventeenth-Century Crisis', in G. Parker and L. M. Smith (eds), *The General Crisis of the Seventeenth Century* (1978) pp. 27–42.
35. J.-P. Labatut, *Les Ducs et pairs de France au XVIIe siècle* (Paris, 1972); D. Dessert, *Argent, pouvoir et société au grand siècle* (Paris, 1984). Note the comments of J. H. Elliott, 'Revolution and Continuity' in Parker and Smith, *General Crisis*, p. 130.
36. L. Stone, *The Crisis of the Aristocracy 1558–1641* (abridged edn, Oxford, 1967) pp. 6–7, 10–11; Anderson, *Lineages*, p. 138n.
37. Anderson, *Lineages*, pp. 138–40. See D. Hay *et al.*, *Albion's Fatal Tree: Crime and Society in Eighteenth-century England* (1975). For a severe critique see J. H. Langbein, 'Albion's Fatal Flaws', *Past and Present*, 98 (1983) 96–120.
38. L. Bernard, 'Popular Uprisings under Louis XIV', *French Historical Studies*, III (1964) 468–74; E. Le Roy Ladurie, 'Révoltes et contestations rurales de 1675 à 1788', *Annales ESC*, XXIX (1974) 6–22.
39. See Hartung and Mousnier, 'Quelques problèmes', pp. 9, 36–40.
40. See Brewer, *Sinews of Power*; Anderson ignores 1688, except for a brief mention on p. 106.
41. Anderson, *Lineages*, p. 342; J. Hurstfield, *The Queen's Wards* (1958); below, pp. 90–1.
42. See P. Geyl, *The Netherlands in the Seventeenth Century: II 1648–1715* (1964) and the same author's *Orange and Stuart* (1969).
43. See H. Kamen, 'The Decline of Spain: a Historical Myth?', *Past and Present*, 81 (1978) 24–50.
44. This paragraph is based in large part on my own researches into the provincial estates of Languedoc.
45. See H. Rosenberg, *Bureaucracy, Aristocracy and Autocracy: The Prussian Experience 1660–1815* (Cambridge, Mass., 1956); W. L. Dorn, 'The Prussian Bureaucracy in the Eighteenth Century', three parts, *Political Science Quarterly*, *XLVI–XLVII (1931–2).*
46. See J. C. Rule, 'Louis XIV and Colbert de Torcy', in R. M. Hatton and J. S. Bromley (eds), William iii and Louis XIV: Essays by and for Mark A. Thomson (Liverpool, 1968) ch. 12.
47. The classic study is R. Mousnier, *La Vénalité des offices sous henri IV et Louis XIII* (revised edn, Paris, 1971).
48. P. Mathias and P. O'Brien, 'Taxation in Britain and France, 1715–1810', *Journal of European Economic History*, V (1976) 601–50.
49. The comfortable presumption that the English economy grew faster than that of France in the eighteenth century is open to question: see Brewer, *Sinews of Power*, pp. 180–2.

1. THE IDEA OF ABSOLUTISM *S. H. Burns*

1. Jacques Bénigne Bossuet, *Politique tirée des propres paroles de l'Écriture*

Sainte, III, i: *Oeuvres complètes de Bossuet* (Paris, 1840) vol. IX, p. 743; and for the distinction between 'absolute' and 'arbitrary', IV, i (p. 763) and VIII, ii (p. 913).

2. John Locke, *Two Treatises of Government*, I, i, ed. Peter Laslett (2nd edn, Cambridge, 1967) p. 159.

3. David Hume, *The History of Great Britain: the Reigns of James I and Charles I*, ed. Duncan Forbes (1970) p. 80 n. 1.

4. Ibid., p. 222 n. 4.

5. On *Plenitudo potestatis* see I. S. Robinson in J. H. Burns (ed.), *The Cambridge History of Medieval Political Thought, c. 350–c. 1450* (Cambridge, 1988) pp. 282–8; also K. Pennington, ibid., pp. 430–6. For rulers as 'vicars of Christ', see P. D. King, ibid., pp. 143–4; Janet Nelson, ibid., pp. 235, 240.

6. See J. H. Burns, '*Politia regalis et optima*: The Political Ideas of John Mair', *History of Political Thought*, II (1981) 40 at n. 46.

7. Ibid., 40 n. 44.

8. *Summa Theologiae*, Ia IIae, q. 90.

9. See Burns, '*Politia regalis et optima*', 36 at n. 25.

10. Hume, *History*, pp. 222–3 n. 4.

11. See W. H. Greenleaf, *Order, Fmpiricism and Politics: Two Traditions in English Political Thought, 1500–1700* (Oxford, 1964) ch. VII.

12. Jean Bodin, *Six Books of the Commonwealth*m ed. M. J. Tooley (Oxford, n.d.) p. 25. Further page references are to this abridged translation.

13. See M. Wolfe, 'Jean Bodin on Taxes: the Sovereignty-Taxes Paradox', *Political Science Quarterly*, LXXXIII (1968) 268–84.

14. See J. H. Burns, 'Sovereignty and Constitutional Law in Bodin', *Political Studies*, VII (1959) 174–7.

15. See, e.g. A. Black, *Monarchy and Community: Political Ideas in the Later Conciliar Controversy 1430–1450* (Cambridge, 1970) pp. 53–84.

16. See M. Bloch (trans. J. E. Anderson), *The Royal Touch: Sacred Monarchy and Scrofula in England and France* (1973).

17. *The Basilicon Doron of King James VI*, ed. J. Craigie, 2 vols (Edinburgh, 1944–50) vol. I, p. 4.

18. See Filmer, *Patriarcha and other Political Writings*, ed. P. Laslett (Oxford, 1949).

19. See D. Wootton (ed.), *Divine Right and Democracy: an Anthology of Political Writing in Stuart England* (1986) pp. 31–2.

20. See F. Oakley, *Omnipotence, Covenant, and Order: An Excursion in the History of Ideas from Abelard to Leibniz* (Ithaca and London, 1984) esp. ch. 4.

21. See K. Pennington in *Cambridge History of Medieval Political Thought*, pp. 435–6; J. P. Canning, ibid., pp. 455–6.

22. See N. Round, *The Greatest Man Uncrowned: a Study of the Fall of Don Alvaro de Luna* (1986) ch. 4.; A. Ryder, *The Kingdom of Naples under Alfonso the Magnificent: the Making of a Modern State* (Oxford, 1976).

23. Bossuet, *Oeuvres*, vol. ix, pp. 779–801.

24. See J. Dunbabin in *Cambridge History of Medieval Political Thought*, pp. 501–4; J. Quillet, ibid., pp. 545–54.

25. See G. Oestreich, *Neostoicism and the early modern State* (Cambridge, 1982) esp. chs 3–4.

26. See U. P. Burke in J. H. Burns and M. Goldie (eds), *The Cambridge History of Political Thought, 1450–1700* (Cambridge, forthcoming, 1990) ch. 16.

27. Oestreich, *Neostoicism*, pp. 114–15.

28. Thomas Hobbes, *Leviathan*, ed. W. G. Pogson Smith (Oxford, 1909) p. 222. Further page references are to this edition.

29. See the preface to his *Observations concerning the Originall of Government* (1952): *Patriarcha and other Political Writings*, ed. Laslett, p. 239–40.

2. FRANCE *Roger Mettam*

1. Roland Mousnier, *La Vénalité des offices sous Henri IV et Louis XIII* (Rouen, 1945).

2. For example: William Beik, *Absolutism and Society in seventeenth-century France – State Power and Provincial Aristocracy in Languedoc* (Cambridge, 1985); Daniel Dessert, *Argent, pouvoir et société au grand siècle* (Paris, 1984); Jonathan Dewald, *The Formation of a Provincial Nobility – the Magistrates of the Parlement of Rouen, 1499–1610* (Princeton, 1980); Barbara B. Diefendorf, *Paris City Councillors in the Sixteenth Century – the Politics of Patrimony* (Princeton, 1983); Robert R. Harding, *Anatomy of a Power Elite – the Provincial Governors of Early Modern France* (New Haven, 1978); Sharon Kettering, *Judicial Politics and Urban Revolt in Seventeenth-century France – the Parlement of Aix, 1629–1659* (Princeton, 1978); James B. Wood, *The Nobility of the Election of Bayeux, 1463–1666 – Continuity through Change* (Princeton, 1981).

3. For example: Sharon Kettering, *Patrons, Brokers and Clients in Seventeenth-century France* (Oxford, 1986); Roger Mettam, *Power and Faction in Louis XIV's France* (Oxford, 1988).

4. Nevertheless, with this warning, some of them provide useful résumés of early modern French political ideas, for example: William Farr Church, *Constitutional Thought in Sixteenth-century France – a Study in the Evolution of Ideas* (Cambridge, Mass., 1941); Herbert H. Rowen, *The King's State – Proprietary Dynasticism in early modern France* (New Brunswick, NJ, 1980).

5. See the excellent article by David Parker, 'Sovereignty, Absolutism and the Function of the Law in Seventeenth-century France', *Past and Present*, 122 (February 1989); for earlier stimulating contributions to the debate on 'absolutism', see the articles by E. H. Kossmann, 'The Singularity of Absolutism', G. Durand, 'What is Absolutism?', and François Dumont, 'French Kingship and Absolute Monarchy in the Seventeenth Century', all in Ragnhild Hatton (ed.), *Louis XIV and Absolutism* (1976).

6. See Albert N. Hamscher, *The Parlement of Paris after the Fronde, 1653–1673* (Pittsburgh, 1976) esp. ch. IV.

7. These powers, and their historical antecedents, are admirably and briefly summarised by Richard Bonney, *L'absolutisme*, 'Que sais-je?', no. 2486 (Paris, 1989).

8. Jacques-Bénigne Bossuet, *Politique tirée des propres paroles de l'Écriture-sainte*, 2 vols (Paris, 1709); the quotation is from part I, book v, article iv, proposition 1.

9. See James E. King, *Science and Rationalism in the Government of Louis XIV* (Baltimore, 1949), although its early date means that it does not consider all the issues raised in the modern debate on 'absolutism'.

10. Their writings are well summarised in two books by Charles Woolsey Cole: *French Mercantilist Doctrine before Colbert* (New York, 1931); and *Colbert and a Century of French Mercantilism*, 2 vols (New York, 1939; reprinted London, 1964), especially vol. I, chs I–VI.

11. Albert N. Hamscher, 'The conseil privé and the parlements in the age of Louis XIV – a study in French absolutism', *Transactions of the American Philosophical Society*, LXXVII, part II (1987).

12. For two lengthy discussions of the aristocratic arguments, see: Paul Bénichou, *Morales du grand siècle* (Paris, 1948) pp. 13–111; and F. E. Sutcliffe,

Guez de Balzac et son temps – littérature et politique (Paris, 1959) esp. pp. 57–212; for a briefer summary see Roger Mettam, 'Definitions of Nobility in Seventeenth-century France', in Penelope J. Corfield (ed.), *Language, History and Class* (Oxford, 1990).

13. An excellent examination of these issues, in the context of the 1650s, is the work by Richard M. Golden, *The Godly Rebellion – Parisian Curés and the Religious Fronde, 1652–1662* (Chapel Hill, NC, 1981); equally effective on the later period is B. Robert Kreiser, *Miracles, Convulsions, and Ecclesiastical Politics in early Eighteenth-century Paris* (Princeton, 1978).

14. See R. J. Knecht, *Francis I* (Cambridge, 1982) pp. 51–65.

15. See: on the sixteenth century, Church, *Constitutional Thought*; and on the ideological disputes between the Huguenots and the crown under Henri IV and Louis XIII, David Parker, *La Rochelle and the French Monarchy: Conflict and Order in Seventeenth-century France* (1980) pp. 151–70.

16. Jean Bodin, *Les six livres de la république* (1576); the greater part of the work is concerned with the nature of sovereignty and monarchy; Bodin allowed that, while a subject should never lift his hand against his sovereign, he had the moral right to refuse to obey any of his commands which were immoral or unnatural, although he had to be prepared to go into exile or hiding, or face death, if he did so.

17. See: on the Protestant opposition to Louis XIV, Guy Howard Dodge, *The Political Theory of the Huguenots of the Dispersion, with Special Reference to the Thought and Influence of Pierre Jurieu* (New York, 1947); on the aristocratic theorists, there being no reliable modern survey, it is necessary to consult the original tracts, especially F. de Fénelon, *Écrits et lettres politiques*, ed. Charles Urbain (Paris, 1920; reprinted Geneva, 1981); the duc de Saint-Simon, *Projets de gouvernement du duc de Bourgogne* (Paris, 1860), and his 'Lettre anonyme au roi (avril 1712)', in M. P. Faugère (ed.), *Écrits inédits de Saint-Simon*, 8 vols (Paris, 1880–93) vol. IV.

3. CASTILE *I. A. A. Thompson*

1. P. Croft, 'Annual Parliaments and the Long Parliament', *Bulletin of the Institute of Historical Research* (1986) 155–71, at p. 166.

2. J. Beneyto Pérez, *Los orígenes de la ciencia política en España* (Madrid, 1949) p. 285, n. 103.

3. J. A. Maravall, *Estudios de historia del pensamiento español*, vol. 3 (Madrid, 1975) p. 193.

4. *Journal of a Younger Brother. The Life of Thomas Platter* (1963) p. 226.

5. Diego de Covarrubias y Leyva, *Textos jurídico-políticos*, ed. M. Fraga Iribarne (Madrid, 1957) p. 282.

6. J. A. Maravall, *La philosophie politique espagnole au XVIIe siècle* (Paris, 1965) p. 256.

7. B. Hamilton, *Political Thought in Sixteenth-Century Spain* (Oxford, 1963) p. 145. The expression 'rey propietario', commonly taken to mean 'king and owner', should be understood to mean 'proprietary king', the ownership applying, that is, not to the kingdom, but to the office, in the same way that other offices were said to be held 'en propiedad', and not by proxies, substitutes, or lessees.

8. A. González Palencia, *La Junta de Reformación, 1618–1625*, Archivo Histórico Español, vol. 5 (Valladolid, 1932) p. 86, 23 May 1621; Hamilton, *Political Thought*, p. 57.

9. J. H. Elliott, 'The Court of the Spanish Habsburgs: a peculiar institution?', in P. Mack and M. C. Jacob (eds), *Politics and Culture in Early-Modern Europe*

(Cambridge, 1987) pp. 5–24, and 'Philip IV of Spain, Prisoner of Ceremony', in A. G. Dickens (ed.), *The Courts of Europe. Politics, Patronage and Royalty 1400–1800* (1977) pp. 169–89; J. Brown, 'Enemies of Flattery: Velázquez's Portraits of Philip IV', *Journal of Interdisciplinary History*, XVII, 1 (Summer 1986) 137–54.

10. J. Jacobs (ed.), *The Familiar Letters of James Howell* (1890) p. 156; T. Ruiz, 'Une royauté sans sacre, la monarchie castillane du bas moyen age', *Annales ESC*, 39, 3 (May–June 1984) 429–53.

11. It is clear, for example, that a major purpose of the writings of the Spanish Jesuits on the subject of taxation was to provide pastoral guidance for confessors in their spiritual counsel to actual, or potential, defaulters, v. J. Laures, *The Political Economy of Juan de Mariana* (New York, 1928), p. 215.

12. D. Juan de Hinestrosa in *ayuntamiento* of Cuenca, 30 Jan. 1655. For one statement that encapsulates them all, D. Francisco López de Arriaga, Burgos, 19 Nov. 1625, 'que su real pecho se compone de los mas santos efetos que asta oy se an visto en Principe Cristiano, pues en lugar de acudir a sus entretenimientos y a mirar por su salud . . . ofrece vertir [su sangre] por la conservacion, defensa y alivio de sus naturales subditos y vasallos', and so 'le ofrece un reconocido y fiel afecto de servirle con su persona, con su sangre y con la de sus hijos', A. M. Burgos, Sección Histórica no. 800.

13. AGS Patronato Real 85', f.87, 'no lo manda Su Majestad sino lo ruega, y que si Su Majestad lo mandase que lo harian'.

14. B. González Alonso, 'La fórmula "Obedézcase, pero no se cumpla" en el Derecho castellano de la Baja Edad Media', *Anuario de Historia del Derecho Español* (1980) 469–87.

15. 'Las leyes de los Principes siempre se entienden que se han de guardar al pie de la letra cuando y donde y como conviene a la honra y provecho del Príncipe y su República, y como las virtudes de la prudencia, justicia y epickeia, etc., lo ordenaren', F. Juan de Victoria, OP, 'Noticias de la Invencible', *CODOIN* vol. 81, p. 231, condemning Medina Sidonia and Diego Flores for their handling of the Armada and countering the defence that they were simply adhering to the king's instructions. 'Epickeia' is the principle that discretion must be applied in obeying superior orders. For the assumption in the Golden Age theatre that the exercise of such 'discreción' was an obligation on every man, A. Gómez-Moriana, *Derecho de resistencia y tiranicidio. Estudio de una temática en la 'comedias' de Lope de Vega* (Santiago de Compostela, 1968) pp. 108, 117.

16. Note the comments of Domenico Zane, the Venetian ambassador in Madrid between 1655 and 1659, 'come che i consiglieri sieno puramente legisti non pensano altro che il summum jus, senza l'uso delle convenienze, da che ne nascono poi quelli scandalosi disordini che danno chiaramente a conoscere che per governare il mondo sono assai migliori gli uomini savi che li saputi', N. Barozzi and G. Berchet (eds), *Relazioni . . . dagli ambasciatori veneti nel secolo decimosettimo*, serie 1, vol. 2 (Venice, 1860) p. 280. For the constitutional role of the councils, P. Fernández Albaladejo, 'Monarquía, Cortes y "cuestión constitucional" en Castilla durante la edad moderna', *Revista de las Cortes Generales*, vol. 1 (1984) pp. 11–34, and B. Cárceles, 'The Constitutional Conflict in Castile between the Council and the Count-Duke of Olivares', *Parliaments, Estates and Representation*, 7 (1987) 51–9.

17. Forcefully expressed in a *consulta* of the Council of Castile, 26 Mar. 1669, 'Y aviendose cumplido por parte del Reyno con lo que la ha tocado en observanzia de lo capitulado, pareze obligazion prezisa de Vuestra Magestad, siendo este Contracto reziproco, observar el pacto y condizion en que Su Magestad, que sea en gloria, quiso estrechar su potestad . . . Y la mayor grandeza de los Reyes es el confessar sujeta su potestad a el vinculo de estos Contractos, y no concurriendo causa publica ynduvitablemente que obligue a su alterazion, es preziso en las consideraciones de

Justizia que la ley, que en ellos se dio, se cumpla sin violazion alguna', British Library, Egerton 332, f.302v.

18. This is one of the main contentions of J. A. Maravall's *Estado moderno y mentalidad social, siglos XV a XVII*, 2 vols (Madrid, 1972).

19. F. Vermúdez de Pedraza, *El Secretario del Rey* (1620) (Madrid, 1973) p. 20: 'ni aun qualquier escritura de España tiene autoridad en estos Reynos, sino va refrendada de sus secretarios, aunque sean de personas Reales, ni los despachos de gracia, ni de justicia aunque intervenga firma de Vuestra Majestad no se cumplen, sino van refrendados del Secretario.'

20. AGS GA 865, Junta de Galeras 30 Nov. 1621.

21. See, for example, the part played by the Council of Castile and the Chancillería of Granda in bringing an end to the sale of common wastes in Andalusia in the 1640s, A. Domínguez Ortiz, 'La comisión de D. Luis Gudiel para la venta de baldíos de Andalucía, *Estudios de historia económica y social de España* (Granada, 1987) pp. 89–103.

22. *Nueva Recopilacílon*, ley 1, título vii, libro VI.

23. C. Jago, 'Habsburg Absolutism and the Cortes of Castile', *American Historical Review*, 86 (1981) 307–26; I. A. A. Thompson, 'Crown and Cortes in Castile, 1590–1665', *Parliaments, Estates and Representation*, 2, no. 1 (June 1982) 29–45, and 'The End of the Cortes of Castile', ibid., 4, no. 2 (Dec. 1984) 125–33.

24. Sir Ralph Winwood, *Memorials of Affairs of State*, ed. E. Sawyer (1725) vol. 2, p. 69.

25. Among other instances, over the *excusado* in 1628, the salt tax in 1631, the *medio dozavo* in 1634, the *papel sellado* in 1636, the *subsidio* in 1656, the Millones in 1669 and 1686.

26. A. Domínguez Ortiz, *Las clases privilegiadas en la España del Antiguo Régimen* (Madrid, 1973) p. 371. Consider the judgement of a Junta of 1621 on the nature of the king's rights over appointments to the Council of the Inquisition: 'que a Vuestra Majestad no le pertenesce otro ningun derecho en esta materia sino solo la nominacion de la persona, y que la aprobazion de su calidad ... perteneze a la general Inquisicion como a tribunal competente que en materia mero eclesiastico tiene pribativamente delegada la jurisdicion de Su Santidad, la qual Vuestra Majestad no querra suplir, reformar i menos usurpar. Por que seria pecado mortal y de perniziosa consequenzia atribuirse a V.Md. jurisdicion eclesiastica sin authoridad appostolica ...', British Library, Egerton MS 345 f.87.

27. Domínguez Ortiz, *Clases privilegiadas*, p. 380, and *La sociedad española en el siglo XVII*, vol. 2, *El estamento eclesiástica* (Madrid, 1970) pp. 249–51, 3 Aug. 1693. For the judicial, financial and patronal rights of the Nuntio, N. García Martín, 'Secciones, emolumentos y personal de la Nunciatura española en tiempos de Cesar Monti (1630–1634)', *Anthologica Annua*, 4 (Rome 1956) 283–339.

28. Domínguez Ortiz, *Clases privilegiadas*, p. 419.

29. Maravall, *Philosophie politique espagnole*, pp. 180, 120, 151, 169, 118, 72, 78.

30. 'El mandato del principe es ley, como está promulgada en la nueva recopilacion', *corregidor* of Cuenca, in *ayuntamiento* of 30 Jan. 1655; 'Su Majestad es dueño absoluto para mandarlo y que no se admita excusa ni dilacion', *corregidor* of Cuenca, in *ayuntamiento* of 8 July 1660; 'sera preciso obedecerle en servirle como dueño y señor absoluto y despótico que es de nuestras personas y aziendas', D. Francisco Velázquez in *ayuntamiento* of Salamanca, 18 Mar. 1697.

31. AHN Consejos leg. 4428, 1642, no. 11.

32. For example, Eugenio Conejero de Pedraza in *ayuntamiento* of Cuenca, 17 June 1638, 'los Reyes de Castilla por su boluntad se an dexado suxetar en la materia de servicios a que ayan de ser por otorgamiento de los Procuradores de las

Ciudades ... mas ni por esto se a de entender que el Reino pueda por su libre voluntad prevalecer justificadamente contra lo de Su Magestad en caso que ordenare otra cosa ... si faltase el Reino a la obligacion connatural o civil de consentir en lo justo que Su Magestad manda, podra muy vien su Real Magestad acer sin ellos y restituirse a la primera ynmunidad de su señorio', AM Cuenca, leg. 271, exp. 1, ff. 101v–103v.

33. Jacobo Sobieski, in J. García Mercadal (ed.), *Viajes de extranjeros por España y Portugal*, vol. 2 (Madrid, 1959) p. 332. There were complaints that under Philip IV too 'los Consejos no solo se llaman los señores, sino que en la verdad lo son, avasallando la voluntad de su príncipe a las resoluciones de su alvedrío', A. Núñez de Castro, *Libro histórico-político. Solo Madrid es Corte* (Madrid, 1675) p. 121; and under Charles II, the Marquis de Villars was writing of 'the domination of the Councils over the king', especially of the Council of State, without which neither king nor chief minister dare do anything (1681), García Mercadal, *Viajes*, vol. 2, p. 881.

34. Duque de Montalto to D. Pedro Ronquillo, Madrid, 1 Aug. 1685, 'no es otra cosa este Gobierno que un Seminario de muchachos sin Rector a quien respetan, con que cada uno hace lo que se le antoja', *CODOIN*, vol. 79, p. 359.

35. A. Pellegrini, *Relazioni inedite di ambasciatori lucchesi alla corte di Madrid (sec. XVI–XVII)* (Lucca, 1903) p. 81, 3 Aug. 1649. Antoine Brunel (1655), 'Never has there been a prince who has allowed himself to be ruled more absolutely by his ministers than this one', García Mercadal, *Viajes*, vol. 2, p. 412.

36. J. H. Elliott and F. de la Peña, *Memoriales y Cartas del Conde Duque de Olivares*, vol. 2 (Madrid, 1978) p. 231 (Guidi); Pellegrini, *Relazioni lucchesi*, p. 90, 12 July 1674; García Mercadal, *Viajes*, vol. 2, p. 918 (Villars); *CODOIN*, vol. 67, p. 71 (Godolphin); Lord Mahon, *Spain under Charles the Second* (1844) p. 18 (Stanhope).

37. H. Kamen, *Spain in the later Seventeenth Century* (1980) p. 16.

38. F. Tomás y Valiente, *El derecho penal de la Monarquía Absoluta (siglos XVI–XVII–XVIII)* (Madrid, 1969) p. 44; M. R. Weisser, *The Peasants of the Montes* (Chicago, 1976) p. 106.

39. British Library, Egerton MS 332, ff.286–92v, Consejo de Castilla, Nov. 1654; British Library, Egerton MS 347, ff.188–94v, Consejo de Estado, 17 July 1663; *CODOIN*, vol. 79, p. 338 – Montalto was a close relative of the chief ministers, Oropesa and Los Vélez, and later himself a Councillor of State.

40. M. Danvila, 'Nuevos datos para escribir la historia de las Cortes de Castilla en el reinado de Felipe III', *Boletín de la Real Academia de Historia* 8 (1886) 273; British Library, Egerton MS 332, f.288v.

41. R. L. Kagan, *Lawsuits and Litigants in Castile 1500–1700* (Chapel Hill, NC, 1981) pp. 216, 219.

42. Pedro Diaz Márquez, 'Memorial', Real Academia de la Historia, Col. Jesuitas, vol. 5, ff.123–4; British Library, Add MSS 9936, ff.214–15, c. 15 Apr. 1649.

43. A. Domínguez Ortiz, *Política y hacienda de Felipe IV* (Madrid, 1960) p. 223, n. 11; Ortiz, 'Ventas y exenciones de lugares durante el reinado de Felipe IV', *Anuario de Historia del Derecho Español* (1964) 163–207.

44. AHN Consejos leg, 4427, 1639, n. 35; leg. 7162, Consejo de Castilla 3 Feb. 1652.

45. Elliott and de la Peña, *Memoriales y Cartas*, vol. 2, p. 171.

46. F. Tomás y Valiente, *Los validos en la Monarquía Española del siglo XVII* (Madrid, 1963) p. 208; British Library, Egerton MS 347, f.186; Mahon, *Spain under Charles the Second*, p. 68.

47. C. Weiss, *L'Espagne depuis le règne de Philippe II jusqu'à l'avènement des Bourbons* (Paris, 1844) vol. 2, p. 55.

48. Covarrubias y Leyva, *Textos jurídico-políticos*, p. 169.

49. F. Tomás y Valiente, 'El gobierno de la Monarquía y la administración de los reinos en la España del siglo XVII', ch. 1 of R. Menéndez Pidal, *Historia de España, tomo xxv, La España de Felipe IV. El gobierno de la Monarquía, la crisis de 1640, y el fracaso de la hegemoniía europea* (Madrid, 1982) p. 14.

50. J. Vicens Vives, 'The Administrative Structure of the State in the Sixteenth and Seventeenth Centuries', in H. J. Cohn (ed.), *Government in Reformation Europe 1520–1560* (1971) p. 69; T. Wittman, 'Sobre el presunto carácter "turco" del absolutismo español del Siglo de Oro', *Estudios económicos de Hispano-América colonial* (Budapest, 1979) pp. 11–18; A. Domínguez Ortiz, 'La crise intérieure de la Monarchie des Habsburgs espagnols sous Charles II', in J. A. H. Bots (ed.), *The Peace of Nijmegen 1676–1678/79. La Paix de nimègue* (Amsterdam 1980) pp. 157–67; I. A. A. Thompson, *War and Government in Habsburg Spain, 1560–1620* (1976).

51. B. Yun Casalilla, 'La aristocracia castellana en el seiscientos. ¿Crisis, refeudalización u ofensiva política?', *Revista Internacional de Sociología*, 2a época, 45 (1987) 77–104.

52. P. Anderson, *Lineages of the Absolutist State* (1974) p. 18; Tomás y Valiente, 'El gobierno de la Monarquía', p. 72, 75; Maravall, *Estado moderno*, vol. 1, pp. 300–10.

53. B. Clavero, 'Institución política y derecho: Acerca del concepto historiográfico de "Estado Moderno"', *Revista de Estudios Políticos*, 19 (1981) 43–57, for the view that the power of the crown was but one power among many. For the general argument, H. Kamen, *Spain 1469–1714; a Society of Conflict* (1983).

54. For a general discussion of these various positions, see S. de Dios 'Sobre la génesis y caracteres del estado absolutista en Castilla', *Studia Histórica-Historia Moderna*, 3 (1985) 11–46, and 'El Estado Moderno ¿un cadáver historiográfico?', in A. Rucquoi, *Realidad e Imágenes del Poder. España a fines de la Edad Meida* (Valladolid, 1988) pp. 389–408.

55. C. Rahn Phillips, *Six Galleons for the King of Spain* (Baltimore, 1986).

56. B. González Alonso, 'Notes sobre las relaciones del estado en la administración señorial en la Castilla moderna', *Anuario de Historia del Derecho Español* (1983) 365–94.

57. I. Atienza Hernández, "Refeudalización" en Castilla durante el Siglo XVII: ¿Un tópico?', *Anuario de Historia del Derecho Español* (1986), 889–919; J. M. de Bernardo Ares, 'Los juicios de residencia como fuente para la Historia Urbana', *Andalucía Moderna, Actas II Coloquios Historia de Andalucía*, vol. 2 (Córdoba, 1983) pp. 1–24.

58. Vicens Vives, 'Administrative Structure of the State', p. 64.

4. SWEDEN *A. F. Upton*

1. S. Hildebrand (ed.), *Karl XIs almanackanteckningar: från originalen ånyo angivne* (Stockholm, 1918) p. 110.

2. M. Roberts, *Sweden as a Great Power 1611–1697: Government: Society: Foreign Policy* (1968) p. 15.

3. Å. Helmback and E. Wessen (eds), *Magnus Erikssons landslag* (Lund, 1962) p. xiii.

4. C. E. Normann, *Prästerskapet och det Karolinska enväldet* (Lund, 1948) p. 13.

5. Roberts, *Sweden as a Great Power*, p. 9.

6. E. Hildebrand (ed.), *Sveriges regeringsformer 1634–1809* (Stockholm, 1891) pp. 1f.

7. Roberts, *Sweden as a Great Power*, p. 102.

8. Hildebrand, *Sveriges regeringsformer*, pp. 214 f11.
9. G. Barudio, *Absolutismus – Zerstörung der 'libertären Verfassung': Studien zur 'Karolinscher Eingewalt' in Schweden zwischen 1680 und 1693* (Frankfort, 1967) p. 42.
10. Ibid., p. 29.
11. F. F. Carlson, *Sveriges Historia under konungarna af Pfalziska huset: Carl XI*, vol. I (Stockholm, 1885) p. 421.
12. Ibid., vol. II, p. 17.
13. Ibid., vol. I, p. 469.
14. Riksarkivet, Stockholm, *Wattrang rådsprotokoll 1680–1681*, 4 Nov. 1680.
15. Riksarkivet, Stockholm, *Rådsprotokol 72*, 4 Dec. 1680.
16. A. A. Stiernman (ed.), *Alla riksdagens och mötens beslut*, vol. II, 1632–1680 (Stockholm, 1729) p. 1873.
17. Roberts, *Sweden as a Great Power*, pp. 81–3.
18. Riksarkivet, Stockholm, *Sekreta utskotts protokoll 1686*, 27 Sept. 1686.
19. Roberts, *Sweden as a Great Power*, p. 89.
20. C. G. Styffe, *Samling af Instruktionen rörande den civila förvaltningen i Sverige och Finland* (Stockholm, 1856) p. 124.
21. Normann, *Prästerskapet* . . ., p. 169.
22. *Sveriges riddarskaps och adels riksdags protokoll*, vol. XV (Stockholm, 1855–), p. 242.
23. S. Loenbom, *Handlingar til konung Carl XI:tes historia*, vol. XIV (Stockholm, 1763) p. 180.
24. Roberts, *Sweden as a Great Power*, p. 91.
25. A. Fryxell, *Handlingar rörande Sveriges historia ur utrikes arkiver samlade*, vol. II (Stockholm, 1836) p. 193.

5. BRANDENBURG-PRUSSIA *H. W. Koch*

1. R. Vierhaus, *Propyläen Geschichte Deutschlands*, vol. 5, *Staaten und Stände. Vom Westfälischen Frieden zum Hubertusburger Frieden 1648–1763* (Berlin, 1984) p. 9.
2. See H. W. Koch, *A History of Prussia* (1978) ch. 1 passim.
3. G. Oestreich, 'Strukturprobleme des europäischen Absolutismus', *Antrittsvorlesung*, p. 329, copy in author's possession.
4. So F. L. Carsten in his *Origins Of Prussia* (1954) and even more pronounced in his essay 'Prussian Despotism at its Height' now in Carsten, *Essays in German History* (1985) pp. 145ff. Much the same tenor is adopted by Hans Rosenberg in his *Bureaucracy, Aristocracy and Autocracy. The Prussian Experience 1660–1815* (Cambridge, Mass., 1958) passim.
5. *The New Cambridge Modern History*, vol. 5, *The Ascendancy of France*, ed. F. L. Carsten (Cambridge, 1961).
6. For the best recent analysis of early socialist thought, showing up entirely new and hitherto neglected aspects and perspectives see E. Nolte, *Marxismus und Industrielle Revolution* (Stuttgart, 1983) chs 1–5.
7. W. Sombart, *Der moderne Kapitalismus*, 3 vols, published in six parts (reprinted Munich, 1987) and *Sombarts 'Moderner Kapitalismus'. Materialien zur Kritik und Rezeption*, ed. and introduced B. v. Brocke (Munich, 1987) ch. 1.
8. M. Bloch, *Feudal Society* (1961); H. Pirenne, *Histoire de l'Europe. Des invasions au XVIe siècle* (Brussels, 1936); J. Huizinga, *The Waning of the Middle Ages* (1965); F. L. Ganshof, *Qu'est-ce que la féodalité?* (Paris, 1982).
9. Barrington Moore Jr, *Social Origins of Dictatorship and Democracy. Lord and Peasant in the Making of the Modern World* (1967) p. 419.

10. G. Barudio, *Der Teutsche Krieg 1618–1648* (Frankfurt/Main, 1985) p. 35.
11. Th. Schieder, 'Wandlungen des Staats in der Neuzeit', in *Historische Zeitschrift*, 216 (1973) p. 269.
12. For a recent discussion of the 'Germanic' concept of *Treue* see Walter Kienast, 'Germanische Treue und "Königsheil"' in *Historische Zeitschrift*, 227, (1978) p. 265 and esp. 320f.
13. Fr. Gruaus, 'Über die sogenannte germanische Treue', in *Historia*, I (Prague, 1959) p. 307.
14. *Sachsenspiegel*, III, paragraph 42, No. 6, cited by G. Franz, *Deutsches Bauerntum*, vol. 1 (Darmstadt, 1940) p. 164.
15. G. Franz, *Der deutsche Bauernkreig*, vol. 1 (Darmstadt, 1977) p. 2.
16. K. Kaczerowsky (ed.), *Flugschriften des Bauernkrieges* (Hamburg, 1970) Weigandts Reichsreformentwurf vom 18 Mai 1525, pp. 65 ff.
17. Jacob Burckhardt, *The Civilisation of the Renaissance in Italy* (1960) pp. 2 ff.
18. Ibid.
19. See note 2 above; for the most recent study of the order see H. Boockmann, *Der Deutsche Orden. Zwölf Kapital aus seiner Geschichte* (Munich, 1981) pp. 17 ff., 38 ff., 66 ff. and 181 ff.; M. Burleigh's *Prussian Society and the German Order* (Cambridge, 1984) deals with the later phase of the order and although not without usefulness is more of a distillate of previous secondary works.
20. G. P. Gooch, *Studies in German History* (1948) p. 1.
21. Zara Steiner in *International Relations*, VIII, 3 (May 1985) 300, in a review of a volume edited by H. W. Koch.
22. F. Schnabel, *Deutsche Geschichte im neunzehnten jahrhundert*, vol. 1, *Die Grundlagen* (Munich, 1987) pp. 35 ff., 80 ff.
23. Ibid., p. 81.
24. O. Büsch and O. Neugebauer (eds), *Moderne Preussische Geschichte*, 3 vols (Berlin, 1981); Kurt Hinze, 'Die Bevölkerung Preussens im 17. und 18. Jahrhundert nach Quantität und Qualität', vol. 1, pp. 281 ff.; P. Baumgart, 'Zur Geschichte der kurmärkischen Stände im 17. und 18. Jahrhundert', vol. 2, pp. 509 ff.; G. Schmoller, 'Die ländliche Kolonisation des 17. und 18. Jahrhunderts', pp. 911 ff.
25. H. Aubin and W. Zorn (eds), *Handbuch der deutschen Wirtschafts- und Sozialgeschichte*, 2 vols (Stuttgart, 1971) vol. 1, pp. 414 ff., 541 ff.
26. See note 4 above; F. L. Carsten, 'The Origins of the Junkers', pp. 17 ff.
27. As does Carsten.
28. Like 'absolutism' so the term 'Junker' belongs to the vast stock of vocabulary with which the liberals of the nineteenth century enriched our vocabulary for the purposes of political debate. The term is of middle High German origin, *juncherre*, i.e. young master, and has retained the meaning in Dutch, *jonker* to this day. During the Middle Ages it defined a young man of noble blood who was, so to speak, learning the knight's trade before actually being elevated to this status. In its more modern version it referred to the son of a nobleman, or noble estate owner, as well as to a young nobleman entering the army, but being as yet not in possession of a commission, i.e. *Fahnenjunker*. See *Duden. Das Herkunftswörterbuch*, vol. 7 (Mannheim, 1963) p. 298.
29. So H.-U. Wehler in the works written or edited by him.
30. E. Krippendorff, *Staat und Krieg. Die historische Logik politischer Unvernunft* (Frankfurt/Main, 1985) p. 273.
31. This is the thesis put forward by Barudio in *Der Teutsche Krieg*, pp. 13 ff. as well as in his handbook *Das Zeitalter des Absolutismus und der Aufklärung 1648–1779* (Frankfurt/Main, 1985) passim.
32. F. Dickmann, 'Rechtsgedanke und Machtpolitik Richelieus', *Historische Zeitschrift*, 196 (1963); Dickmann, *Der Westfälische Frieden* (Münster, 1977).

33. O. Brunner, W. Conze and R. Koselleck (eds), *Geschichtliche Grundbegriffe. Historisches Lexikon zur politisch-sozialen Sprache in Deutschland*, vol. 1 (Stuttgart, 1979). (However, it does have a lengthy entry for *Anarchie*!)

34. K. Fuchs and H. Raab (eds), *dtv Wörterbuch zur Geschichte*, vol. 1 (Munich, 1987) p. 19.

35. Jean Bodin, *De la république* (n.p., 1576) p. 341.

36. E. Opgenoorth, *Friedrich Wilhelm. Der Grosse Kurfürst von Brandenburg*, 2 vols (Göttingen, 1971–8) vol. 1, pp. 23 ff., 29 ff., 33 ff.

37. P. Geyl, *The Revolt of the Netherlands 1555–1609* (1980) pp. 271 ff.

38. Ibid., p. 272.; G. Oestreich, *Strukturprobleme der frühen Neuzeit. Ausgewählte Aufsätze*, ed. B. Oestreich (Berlin, 1980); 'Fundamente preussischer Geistesgeschichte. Religion und Weltanschauung in Brandenburg im 17 Jahrhundert', pp. 275 ff., 'Das politische Anliegen von Justus Lipsius' De constantia . . . in publicis malis (1584)', pp. 298 ff., 'Justus Lipsius als Universalgelehrter zwischen Renaissance und Barock', pp. 318 ff., 'Die antike Literatur als Vorbild der praktischen Wissenschaften im 16. und 17 Jahrhundert', p. 358 ff.

39. *Moderne Preussische Geschichte*, vol. 3, G. Oestreich, 'Calvinismus, Neustoizismus und Preussentum', pp. 1268 ff.

40. J. Bohatec, *Calvins Lehre vom Staat und Kirche, mit besonderer Berücksichtigung des Organismusgedankens* (Breslau, 1937); Bohatec, *Budé und Calvin, Studien zur Gedankenwelt des französischen Frühhumanismus* (Graz, 1950).

41. Koch, *History of Prussia*, p. 80.

42. M. Weber, *The Protestant Ethic and the Spirit of Capitalism* (1974) chs II, III, IV, V; R. H. Tawney, *Religion and Rise of Capitalism* (1961) passim.

43. A. Mörath (ed.) *Beiträge zur Korrespondenz des Kurprinzen Friedrich Wilhem von Brandenburg mit dem Grafen Adam zu Schwarzenberg, 1634–1640* (1896) p. 5 ff., 10 ff; G. Oestreich, *Der Grosse Kurfürst* (Göttingen, 1971) pp. 15 ff.

44. See T. v. Moerner (ed.), *Kurbrandenburgs Staatsverträge 1601–1700* (Berlin, 1867) and J. Kretschmar, 'Die Allianzverhandlungen Gustav Adolfs mit Kurbrandenburg im Mai und Juni 1631', in *Forschungen zur Brandenburgischen-Preussischen Geschichte*, No. 17 (1904); *Urkunden und Aktenstücke zur Geschichte des Kurfürsten Friedrich Wilhelm von Brandenburg*, 23 vols (Berlin, 1864–1930) vol. 1, *Schwarzenberg an Kurfürsten, 2. Januar 1641*, pp. 391 ff.

45. A point overlooked by P.-M. Hahn, 'Landesstaat und Ständetum im Kurfürstentum Brandenburg während des 16. und 17. Jahrhunderts', in P. Baumgart and J. Schmädeke (eds), *Ständetum und Staatsbildung in Brandenburg-Preussen* (Berlin, 1983) pp. 41 ff.; M. Hass, *Die kurmärkischen Stände im letzten Drittel des des sechszehnten Jahrhunderts* (Munich-Leipzig, 1913) pp. 173 f.; J. Schultze, *Die Mark Brandenburg*, vol. 4, *Von der Reformation zum Westfälischen Frieden* (Berlin, 1964), pp. 202 ff., 294 ff., though the estates of Brandenburg between 1601 and 1640 deserve still closer attention by the historian. See H. Rössler (ed.), *Deutscher Adel 1555–1740. Büdinger Vorträge 1964* (Darmstadt, 1965); G. Heinrich, 'Der Adel in Brandenburg-Preussen', pp. 285 f.

46. Hass, *Die kurmärkischen Stände . . .*, pp. 173 ff.

47. Opgenoorth, *Friedrich Wilhelm*, vol. 1, pp. 57 ff.

48. O. Meinardus (ed.), *Protokolle und Relationen des Brandenburgischen Geheimen Rates aus der Zeit des Kurfürsten Friedrich Wilhelm von Brandenburg*, 7 vols; vol. 7, part 1 has been posthumously edited by E. Müller (Leipzig, 1889–1919) vol. III, No. 181.

49. H. Rachel, 'Der Grosse Kurfürst und die ostpreussischen Stände', in *Staats- und sozialwissenschaftliche Forschungen*, ed. by G. Schmoller and M. Sering, vol. 24 (Leipzig, 1909) pp. 7 ff., 215 ff.

50. O. Hintze, *Die Hohenzollern und ihr Werk* (Berlin, 1915) pp. 158 ff.

51. G. Franz, *Der Dreissigjährige Krieg und das deutsche Volk* (Stuttgart, 1961) pp. 8 ff.; G. Engelbert, 'Der Hessenkrieg am Niederrhein' in *Annalen des Historischen Vereins des Niederrheins* (1959–61) pp. 161 ff.

52. Franz, *Der Dreissigjährige Krieg...*, p. 8.

53. Dickmann, *Der Westfälische Friede*, p. 43.

54. Franz, *Der Dreissigjährige...*; E. Keyser, *Bevölkerungsgeschichte Deutschlands* (n.p. 1943) pp. 339 f.; F. Schroer, *Das Havelland im dreissigjährigen Krieg* (Cologne, 1967) passim.

55. Curt Jany, *Geschichte der Preussischen Armee vom 15. Jahrhundert bis 1914*, vol. 1 (Osnabrück, 1967) books I and II passim.

56. Meinardus (ed.), *Protokolle und Relationen...*, vol. 1, No. 51.

57. Ibid., No. 51.

58. Ibid., No. 211 on Schwarzenberg's death; S. v. Pufendorf, *De rebus gesti Friderici Wilhelmi Magni Electoris Brandenburgici commentariorum libri 19* (Berlin, 1695) abbreviated German translation *Friedrich Wilhelms ... Leben und Thaten* (Berlin/Frankfurt a.d. Oder, 1710) p. 5.

59. Jany, *Geschichte der Preussischen Armee*, p. 98.

60. Meinardus (ed.), *Protokolle und Relationen...*, vol. III, nos. 256, 284.

61. Moerner, *Staatsverträge*, No. 64.

62. Jany, *Geschichte der Preussischen Armee*, p. 102.

63. Ibid.; H. Delbrück, *Geschichte der Kriegskunst im Rahmen der politischen Geschichte*, vol. 4 (Berlin, 1962) pp. 273 ff.

64. Jany, *Geschichte der Preussischen Armee*, p. 103.

65. See note 3, Hintze quoted by Oestreich. See also F. Gilbert (ed.) *The Historical Essays of Otto Hintze* (Oxford, 1975) pp. 180 ff.

66. Delbrück, *Geschichte der Kriegskunst*, vol. 4, p. 304 ff.; Jany, *Geschichte der Preussischen Armee*, pp. 164 ff., 169 ff., 175 ff.; E. v. Frauenholz (ed.), *Entwicklungsgeschichte des deutschen Heerwesens*, vol. 4 (Munich, n.d.) pp. 23 ff., 30 ff.

67. F. Redlich, *The German Military Enterpriser and his Work Force. A Study in European Economic and Social History*, vol. 2 (Wiesbaden, 1965) pp. 237 ff.

68. Ibid., p. 45.

69. Ibid.

70. Oestreich, *Der grosse Kurfürst*, p. 14.

71. Aubin and Zorn (eds), *Handbuch*, vol. 1, pp. 445, 564.

72. So Michael Roberts and his lecture 'The Military Revolution'.

73. The best recent biography is that by Hellmut Diwald, *Wallenstein* (Munich, 1969) in which the military and political aspect receives prominent attention. Golo Mann's *Wallenstein* (Frankfurt/Main, 1971) has the advantage of being available in an English translation, but otherwise is more 'Mann' than 'Wallenstein'. Perhaps more important is the fact that Diwald is a Slavicist which Mann is not. Ricarda Huch's *Der grosse Krieg in Deutschland* has held its interpretation surprisingly well with the current state of research, though written by a non-professional historian, and literary-novelistic in its approach. Originally published in 1931 it has been republished in Berlin (1980).

74. Meinardus (ed.), *Protokolle und Relationen...*, vol. III, No. 228 and *Urkunden* (see note 44), vol. 1, pp. 373 ff.

75. See the Hahn reference in note 45 and U. Arnold, 'Ständeherrschaft und Ständekonflikte im Herzogtum Preussen', in Baumgart and Schmädeke (eds), *Ständetum und Staatsbildung*, pp. 80 ff.

76. Rosenberg, *Bureaucracy...*, passim; Opgenoorth, *Friedrich Wilhelm*, passim; S. Isaacsohn, *Geschichte des Preussischen Beamtentums*, vol. 1 (Berlin, 1874); Wolfgang Neugebauer, 'Zur neuren Deutung der preussischen Verwaltung im 17.

und 18. Jahrhundert in vergleichender Sicht', in *Moderne Preussische Geschichte*, vol. 2, pp. 541 ff.; Otto Hintze, *Beamtentum und Bürokratie* (Göttingen 1981) passim.

77. Koch, *History of Prussia*, p. 47.

78. G. Küntzel and M. Hass (eds), *Die politischen Testamente der Hohenzollern*, vol. 1, *Politisches Testament des Grossen Kurfürsten von 1667* (Berlin, 1919) pp. 41 ff.

79. *Urkunden*, vol. V, pp. 536 ff., 568 ff.

80. O. Behre, *Geschichte der Statistik in Brandenburg-Preussen bis zur Gründung des kgl. Statistischen Bureaus* (Berlin, 1905) pp. 65, 62, 53, 133, 68; H. v. Petderdorff, 'Beiträge zur Wirtschafts-, Steuer- und Heeresgeschichte der Mark im 30jährigem Kriege', in *Forschungen zur brandenburgischen und preussischen Geschichte*, vol. 2 (1889) p. 3.

81. Behre, *Geschichte der Statistik*, pp. 53, 68.

82. E. Fedicin, *Historisch-diplomatische Beiträge zur Geschichte der Stadt Berlin*, vol. 5 (Berlin, 1842) p. 516; J. P. Süssmilch, *Der Königlichen Residentz Berlin schneller Wachsthum und Erbauung* (Berlin, 1752) pp. 24, 26; F. Stiller, 'Das Berliner Armenwesen vor dem Jahre 1820', in *Forschungen zur Brandenburgischen Geschichte*, vol. 20 (1908) p. 186; W. Mila, *Berlin oder die Geschichte des Ursprungs, der allmählichen Entwicklung und des jetzigen Zustandes dieser Hauptstadt* (Berlin, 1829) p. 155; Ch. F. Nicolai, *Beschreibung der königlichen Residenzstädte Berlin und Potsdam und aller daselbst befindlicher Merkwürdigkeiten. Nebst Anhang, enthaltend das Leben aller Künstler, die seit Churfürst Friedrich Wilhelms des Grossen Zeiten in Berlin gelebt haben, oder deren Kunstwerke daselbst befindlich sind*, vol. 1 (Berlin, 1786) p. XLII and passim.

83. Extracted from Süssmilch, *Der Königlichen Residentz*.

84. For a general overview as well as analysis see relevant parts of F. Braudel's *The Structures of Everyday Life* (1981); Braudel, *The Wheels of Commerce* (1982); and Braudel, *The Perspective of the World* (1984). The work as a whole is also a signpost to what extent its author has detached himself from the maxims of the 'Annales'-school which he himself in his younger years had helped to fashion decisively.

85. G. Landau, 'Die materiellen Zustände der unteren Classen in Deutschland sonst und jetzt', in E. M. Arndt, *Germania*, vol. 2 (Leipzig, 1851) p. 344.

86. Ibid., p. 351; Ch. O. Myllius (ed.), *Corpus Constitutionum Marchicarum, Oder Königl. Preuss. und Churfürst. Brandenburgischer, sonderlich in der Chur- und Marck Brandenburg, auch incorporirten Landen publicirte und ergangene Ordnungen Edicta, Mandaata, Rescripta etc.*' 6 parts, 4 continuation and 1 supplementary volume (Berlin-Halle, 1737–51), vol. 5, part 5, ch. 1, nos. 20, 121. See also K. Kumpmann, 'Arbeitslosigkeit und Arbeitslosenversicherung', in L. Elster, A. Weber and F. Wieder (eds), *Handwörterbuch der Staatswissenschaften*, vol. 1 (Jena, 1925) p. 792.

87. E. Hoffmann-Krayer (ed.), *Handwörterbuch des deutschen Aberglaubens*, vol. 1 (Berlin, 1927) p. 66.

88. J. Delumeau, *La Peur en Occident (XIVe–XVIIIe siècles). Une cité assiégée* (Paris, 1978). A valuable work in spite of the frequently undifferentiated examples cited to support his argument and the leaps he makes from one epoch to another which culminate in a somewhat rough picture of general European development. Quite apart from that, many of the sources cited actually conflict with his own conclusions.

89. *Urkunden*, vol. 15, p. 552.

90. Ibid. p. 556.

91. Ibid. p. 487 ff.

92. Ibid.

93. Hintze, ... *Hohenzollern*, pp. 213 ff.

94. J. G. Droysen, *Geschichte der Preussischen Politik*, vol. 3, part 2 (Berlin, 1865), p. 5.

95. Oestreich, 'Struckturprobleme des europäischen Absolutismus', p. 335.

96. Ibid., p. 336; F. Hartung and R. Mousnier, 'Quelques problèmes concernant la monarchie absolue', in *Relazioni del X congr. internaz. di scienze storiche*, vol. 4 (1955); see also Vierhaus, *Propyläen Geschichte Deutschlands*.

97. K. Rieker, *Die rechtliche Stellung der evangelischen Kirche Deutschlands* (Leipzig, 1893) pp. 255 ff.; O. Hintze, 'Die Epochen des evangelischen Kirchenregiments in Preussen', in *Moderne Preussische Geschichte*, vol 3, pp. 1217 ff.

98. Carsten, *Essays*..., p. 133; D. J. Cohen, 'Die Landjudenschaften der brandenburgisch-preussischen Staaten im 17. und 18. Jahrhundert – Ihre Beziehungen untereiander aufgrund neuerschlossener jüdischer Quellen', in *Ständetum und Staatsbildung*..., pp. 208 ff.; B. Schedlitz. *Leffmann Behrens. Unsuchungen zum Hofjudentum im Zeitalter des Absolutismus* (Hildesheim, 1984). Although concentrating on Hanover, it does contain valuable insights with regard to Brandenburg-Prussia.

99. See R. v. Thadden and M. Magdelaine, *Die Hugenotten* (Munich, 1986) passim

100. O. Büsch, *Militärsystem und Sozialleben im alten Preussen* (Berlin, 1962) passim.

101. See W. Neugebauer, *Absolutistischer Staat und Schulwirklichkeit in Brandenburg-Preussen* (Berlin, 1985) passim.

102. J. Wallmann, *Philipp Jakob Spener und die Anfänge des Pietismus* (Tübingen, 1986); K. Deppermann, *Der Hallesche pietismus und der Preussische Staat unter Friedrich III* (Göttingen, 1961); C. Hinrichs, *Preussen als historisches Problem*, (Berlin, 1964) pp. 171 ff.; Hinrichs, *Preussentum und Pietismus. Der Pietismus in Brandenburg-Preussen als religiös-soziale Reformbewegung* (Göttingen, 1971).

103. *Zentrales Staatsarchiv*, Merseburg (*ZStA*), Rep. 19, No. 59 b fasc. 1; H. Rachel, 'Handel und Handelsrecht von Königsberg in Preussen im 16.–18. Jahrhundert', in *Forschungen zur Brandenburgischen und Preussischen Geschichte*, vol. 22 (1909).

104. *ZStA*, Merseburg, Rep. 19, No. 26 d, fasc. 8; Meinardus, *Protokolle*..., vol. 6, Nos 263, 378, 408, 544, 583, 602, 653, 779; F. Blaich, *Die Wirtschafts politik des Reichstags im Heiligen Römischen Reich* (Stuttgart, 1970) pp. 193 ff.; E. Heyck, 'Brandenburgisch-deutsche Kolonisationspläne. Aus den Papieren des Markgrafen von Hermann von Baden-Baden', in *Zeitschrift für die Geschichte des Oberrheins*, vol. 41 (1887).

105. See Rachel, 'Handel und Handelsrecht', pp. 341 ff.; also Heyck 'Brandenburgisch-deutsche Kolonisations plane'; C. Voigt, 'Admiral Gijsels van Lier', in *Brandenburgische Jahrbücher*, vol. II (1938); H. Saring, 'Schiffahrtspolitik des Grossen Kurfürsten', ibid.

106. See *Urkunden*, vol. 12, pp. 623 ff.; H. Szymanski, *Brandenburg-Preussen zur See 1605–1815* (Leipzig, 1939) pp. 22 f.

107. Ibid., Szysmanski, passim; H. Peter, *Die Anfänge der Brandeburgischen Marine* (Berlin, 1877) passim; P. Schück, *Brandenburg-Preussens Kolonialpolitik unter dem Grossen Kurfürsten und seinen Nachfolgern*, 2 vols (Berlin, 1889).

108. Szysmanski, *Brandenburg-Preussen zur See*, pp. 32 ff; Schück, *Brandenburg-Preussens Kolonial politik*, pp. 113 ff.

109. Schück, pp. 142 ff., 157 ff., 341 ff.; K. Liesegang, 'Die Goldgewinnung an der Guineaküste in alter Zeit und die ersten deutschen Bergwerke in der brandenburgisch-preussischen Kolonie Grossfriedrichsburg', in *Koloniale Rund-*

schau, 34 (1943); *Urkunden*, vol. 3, pp. 600, 629 ff., 793 ff.; Moerner, *Staatsverträge*, No. 259; P. Boissonnade, *Histoire des premier essais des relations économiques directes entre la France et l'état prusse pendant le règne de Louis XIV, 1643–1715* (Paris, 1912) pp. 290 ff.; *ZStA* Merseburg Rep. 85 Nos 6 to 12.

110. *Urkunden*, vol. 5, p. 952.

111. Rachel, 'Handel und Handelsrecht', p. 463; K. Spannagel, *Minden und Ravensberg unter brandenburgisch-preussischer Herrschaft 1648–1719* (Hanover, 1894), pp. 22 ff.

112. *ZStA*, Merseburg, Rep. 21, No. 24 a fasc. 7, Elector to Magistrate Berlin, 3 Feb. 1850; ibid., Rep. 14, F Nos 8 and 9; A. Geyer, 'Zur Baugeschichte des königlichen Schlosses in Berlin', in *Hohenzollern-Jahrbuch*, 1 (1897); *ZStA*, Merseburg, Rep. 21 Nos 13[c]d.; Rep. 92, No. 5; Rep. 35, N. I, 7; Rep. 9, E 15 fasc. 3; W. Boeck, *Oranienburg* (Berlin, 1938) pp. 16 ff, 18 ff.

113. Opgenoorth, *Friedrich Wilhelm*, vol. 2; p. 70.

114. E. Kehr, 'Zur Genesis der preussischen Bürokratie und des Rechtsstaats', in H.-U. Wehler (ed.), *Eckart Kehr. Der Primat der Innenpolitik* (Berlin, 1965) p. 40.

115. See note 102 above.

116. P. Baumgart, 'Die preussische Königskrönung von 1701, das Reich und die europäische Politik', in O. Hauser (ed.), *Preussen, Europa und das Reich* (Cologne, 1987), pp. 65 ff.

6. THE AUSTRIAN LANDS: HABSBURG ABSOLUTISM UNDER LEOPOLD I *Jean Bérenger*

1. Robert J. W. Evans, *The Making of the Habsburg Monarchy* (Oxford, 1979) pp. 157–8.

2. Gerhard Oestreich, *Geist und Gestalt des frühmodernen Staates* (Berlin, 1969), pp. 80–100.

3. Jean Berenger, *Finances et absolutisme autrichien dans la seconde moitié du XVIIème siècle* (Paris, 1975).

4. Emperor Leopold to the Nuncio, 29 May 1666, Nuntiaturberichte aus Deutschland, ed. Arthur Levinson, *Archiv für oesterreichische Geschichte*, 103, p. 800.

5. Emperor to the Nuncio, 4 July 1666, ibid., p. 803.

6. Quoted by Ernest Denis, *La Bohême après la Montagne Blanche* (Paris, 1903) p. 21.

7. J. W. Bromlej, 'Zur Frage über die Einstellung der Reformation in den Kroatischen Gebieten', *Studia Historica* (Budapest, 1963) 253–69.

8. Justus Lipsius, *Monita et exempla politica* (Leuven, 1605).

9. *Est igitur vinculum et firmamentum reipublicae Religio*, quoted by Anna Coreth, *Pietas Austriaca* (Vienna, 1956) p. 12.

10. Kurt Piringer, *Ferdinand III. Katholische Restauration* (Vienna, 1951) p. 137.

11. David Kaufmann, *Die letzte Vertreibung der Juden aus Wien* (Vienna, 1889).

12. *Landtagsproposition*, November 1651, published in *Theatrum Europaeum* (Frankfurt/Main) VII, p. 30.

13. Kamil Krofta, *Dějiny Selkého stavu v Čechach* (Prague, 1919).

14. Statni Ustredni Archiv, Prague, Artikulove Sněmovni, Karton 1677–94, Session of 1677, 'Von denen ewa noch uncatholischen Unterthanen'.

15. SUA Prague, ibid. '... in denen von Gott Ihro anvertrauten Erbkönigreich und Landen, die Ehre des Allerhöchsten befördert und die Reinigkeit des alleinseeligmachenden Glaubens, so ein Fundamentalgesetz dieses dero Erbkönigreichs Böheimb ist, erhalten und stabiliret werde'.

16. Piringer, *Katholische Restauration*, p. 48.
17. 'Specification welchen Herrn Inwohnern wegen bestellung der öden und wüsten Pfarren zugeschrieben worden und welche darauff geantwortet', Prague, 11 March 1669, SUA, Prague, Staré Manipulacé, L 34.
18. Ibid., Prague.
19. SUA Prague, Artikulove Snemovni, Karton 1658–76; session of 1664.
20. Ibid., first article: 'Von denen Collaturen und Pfarren'.
21. Ibid., Karton 1694–1708, session of 1697.
22. 'Gutachtlicher Bericht...', Prague, 11 March 1669, SUA, Prague, Staré Manipulacé L 34, Karton 1667–9.
23. Ibid., Artikulove Snemovni, Karton 1677–94, session of 1677, 'Von denen Collaturen und Pfarren'.
24. Ibid., session of 1681.
25. Ibid., session of 1682: 'Von Einrichtung der Collaturen und Pfarren'.
26. Joseph Wisnicki, 'Die Geschichte der Abfassung der *Tractatus de juribus in corporalibus*', *Jahrbuch für Landeskunde Niederösterreichs* (Vienna, 1927).
27. Elisabeth Ducreux, 'Lire à en mourir: livres et lecteurs en Bohême au XVIIIème siècle', in *Les usages de l'imprimé*, Roger Chartier (ed.) (Paris, 1987) pp. 253–303.
28. Report from Grémonville to Louis XIV, Vienna, 7 April 1667, Archives des Affaires Etrangères, Paris, Correspondance politique Autriche, 26, fo. 197.
29. Report from Sagredo to the Senate of Venice, Archivio di Stato, Venice Senato, Segreta, Dispacci di Germania, 121, 9 September 1662.
30. Jan Oberuc, *Les Persécutions des Luthériens en Slovaquie* (Strasbourg, 1927) pp. 66–8.
31. Bela Obal, *Die Religionspolitik in Ungarn nach dem Westfälischen Frieden* (Halle, 1910).
32. J. Bérenger, 'Francia-Magyar kapcsolatok Wesselényi összeésküvésé idején', *Történelmi Szemle*, 10 (Budapest, 1967) 275–91.
33. Gyula von Pauler, *Wesselényi Ferenc Nador és tarsainak összeésküvése* (Budapest, 1873).
34. J. Bérenger, 'An attempted rapprochement between Louis XIV and the Emperor', in *Louis XIV and Europe*, Ragnhild Hatton (ed.) (1976) pp. 133–52.
35. Gottlieb Eucharius Rinck, *Leopolds des Grossen Leben und Thaten* (Leipzig, 1708) II, p. 204.
36. Diploma Regis, published in *Articuli Universorum Statuum et Ordinum Inclyti Regni Hungariae* (1608–59) (Pottersdorf, 1668) pp. 639–40.
37. George Barsony, *Veritas toti Mundo declarata* (Sopron, 1681).
38. Istvan Werböczi, *Opus tripartitum Juris consuetudinarii Inclyti Regni Hungariae* (1st edn, Vienna, 1517).
39. 'Hungaros perdidisse omnia privilegia etiam jure belli et hodie esse subditos hereditarios quanquam id concedere nollent', quoted by Esaias Pufendorf, *Tagebuch*, 18 June 1673, Vienna, *Haus, Hof und Staatsarchiv* Manuscript W 324, fo. 429.
40. Nuncio's report, Vienna, 31 January 1672, *Nuntiaturberichte*..., A. Levinson (ed.), *Archiv für österreichische Geschichte*, 106, p. 607.
41. Oberuc, *Persécutions des Luthériens*, pp. 104–36.
42. Franz von Krones, 'Zur Geschichte Ungarns (1671–83) mit besonderer Rücksicht auf der Tätigkeit des Jesuitenordens', *Archiv für österreichische Geschichte*, 80.
43. Raimondo Montecuccoli, 'L'Ungheria nell'anno 1677', in *Ausgewählte Schriften* ed. Aloïs Veltze (Vienna, 1897) III, pp. 454–8.
44. Report from Grémonville to Louis XIV, Vienna, 4 October 1672, AE, Paris, CP Autriche, 43, fo. 197.

45. Nuncio's report, Vienna, 27 December 1676, *Nuntiaturberichte . . ., Archiv für österreichische Geschichte*, 106, pp. 188.

46. J. Bérenger, 'Le Royaume de France et les "Malcontents" de Hongrie', *Revue d'Histoire diplomatique* (1973) 3, 1–43.

47. Contarini's report to the Senate of Venice, Vienna, 13 July 1681, Archivio di Stato, Venice, Senato, Segreta, Dispacci di Germania, 155.

48. J. Bérenger, *Les 'Gravamina', Doléances de la Diète hongroise, 1655–1681*, (Paris, 1973), pp. 269–80.

49. I. Katona, *Historia Regum Hungariae*, (Pesth 1798) xxxv, pp. 455–61.

50. Oberuc, *Persécutions des Luthériens*.

51. Sébeville's report to Colbert de Croissy, Vienna, 3 January 1682, AE Paris, CP Autriche, 52, fo. 37.

52. E. Hellbling, *Verfassung und Verwaltungsgeschichte* (Vienna, 1956) p. 230.

53. Gyözö Ember, *Az ujkori közigazgatas története* (Budapest, 1946).

54. Leopold Cardinal Kollonich, *Das Einrichtungswerk des Königreiches Ungarn*, Vienna, Hofkammerachiv, Manuscript 382. This main work of Kollonich was never published.

55. Evans, *Making of the Habsburg Monarchy*, pp. 235–74.

7. THE EMERGENCE OF ABSOLUTISM IN RUSSIA Philip Longworth

1. E.g. Marc Szeftel, 'The Title of the Muscovite Monarch', *Canadian-American Slavic Studies*, 13, nos 1–2 (1979) 59–81. However, the view has been challenged by Isabel de Madariaga, 'Autocracy and Sovereignty', ibid., 16, nos 3–4 (1982), 369–87, esp. n. 11.

2. For a critique of Soviet views on the subject, see S. M. Troitskii, *Rossiia v xviii veke* (Moscow, 1982) esp. pp. 25–47.

3. Perry Anderson, *Lineages of the Absolutist State* (New York 1979) p. 17. But see note 40 below.

4. M. Ya. Volkov, 'O stanovlenii absoliutizma v Rossii', *Istoriia SSSR*, 1 (1970) 90–104.

5. This development has been well described by Ye. I. Kolycheva, *Agrarny stroi Rossii xvi veka* (Moscow 1987).

6. Troitskii, *Rossiia v xvii veke*, p. 10.

7. The traditional date for the end of Mongol suzereinty is 1480. The rise of Moscow to pre-eminence among the Russian principalities owed much to its role as chief tribute-collector for the Mongols. However, the Mongol influence on Russia, which has often been held to explain the despotic nature of the Russian state, should not be exaggerated. See Charles J. Halperin, *Russia and the Golden Horde* (1987).

8. R. E. F. Smith, *The Enserfment of the Russian Peasantry* (Cambridge, 1968) p. 17. See also G. Alef, *The Origins of the Muscovite Autocracy* (Munich, 1986).

9. Kolycheva, *Agrarny stroi Rossii*, pp. 202–4.

10. On this and related matters see G. Alef, 'Aristocratic Politics in Muscovy in the late Fifteenth and early Sixteenth Centuries', *Forschungen zur Osteuropäischer Geschichte*, 27 (1980) 77–99. Generally on Ivan IV's reign, see R. G. Skrynnikov, *Ivan Groznyi* (Moscow, 1975).

11. The transfer of the Orthodox Metropolitan from Vladimir (and originally Kiev) to Moscow, also helped the latter to gain pre-eminence. After 1453 Moscow had also become a major source of financial patronage for the Orthodox Patriarchs under Ottoman rule.

12. Robert Croskey, 'Byzantine Greeks in late Fifteenth- and early Sixteenth Century Russia', L. Clucas (ed.), *The Byzantine Legacy in Eastern Europe* (Boulder, 1988) pp. 35–56. See also A. Lappo-Danilevskij, 'L'Idée de l'état et son

évolution en Russie depuis les troubles du xviie siècle jusqu'aux réformes du xviiie', in Paul Vinogradoff (ed.), *Essays in Legal History* (1913) pp. 356–83. The title 'autocrat' (*samoderzhets*) was first used by Ivan III in 1492, though it only became one of the monarch's established titles towards the sixteenth century, see Szeftel reference in note 1 above.

13. Stories about Prince Dracula (Vlad Tepes of Wallachia) were important here – see Matei Cazacu, 'Aux sources de l'Autocratie Russe', *Cahiers du monde russe et soviétique*, XXIV, 1–2 (1983) 7–41. How far knowledge of the Tudor monarchy, brought by English merchants from the later sixteenth century, might have had an influence is as yet unexplored.

14. R. E. F. Smith, *Peasant Farming in Muscovy* (Cambridge, 1977) p. 233.

15. Philip Longworth, *The Cossacks* (1969).

16. There was to be a succession of pretenders into the eighteenth century and beyond – see Longworth, 'The Pretender Phenomenon in Eighteenth Century Russia' *Past and Present*, 66 (1975) 61–83.

17. See L. V. Cherepnin, *Zemskie sobory russkogo gosudarstva v xvi–xvii vv.* (Moscow, 1978) pp. 149–67. The Swede Fokkerot mentions a ban on the imposition of new taxes without consent while Strahlenberg (in the early eighteenth century) mentions a ban on suspending the laws – see M. Kovalevsky, *Modern Customs and Ancient Laws of Russia* (1891) pp. 180–1.

18. A recent study of a manuscript dating from the reign of Boris Godunov shows that the state apparatus continued to be extended after Ivan's death with, for example, the establishment of a new chancery to administer Siberia – see Maria Salomon, 'An Edition and Analysis of the "Lawes of Russia" Manuscript, with particular Reference to the Bureaucratic Apparatus of the Muscovite State', MA thesis, McGill University (1988); also S. B. Veselovskii, *D'iaki i pod'iachie xvi–xvii vv* (Moscow, 1975).

19. Curiously, Ivan IV was also remembered fondly in popular songs and legends, a phenomenon that owed something to his own (and later Alexis) propagandising efforts – see Maureen Perrie, *The Image of Ivan the Terrible in Russian Folklore* (Cambridge, 1987).

20. Raymond H. Fisher, *The Voyage of Simeon Dezhnev* (Hakluyt Society, 1981).

21. See Philip Longworth, *Alexis, Tsar of All the Russias* (1984) pp. 29, 53, 231 and n. 19, p. 257.

22. See R. J. W. Evans, *The Making of the Habsburg Monarchy 1550–1700* (Oxford, 1979) pp. 39–116.

23. Longworth, *Alexis*, pp. 30–2, 35.

24. *Akty sobrannye v bibliotekakh i arkhivakh rossiiskoi imperii*, IV (St Petersburg, 1836) pp. 149–50.

25. See *Life of the Archpriest Avvakum*, trans. J. Harrison and Hope Mirrlees (1924).

26. Cases are cited in Longworth, *Alexis*, pp. 34, 81 and 69–70.

27. Constantine Porphyrogenitus, *Le livre des cérémonies*, ed. A. Vogt, I (Paris, 1935).

28. E.g. in his rule book on falconry. For a partial translation of this see *Slavonic and East European Review* (1924) and Longworth, *Alexis*, pp. 118–20.

29. *Dopolneniia k aktam istoricheskim*, VI (St Petersburg, 1875) pp. 204–6.

30. W. Ryan, 'The *Secreta Secretorum* and the Muscovite Autocracy', in *Pseudo Aristotle: The Secret of Secrets, Sources and Influences*, W. S. Ryan and Charles D. Schmidt (eds), Warburg Institute Surveys, No. 9 (1982) pp. 114–23.

31. Not Dracula as portrayed by Bram Stoker, however, See the Cazacu reference in note 13 above; also his recent book, *L'Histoire du Prince Dracula* (Geneva 1988).

32. Longworth, *Alexis*, pp. 72–3.

33. See the portrait of Alexis by Daniel Wuchters in the State Russian Museum, Leningrad (reproduced on the dust-jacket of Longworth, *Alexis*).

34. For the circumstances see Longworth, *Alexis*, pp. 71, 97.

35. A. I. Rogov, 'Shkola i prosveshcheniia' in A. V. Artsikhovskii (ed.), *Ocherki iz russkoi kul'tury xvii v.*, II (Moscow, 1979) p. 150.

36. The Private Office was disbanded in 1676 but revived by Peter I under a different name (*Preobrazhenskii Prikaz*). Of the major works on the Private Office I. Ya. Gurliand's *Prikaz velikogo gosudaria taiugkh del* (Jaroslavl, 1908) views it from a legal perspective while A. I. Zaozerskii's *Tsarskaia votchine xvii v* (Moscow, 1937), emphasises its economic role.

37. *Tsentral'nyi gosudarstvennyi arkhiv drevnikh aktov*, Moscow, Fond 27 shows the range of his concerns. It also disposes of Professor Szeftel's contention (see note 1 above) that Alexis 'did not decide a single important case without the *Duma*'. For further evidence see below. Szeftel's notion, following Kliuchevskii, that the tsar had power over individuals but not institutions does not hold for this period either. As de Madariaga (note 1 above) rightly observes, the Russian political system corresponded closely with royal absolutism in France, Denmark and Sweden by the end of the century.

38. For a new critical edition of the Code see A. G. Man'kov *et al.* (eds), *Sobornoe ulozhenie 1649 goda* (Leningrad, 1987) and the new translation by Richard Hellie, volume II of which (forthcoming) will provide annotations. For a brief account of the content see Longworth, *Alexis*, pp. 48–53.

39. Longworth, *Alexis*, pp. 124, 128, 242.

40. Anderson, *Lineages*, p. 195. His treatment of Russia, which suffers from an overly ideological approach not seen in the best of Soviet writing on the subject, is particularly misleading.

41. The peasant's traditional right to terminate his tenancy on St George's Day, in November, after the harvest, had first been suspended on a temporary basis in the late sixteenth century. The suspensions were repeated and their length extended. At the same time the periods within which a runaway peasant could be hunted down and returned to his lord were lengthened. See Smith, *Enserfment*, and Jerome Blum, *Lord and Peasant in Russia from the 9th to the 19th Centuries* (New York, 1967). The code abolished the time limits altogether and placed the peasant under the jurisdiction of his lord. It might be noted that the reasons for enserfing the peasants of Poland were different in so far as the Polish seigneurs wished to exploit the grain-export boom to north-western Europe. The Polish state did not benefit from the development. Grain exports played a negligible role in the Russian case, though a general labour shortage was relevant to the imposition of serfdom in both states. See Blum, 'The Rise of Serfdom in Eastern Europe', *American Historical Review*, 72, no. 4 (1957) 807–36.

42. See. F. Sigel, *Lectures on Slavonic Law* (1902) pp. 45, 48. He is mistaken, however, in concluding that the government's consultation of Assemblies of the Land reflects the idea that law-making lay with the people.

43. For an interesting discussion of *mestnichestvo*, see A. M. Kleimola, 'Boris Godunov and the Politics of *Mestnichestvo*', *Slavonic and East European Review*, No. 53 (1975) 355–70. Also S. O. Shmidt, '*Mestnichestvo i absoliutizm*' in N. M. Druzhinin *et al.* (eds), *Absoliutizm v Rossii (xvii–xviii vv)* (Moscow, 1964) pp. 168–205.

44. Longworth, *Alexis*, p. 190.

45. The term *boiar* is commonly used far too loosely. Though in earlier periods it had denoted a member of the Grand Duke's retinue, in the seventeenth century it denotes a holder of the first of the four Council ranks, equivalent to the rank of Field Marshal and its civilian parallels in Peter I's Table of Ranks.

46. A. Barsukov, *Rod Sheremetevykh*, 8 vols (St. Petersburg, 1881–1904) V, pp. 13–15.

47. Robert Crummey, 'The Origins of the Noble Official' in W. Pintner and K. Rowney (eds), *Russian Officialdom* (1980) pp. 46–75, esp. Table III–I.

48. Longworth, *Alexis*, p. 236.

49. Grigorii Kotoshikhin, *O Rossii v tsarstvovanie Alekseia Mikhailovicha* (St Petersburg, 1906) VIII. Kotoshikhin was a bureaucrat, quite close to the centre of power. His (generally hostile) account of Russia was written for the Swedish government after his defection.

50. The fullest treatment is Cherepnin, *Zemskie sobory*...

51. See Alexis' letter to the dead saint which was read aloud over the grave before its disinterment and translation to Moscow, Longworth, *Alexis*, pp. 80–2.

52. A major reason for Alexis' breach with Nikon was the Patriarch's refusal to instal a new Metropolitan of Ukraine, which acceded to Muscovy in 1654, on the ground that jurisdiction over the Ukrainian Church belonged to his senior, the Patriarch of Constantinople.

53. Longworth, *Alexis*, pp. 111–12, 122–30, 177–81.

54. See W. Palmer, *The Patriarch and the Tsar*, vol. I (1871) pp. 1–615.

55. Longworth, *Alexis*, pp. 183, 213.

56. See the Volkov reference in note 4 above. See also Troitskii, *Rossiia v xviii veke*.

57. Richard Hellie, *Enserfment and Military Change in Muscovy* (Chicago, 1971) pp. 169–70.

58. Longworth, *Alexis*, pp. 132, 144, 242.

59. See Hellie, *Enserfment*. Russia's first military historian, Major-General Rusinov, writing in the reign of Catherine II, gave Alexis, not Peter, the credit for laying the foundation 'not only of a standing army but of its organisation according to the rules of military science' – quoted by L. G. Beskrovnyi, *Russkaia armiia i flot xviii v* (Moscow, 1958), p. 7.

60. See V. I. Buganov, *Moskovskoe vosstanie 1662 g.* (Moscow, 1964); and his *Moskovskie Vosstaniia kontsa xvii veka* (Moscow, 1969).

61. Longworth, *Alexis*, pp. 151ff.

62. Ibid., pp. 132–4.

63. See his study of the subject in S. H. Baron, *Muscovite Russia* (1980).

64. Longworth, *Alexis*, p. 223.

65. See the published records of these embassies in N. M. Bantysh-Kamenskii, *Obzor vneshnikh snoshenii Rossii (po 1800 god)*, II (Moscow, 1896) and *Pamiatniki doplomaticheskikh snoshenii drevnei Rossii s derzhavami inostrannymi*, vol. X (St Petersburg, 1871). See also note 66 below.

66. See Longworth, *Alexis*, pp. 120–1; also I. Ya. Gurliand, 'Ivan Gebdon – Kommissarius i Rezident', *Materialy po istorii administratsii Moskovskogo gosudarstva vtoroi poloviny xvii v* (Jaroslavl, 1903) pp. 37–49.

67. See Baron's several contributions on the *gosti* in his *Muscovite Russia*.

68. Longworth, *Alexis*, pp. 115–16, 146.

69. See the account by one of the Dutchmen recruited by the Russian government, Jan Struys, *The Perillous and Most Unhappy Voyages of John Struys* (1684).

70. See N. A. Baklanova, *Ocherki po istorii torgovli i promyshlennosti* (Moscow, 1928); T. Rainov, *Nauka v Rossii xi–xvii vekov* (Moscow-Leningrad, 1940); also Longworth, *Alexis*, pp. 204–6.

71. On the history of the salt industry, see R. E. F. Smith and David Christian, *Bread and Salt: A Social and Economic History of Food and Drink in Russia* (Cambridge, 1984) pp. 27–73. The work is also useful on the role of alcohol in the seventeenth-century economy, pp. 109–72.

72. Longworth, *Alexis*, pp. 156–9, 269–70; A. I. Zaozerskii, *Tsarskaia votchina xvii v*. (Moscow, 1937).

73. The experiment was not entirely successful. For discussion of this see S. M. Solov'ev, *Istoriia Rossii s drevneishikh vremen*, vol. xiii (1894) cols 716–18. On commercial problems in general, see Baron, *Muscovite Russia* and Paul Bushkevich, *The Merchants of Muscovy* (Cambridge, 1980).

74. For the text of the Statute see *Dopolneniia* (note 29 above) pp. 667–91; also the article on Ordyn-Nashchokin by Likhach in *Russkii biograficheskii slovar*.

75. See (*inter alia*). Volkov, note 4 above; and A. G. Man'kov, *Razvitie krepostnogo prava v Rossii vo vtoroi polovine xvii v* (Moscow-Leningrad, 1962).

76. Longworth, *Alexis*, pp. 193–4, 260 n. 40, 275 n. 9.

77. See Marc Raeff, *The Well-Ordered Police State* (New Haven, 1983). However, Raeff only notes the application of these notions to Russia in the eighteenth century.

78. This was suggested by the eminent historian Lappo-Danilevskii (see note 12 above) but has not, apparently, been pursued.

79. Raymond H. Fisher, *The Russian Fur Trade 1550–1700* (Berkeley, 1943) pp. 28 and passim.

80. On the confluence of some of these see V. S. Rumiantseva, 'O krest'ia nakhraskol'nikakh kanuna vosstaniia S. T. Razina', in L. V. Cherepnin (ed.), *Krest'ianskie voiny* (Moscow, 1974) pp. 270–86.

81. I. Ya. Gurliand, *Prikaz velikogo gosudaria tainykh del*, p. 299; also I. P. Kozlovskii, *Perviia pochty i perviie pochtmeistery v. Moskovskom gosudarstve* 2 vols (Warsaw, 1913) and A. Vigilev, *Istoriiaotchest vennoi pochty* (Moscow, 1977).

82. Longworth, *Alexis*, pp. 222–3.

83. Lindsey Hughes, *Russia and the West: The Life of a Seventeenth Century Westernizer, Prince Vasily Vasil'evich Golitsyn (1643–1714)* (Newtonville, 1984).

8. BRITAIN *John Miller*

1. See J. Brewer, *Sinews of Power: War, Money and the English State, 1688–1783* (1989). My debt to Brewer's work is obvious.

2. Note the parallels between the power of the king of Scotland and that of the king of Spain, as analysed by Thompson.

3. See C. Russell, 'The British Problem and the English Civil War', *History*, LXXII (1987) 395–415; Brewer, *Sinews of Power*, pp. 13–14, 132.

4. See J. G. A. Pocock, *The Ancient Constitution and the Feudal Law* (revised edn, Cambridge, 1987).

5. *Calendar of State Papers, Venetian, 1625–6*, p. 528; S. R. Gardiner, *History of England 1603–42*, 10 vols (1883–4) VI.227–8, VIII.211–17, IX.120, 229; J. P. Sommerville, *Politics and Ideology in England 1603–40* (1986) especially chs 1, 4.

6. J. P. Cooper, *Land, Men and Beliefs* (1983) pp. 101, 106.

7. See G. J. Schochet, *Patriarchalism in Political Thought* (Oxford, 1975); J. Daly, 'Cosmic Harmony and Political Thinking in Early Stuart England', *Transactions of the American Philosophical Society*, LXIX/7 (1979).

8. Gardiner, *History of England*, V.434; Sommerville, *Politics and Ideology*, ch. 5.

9. See M. Judson, *The Crisis of the Constitution, 1603–45* (New Brunswick, 1949); A. Sharp, *Political Ideas of the English Civil Wars* (1983).

10. However, the Levellers, fearful of the misuse of power by future Parliaments, proposed that there should be certain 'laws paramount' (such as those guaranteeing frequent elections and religious liberty) which no Parliament could alter.

11. For Locke's debt to the writers of the 1640s, especially George Lawson, see J. H. Franklin, *John Locke and the Theory of Sovereignty* (Cambridge, 1978).

12. See for example *Old Parliamentary History* 23 vols (1751–61) XXII.242, 264–5; *Lords Journals*, XI.238–9, 246–8. See also P. Seaward, *The Cavalier Parliament and the Reconstruction of the Old Regime 1661–7* (Cambridge, 1989) pp. 15–22.

13. See *Calendar of State Papers Domestic 1664–5*, p. 565; *1666–7*, p. 318.

14. See Pocock, *Ancient Constitution*, ch. 10; J. Daly, 'The Idea of Absolute Monarchy in Seventeenth-Century England', *Historical Journal*, XXI (1978) 227–50, especially pp. 244–5 where he argues that Filmer was untypical of Tory thinking.

15. J. P. Kenyon, *The Stuart Constitution* (2nd edn, Cambridge, 1986) pp. 349, 351–2; A. Browning, *English Historical Documents 1660–1714* (1953) pp. 64–5; R. L'Estrange, *The Holy Cheat* (1662, reprinted 1682) pp. 27–9; M. Nedham, *A Pacquet of Advices . . . to the Men of Shaftesbury* (1976) pp. 44–5; L'Estrange, *An Account of the Growth of Knavery* (1678) pp. 44–5; Daly, 'Absolute Monarchy', pp. 239–43.

16. Bodleian Library, Carte MS 72, fo. 508.

17. J. Miller, 'Charles II and his Parliaments', *Transactions of the Royal Historical Society*, 5th series, XXXII (1982) 16–23. Those outside the Commons could prove much less inhibited.

18. Not all those who claimed to act in the name of the people advocated democracy, not least because they feared that 'the people' would not vote for them. Algernon Sidney believed that the main merit of a republic was not that it was representative but that it allowed men of true virtue and talent (like himself) to rise to the top: see J. Scott, *Algernon Sidney and the English Republic 1623–77* (Cambridge, 1988) especially pp. 192–4.

19. See J. P. Kenyon, *Revolution Principles: The Politics of Party 1689–1720* (Cambridge, 1977) pp. 17–19 and passim.

20. Sommerville, *Politics and Ideology*, p. 177.

21. A. Grey, *Debates in the House of Commons, 1667–94* 10 vols (1769), VII.406; C. Russell, *Parliaments and English Politics 1621–9* (Oxford, 1979) pp. 39–41.

22. M. B. Pulman, *The Elizabethan Privy Council in the 1570s* (Berkeley, 1971) pp. 196–225, 249; A. Fletcher, *Reform in the Provinces: The Government of Stuart England* (New Haven, 1986) pp. 43–62; K. Sharpe, 'Crown, Parliament and Locality: Government and Communication in Early Stuart England', *English Historical Review*, CI (1986) esp. pp. 344–6.

23. When the Stuarts did begin to build up a body of professional administrators, their aim was not to increase central influence in the localities but to collect revenue.

24. This point was made by three very different observers in 1675–7: Sir W. Temple, *Works*, 2 vols (1731), I.415–16; A. Browning, *Thomas Earl of Danby*, 3 vols (Glasgow, 1951) II.70; Archives des Affaires Etrangères, Paris, Correspondance Politique Angleterre 117, Ruvigny to Pomponne, 9 Jan. 1676 (new style).

25. A point made by one of the judges in 1627: Kenyon, *Stuart Constitution*, p. 97.

26. See W. J. Jones, *Politics and the Bench: the Judges and the English Civil War* (1971); A. F. Havighurst, 'The Judiciary and Politics in the Reign of Charles II', *Law Quarterly Review*, LXVI (1950), 62–78, 229–52; Havighurst, 'James II and the Twelve Men in Scarlet', ibid., LXIX (1953) 522–46.

27. A. Marvell, *An Account of the Growth of Popery and Arbitrary Government* (Amsterdam, 1677) pp. 66–7.

28. C. Russell, *The Crisis of Parliaments* (Oxford, 1971) p. 278. It is true that the

wars of 1624–30 were fought with limited financial support from Parliament, but the political and administrative strains which this imposed were enormous.

29. S. R. Gardiner, *Constitutional Documents of the Puritan Revolution 1625–60* (3rd edn, Oxford, 1951) p. 95. The best account of Charles I's decision-making in the late 1620s is that in R. P. Cust, *The Forced Loan and English Politics 1626–8* (Oxford, 1987).

30. For a discussion of the Stuarts' kingship, see J. Miller, *Bourbon and Stuart: Kings and Kingship in France and England in the Seventeenth Century* (1987).

31. Gardiner, *History of England*, V.424.

32. Russell, *Parliaments and English Politics*, pp. 379–83; Gardiner, *History of England*, V.410; N. Tyacke, 'Puritanism, Arminianism and Counter-Revolution', in C. Russell (ed.), *Origins of the English Civil War* (1973) ch. 4; J. Fielding, 'Opposition to the Personal Rule of Charles I: The Diary of Robert Woodford', *Historical Journal*, XXXI (1988) 780–4; C. Hibbard, *Charles I and the Popish Plot* (Chapel Hill, NC, 1983); J. Miller, *Popery and Politics in England, 1660–88* (Cambridge, 1973).

33. J. R. Tanner, *Constitutional Documents of the Reign of James I* (Cambridge, 1930) pp. 15–16; J. Chamberlain, *Letters*, ed. N. McClure, 2 vols (Philadelphia, 1939) I.301; Kenyon, *Stuart Constitution*, p. 45; Gardiner, *History of England*, VI.83, 231.

34. For the best recent overview, see D. Hirst, 'Revisionism Revised: The Place of Principle', *Past and Present*, 92 (1981).

35. Sommerville, *Politics and Ideology*, pp. 163–72; Kenyon, *Stuart Constitution*, pp. 104–6.

36. There is no substance to the myth that Henry VII restored the monarchy's finances; on the contrary, by his reliance on politically provocative methods, bordering on extortion, rather than on Parliament, he was leading the crown into a blind alley.

37. Gardiner, *History of England*, IV.21; Chamberlain, *Letters*, I.601–2; L. L. Peck, 'Corruption at the Court of James I', in B. C. Malament (ed.), *After the Reformation: Essays in Honour of J. H. Hexter* (Manchester, 1980) pp. 80–5; M. van C. Alexander, *Charles I's Lord Treasurer* (1975) pp. 194–6.

38. Tanner, *Constitutional Documents*, pp. 340–5, 262; Chamberlain, *Letters*, I.532–3.

39. C. Russell, 'Parliamentary History in Perspective, 1604–29', *History*, LXI (1976) 1–27, esp. p. 12; Russell, *Parliaments and English Politics*, pp 49–51.

40. See Cust, *Forced Loan*.

41. Gardiner, *History of England*, VII.376–7. For conflicting views about the extent of constitutionalist opposition to ship money see J. S. Morrill, *The Revolt of the Provinces, 1630–50* (1976) pp. 24–30; K. Fincham, 'The Judges' Decision on Ship Money: The Reaction of Kent', *Bulletin of the Institute of Historical Research*, LVII (1984) 230–7.

42. Gardiner, *History of England*, VIII.103.

43. Gardiner, *Documents*, p. 206.

44. Gardiner, *History of England*, VII.138–40, VIII.299–301; D. Hirst, *Authority and Conflict: England 1603–58* (1986) pp. 171–5; C. Carlton, *Charles I: The Personal Monarch* (pbk edn, 1984) pp. 111, 118–22, 156–61.

45. R. Ashton, 'From Cavalier to Roundhead Tyranny' in J. S. Morrill (ed.), *Reactions to the English Civil War, 1642–9* (1982) ch. 8; I. Gentles, 'The struggle for London in the Second Civil War', *Historical Journal*, XXVI (1983) 301–2.

46. G. E. Aylmer, *The State's Servants: The Civil Service of the English Republic 1649–60* (1973).

47. One could argue that the regimes of 1642–60 were much the most absolute in seventeenth-century England.

48. C. D. Chandaman, *The English Public Revenue, 1660–88* (Oxford, 1975).
49. S. Pepys, *Diary*, ed. R. C. Latham and W. Matthews, 11 vols (1971–83) VIII.332.
50. Miller, *Popery and Politics*, pp. 148–51.
51. Ibid., ch. 8; J. R. Jones, *The First Whigs* (Oxford, 1961).
52. Havighurst, 'Judiciary and Politics', pp. 240–52; J. Miller, 'The Crown and the Borough Charters in the Reign of Charles II', *English Historical Review*, C (1985) 70–84.
53. *Calendar of State Papers Domestic 1680–1*, p. 660; N. Luttrell, *A Brief Historical Relation of State Affairs*, 6 vols (Oxford, 1857) I.199.
54. Cooper, *Land*, pp. 110–12; Miller, 'Charters', pp. 80–4.
55. See J. Miller, 'The Potential for "Absolutism" in Later Stuart England', *History*, LXIX (1984) 187–207.
56. I have argued the former: Miller, *James II: A Study in Kingship* (1989) pp. 124–8.
57. Havighurst, 'James II', pp. 530–1; Bucks Record Office D135/B2/1/4–5.
58. See the comment cited by A. Coleby, *Central Government and the Localities: Hampshire 1649–89* (Cambridge, 1987) p. 220.
59. British Library, Egerton MS 2543, fo. 270.
60. J. R. Jones, *The Revolution of 1688 in England* (1972) ch. 6; J. Childs, *The Army, James II and the Glorious Revolution* (Manchester, 1980) pp. 106–13.
61. *Commons Journals*, VIII.442–3; Kenyon, *Stuart Constitution*, p. 384.
62. This was true (despite later Whig complaints) even of 1685, when the Tories did best in the most open constituencies: B. D. Henning (ed.), *History of Parliament 1660–90*, 3 vols (1984) I.66.
63. T. Bruce, Earl of Ailesbury, *Memoirs*, ed. W. E. Buckley, 2 vols (Roxburghe Club, 1890) I.151; Kenyon, *Stuart Constitution*, p. 410.
64. Miller, *James II*, pp. 196–7; W. A. Speck, *Reluctant Revolutionaries: Englishmen and the Revolution of 1688* (Oxford, 1988) pp. 130–5.
65. Childs, *The Army*, ch. 4.
66. Brewer, *Sinews of Power*, esp. ch. 4; P. G. M. Dickson, *The Financial Revolution in England, 1688–1756* (1967).
67. See J. Miller, *The Glorious Revolution* (1983).
68. H. T. Dickinson, 'Popular Politics in the Age of Walpole' in J. Black (ed.), *Britain in the Age of Walpole* (1984) p. 57. For an excellent analysis of extra-Parliamentary agitation see K. Wilson, 'Empire, Trade and Popular Politics in mid-Hanoverian Britain: The Case of Admiral Vernon', *Past and Present*, 121 (1988) 74–109.
69. T. Hayter, *The Army and the Crowd in mid-Georgian England* (1978).
70. For valuable introductions see T. C. Smout, *A History of the Scottish People 1560–1830* (1972); R. Mitchison, *Lordship to Patronage: Scotland 1603–1745* (1983).
71. See J. Wormald, 'James VI and I: Two Kings or One?' *History*, LXVIII (1983) 187–209.
72. Mitchison, *Lordship to Patronage*, pp. 14–21.
73. See J. Buckroyd, *Church and State in Scotland, 1660–81* (Edinburgh, 1980).
74. Miller, *James II*, pp. 214–16.
75. See P. W. J. Riley, *The Union of England and Scotland* (Manchester, 1978); T. C. Smout, 'The Road to Union', in G. Holmes (ed), *Britain after the Glorious Revolution 1689–1714* (1969) ch. 8.
76. Note the difference between Cromwell's conduct in Scotland and in Ireland.
77. See H. Pawlisch, *Sir John Davies and the Conquest of Ireland: A Study in Legal Imperialism* (Cambridge, 1985).

78. J. Miller, 'The Earl of Tyrconnell and James II's Irish Policy, 1685–8', *Historical Journal*, xx (1977) 803–23.

79. One possible exception was the extension of excise jurisdiction: Brewer, *Sinews of Power*, pp. 113–14.

Notes on Contributors

JEAN BÉRENGER is a Professor at the Sorbonne (École Pratique des Hautes Études, IVe Section); he was formerly a Professor at the University of Rennes II. He is the author of *Finances et absolutisme autrichien dans la seconde moitié du XVIIe siècle*.

J. H. BURNS has been since 1986 Professor Emeritus of the History of Political Thought, University of London (Reader 1960–6, Professor 1966–86, University College). He was general editor 1961–79 of *The Collected Works of Jeremy Bentham*, editor of *The Cambridge History of Medieval Political Thought* (1988); and, with Mark Goldie, of *The Cambridge History of Political Thought 1450–1700* (1990). He was Hinkley Visiting Professor, Johns Hopkins University in 1987 and Carlyle Lecturer, University of Oxford in 1988.

HANNSJOACHIM W. KOCH is Reader in History and teaches at the University of York. Specialising at first on the Third Reich, the Weimar Republic and Bismarckian and Wilhelmine Germany, on which he published several works translated into German, Dutch, Portuguese, Japanese and Arabic, he has turned the focus of his research back on the eighteenth and nineteenth centuries. He has been awarded the Book of the Month prize of the US Literary Guild and the Ranke-Förderpreis of the Gerda-Henkel-Stiftung, Düsseldorf, for his book *Die Befreiungskriege 1807–1815* (Napoleon against Germany and Europe).

PHILIP LONGWORTH, Professor of History at McGill University, was educated at Oxford and taught at Birmingham University and the Open University before moving to Canada. He is the author of several books, including *The Cossacks*, and of many articles in scholarly journals concerning Russia and Eastern Europe. He has particular interests in the early modern period and in comparative history.

ROGER METTAM was educated at Christ's College and Peterhouse, Cambridge; he lectured at York (1964–70) before becoming Lecturer and subsequently Senior Lecturer in History at Queen Mary and Westfield College, University of London. His writings on French history include *Power and Faction in Louis XIV's France* and *Government and Society in Louis XIV's France*,

JOHN MILLER studied at Jesus College, Cambridge, becoming Research Fellow at Gonville and Caius College, Cambridge. He came to Queen Mary (now Queen Mary and Westfield) College, London, in 1975; was appointed Professor of History in 1989. His main area of research is the politics of later Stuart England, but he has also worked on the provincial estates of Languedoc in the seventeenth century. His books include *James II: A Study in Kingship* and *Bourbon and Stuart: Kings and Kingship in France and England in the Seventeenth Century*. He is currently completing a biography of Charles II.

I. A. A. THOMPSON took his PhD at Cambridge. He taught at Reading and Flinders University of South Australia, then became Senior Lecturer at Keele until 1988. He is now a Fellow of the University of Keele. He is the author of *War and*

Government in Habsburg Spain 1560–1620 and of a chapter on Philip IV in *Historia Global de Espana y America*. His research interests include the Cortes of Castile in the sixteenth and seventeenth centuries, bureaucracy, oligarchy and nobility in Habsburg Castile (on which he has written various articles); he is currently writing a study of Philip II.

ANTHONY F. UPTON is a graduate in history of the Queen's College, Oxford, and Duke University, Durham, North Carolina. He became a university teacher of modern history at Leeds University in 1953 and later moved to St Andrews University, where at present he has a personal chair in Nordic History, and is chairman of the Department of Modern History. He is the author of four books on the history of modern Finland, including *Finland in crisis 1940–41* and *The Finnish Revolution 1917–18*. Recently he has been researching the development of absolutism in seventeenth-century Sweden and intends to publish a study of the reign of Karl XI of Sweden.

Index